BREAD UPON THE WATERS

✳

David Blagrove

Cast thy bread upon the waters;
for thou shalt find it after many days.

Ecclesiastes XI

B

M & M BALDWIN
Cleobury Mortimer, Shropshire
1995

Bibliographic Note

This book was first published by J.M. Pearson & Son (Publishers) Ltd in 1984, and we gratefully acknowledge their co-operation in the publication of this new edition. The original text and illustrations are here reproduced in their entirety, but the opportunity has been taken to correct a number of minor errors detected in the first edition.

Author's acknowledgement to the first edition

The author offers grateful thanks to John Oliphant and Diana Redman for reading through the manuscript, to Anne Booker for patiently converting his 'scrawl' into typing, and to all those people on 'the cut' who made the following so worthwhile.

Dedication

To my Wife - as some sort of explanation...

ISBN 0 947712 27 5

Cover designed by David Miller

Published by M & M Baldwin
24 High Street, Cleobury Mortimer, Kidderminster DY14 8BY

Printed by Severnside Printers Limited
Bridge House, Upton-upon-Severn, Worcs. WR8 0HG

Contents

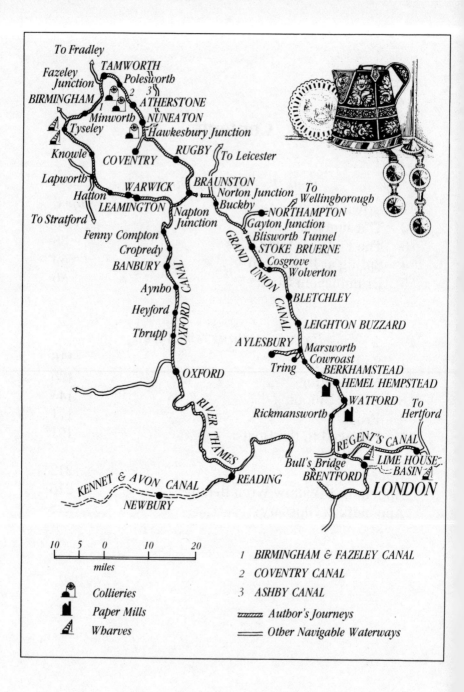

To Fradley
Fazeley TAMWORTH
Junction Polesworth
BIRMINGHAM 2 3
Minworth ATHERSTONE
Tyseley NUNEATON
Hawkesbury Junction
Knowle
Lapworth COVENTRY RUGBY
To Leicester
Hatton WARWICK BRAUNSTON
Leamington Norton Junction
To Stratford LEAMINGTON Buckby
Napton NORTHAMPTON
Junction Gayton Junction
Fenny Compton Blisworth Tunnel
Cropredy STOKE BRUERNE
BANBURY Cosgrove
Aynho Wolverton
Heyford BLETCHLEY
Thrupp LEIGHTON BUZZARD
AYLESBURY Marsworth
OXFORD Cowroast
Tring BERKHAMSTEAD
HEMEL HEMPSTEAD
RIVER THAMES WATFORD
To Hertford
Rickmansworth
KENNET & AVON CANAL READING REGENT'S CANAL
NEWBURY Bull's Bridge LIME HOUSE BASIN
BRENTFORD LONDON

To Wellingborough

GRAND UNION CANAL
OXFORD CANAL

10 5 0   10   20
miles

1 BIRMINGHAM & FAZELEY CANAL
2 COVENTRY CANAL
3 ASHBY CANAL

Collieries
Paper Mills
Wharves

Author's Journeys
Other Navigable Waterways

❧ BOOK 1 ❧
Learning the Job

1

Down River

It was a bitterly cold January morning. I had upended a wastepaper basket over the Chief Clerk and was consequently in search of employment. The buildings and buses of Piccadilly had been lit up against lowering grey clouds when I marched out of the office and crossed Regent Street towards the Underground; now, at Boston Manor Station an easterly wind was whipping the New Year's litter round the forecourt. In the Half Acre at Brentford the trees stood glum and skeletal against a backdrop of gaunt warehouses; half frozen puddles crunched underfoot as I turned right along Brentford High Street. Opposite the "Six Bells" a muddy turning led into Durham Wharf and to my destination, the offices of the Willow Wren Canal Carrying Company.

The office was reached by an iron ladder and turned out to be the loft part of an old stables block. At the top was a glass panelled door on which I knocked. From within a spectacled face regarded me suspiciously. The face's owner shuffled to the door and slipped the latch back. He was a slight, stooping figure wearing pin-striped trousers, black jacket and a wing collar. He had black swept-back hair and a distinctive owl-like expression, enhanced by horn-rimmed spectacles. I glanced furtively to see whether he had a quill pen behind his ear and was disappointed. He greeted me with grave courtesy and inquired my business. I said that I wished to see Mr Morton the manager.

"Oh, er, well, er, have you an appointment?" he asked.

I said that I had not, but that it was a matter of business.

"I will see if he is available," he said grandly, "What name is it?"

I told him and suddenly he grinned broadly, "Oh, I see, I was unaware of your identity. I thought you were another representative."

Leslie Morton's voice roared from inside, "Show the boogger in Stanley!" and I stepped into Willow Wren's nerve centre and Emporium of Commerce.

Less than two hours earlier I had been an employee of an extremely suave West End professional firm, where gentility and office-cleaning were watchwords, where the principals existed in princely splendour amidst finely decorated rooms and even we poor sweated assistants had a carpet on the floor, where a myriad of secretaries and clerks found their niches in life, and where alluring specimens of femininity adorned the typing pool. This was somewhat different. Now I had a month's salary in my pocket and a season ticket valid until February, but no job. I was not exactly regretting the change.

Facing the door was Stanley's desk with an ancient Imperial sit-up-and-beg typewriter on it. Beside him was a telephone and next to that a miniature exchange box with jack plugs—which I later saw used to magnificent effect. On the wall was an enormous graph with curiously named co-ordinates, "Croxley Mills", "Suttons", "Banbury Dairy.", "Marsh Mills". Along these ran lines with names such as "Sandpiper", "Flamingo", "Tern" and symbols stating L. or E. (for loaded or empty). This was the company's boat control board. The room was tastefully panelled in unpainted hardboard with adornments in the shape of distance tables, tide almanacs, a copy of the Shops, Offices and Railway Premises Act and a calendar illustrated by curvaceous women in brief attire. I subsequently found that the monthly adjustment of this and the consequent near revelations were topics of absorbing interest to visiting boatmen.

There was a strong scent of paraffin, mixed with the aroma of Woodbine cigarettes and pipe tobacco and the warmth of this cosy little office was overpowering. Leslie Morton came rolling out of a side door, seized my hand and shook it vigorously. He ushered me into his inner sanctum, which had another flat-topped desk equipped with a telephone and one of those revolting cellular ashtrays, made of Bakelite, which were so popular in the forties and which became completely clogged with ash and cigarette ends. On one wall a framed certificate informed the world that Leslie Noel Morton was a Member of the Institute of Transport. On another hung a large, coloured poster featuring the Company's boats "Redshank" and "Greenshank" tied up abreast, with a leggy blonde straddling the space between the sterns in a suggestive manner.

Leslie Morton was about sixty-five or six. He and Stanley had been together, running Willow Wren for eight years, ever since the day the firm had opened for business in a caravan on the Wharf at Paddington Basin.

Later, when I came to know him better, I learnt that this re-

7

markable man had run away from Public School at thirteen and shipped before the mast in a sailing-ship out of Liverpool. He had been round Cape Horn under sail five times before his sixteenth birthday, survived the sinking of the "Lusitania" and another torpedoing in the 1914-18 war and risen to command in the Mercantile Marine. On coming ashore, he founded a canal carrying business which eventually became the Grand Union Carrying Company—the giant of pre-nationalisation canal fleets. In the thirties, after Company cold feet led to his sacking, he had become an import-export agent, navigated a desk for the Admiralty from 1939 to 1945 and then, at an age when most men consider retiring, had undertaken the running of Willow Wren.

Morton had many faults. He could be a most spiteful old tartar, with a tongue like a lash. He grew boastful and overbearing in his cups but could be most charming, witty and erudite. Slow to take offence, he was quick both to forgive and apologise. Above all, he worshipped his boatmen, whom he ruled over in patriarchal fashion, and they, in turn, respected him. Many, like me, loved him. When he died my great regret was that I did not hear of it until after his funeral. Two of his boatmen hitch-hiked from Wellingborough Mills to his funeral at Epsom, in their words "to foller the old Gaffer".

This winter's day I saw him at his best. He motioned me to sit down, and asked "Well, lad, what can I do for you?" I told him that I had just been sacked and his eyes lit up. "And so you're asking me for a job?" I affirmed this was so. "Well, that's a bloody good recommendation. What did you do to get sacked?" I told him and he roared with laughter. "I got court-martialled once for kicking the skipper down the Bridge companionway," he said. "I don't know as I'd want a wastepaper bin over my head if we had a difference." I pointed out that his being of wickerwork it would not hurt much and he chuckled. "When do you want to start?" I explained that there were many loose ends to be tied and preparations to be made which would take several weeks. "Give me a ring about the end of February then, unless you come up with something else", he said and shook my hand again. The telephone rang in the outer office.

Stanley's voice said, "Willow Wren, Brentford"—pause—"Just one moment please, I'll put you through to our transport department"—click, click from the switchboard and Morton winked at me. Stanley called, "Traffic enquiry, Mr Morton."

"Put 'em through Stan," another click, click. Morton lifted his receiver and said in his most suave voice, "Transport Department, Manager speaking". I retired from his presence thinking what a picture of commercial efficiency the enquirer must have envisaged.

Although my boating career started that day, the foundations had been laid much earlier. All my life I had been aware of the narrowboats which worked the canals of the English Midlands. I had been brought up in Abingdon, a small Thameside town and, like so many youngsters, had fallen under the spell of the river which swept past the ancient stones and bricks.

Some miles upriver, the Oxford Canal joined the Thames, the power station at Osney being supplied with coal by narrow boats, as was Sandford Paper Mill, whilst Oxford Gas Works sent out tar by boat. These activities seemed part of the natural world, unchangeable and immutable.

It was not until my teens, when my family had moved to Reading and I had been sent to boarding school (at a town with no navigable water other than a long-derelict canal) that I began to realise that the rivers and canals of the country were in a parlous condition. I think my early experience of the Thames and the Oxford Canal, both of which were well maintained and seemingly prosperous, had blinded me. It was L.T.C. Rolt's "Inland Waterways of England" which opened my eyes to the system that still existed. I recall reading this book soon after its publication in the early fifties and being struck, both with the quality of its writing, and by the superb photographs—mainly by Angela Rolt—which in retrospect seem to sum up succinctly everything about the Inland Waterways system.

At the 1954/5 Boat Show I visited the stand of the Inland Waterways Association and fell into conversation with one of the pioneers of the canal revival, Mr John James of "Jason". I told him I lived in Reading and that the Kennet and Avon Canal seemed to be in a poor way. His answer to this gratuitous information was to "go and see John Gould at Newbury".

John was a native of Newbury and had lived by, and loved the Kennet and Avon Canal all his life. After the Inland Waterways Association was formed in 1946 he acquired some boats from Harvey Taylor of Aylesbury, a carrier who had ceased trading. Two of these, "Colin" a motor boat and "Iris" its companion unpowered boat or butty, he loaded with paving stones in Birmingham and brought to Newbury. In themselves perhaps unremarkable, when given the hostility towards commercial use of the canals, these attempts proved notable.

When I first met John Gould in 1955 and walked the K. and A. towpath out of Newbury, only Newbury Lock was generally serviceable. Greenham Lock, a mile to the East, was usable with care and navigation was just possible to the head of Bull's Lock, some two miles from Newbury Bridge. Westwards, navigation ended at the tail of Guyers Lock, again about half a mile away. In effect, there was a three mile length with one reasonable lock and two distinctly 'dodgy' ones. This was all that remained, apart from the Bristol to Bath section and about four miles from the Reading end, after five years of official neglect, if not actual sabotage.

Locked in, with no access to boatyards and drydocks, a wooden boat soon deteriorates. However, John Gould fought back. Pleasure trips were to run in "Colin" until the boat became too far gone. A fleet of small rowing dinghies was started, some hiring of houseboats was done, but, most important, legal action was taken against the Authority—now the British Transport Commission. Gould's case was proved and substantial damages awarded against the B.T.C. but the Canal remained closed. At the same time an ex parte injunction to force re-opening was refused and the B.T.C. drafted a Bill to close the Canal.

The law relating to canals was changed by the 1968 Transport Act, but in the early fifties the Railway and Canal Acts of Victorian times were still in force. In order to close a canal permanently its owners had to prove that no navigation had taken place for a year. After this they could apply to the Ministry of Transport (originally the Board of Trade) for a Warrant of Abandonment. The Wilts. and Berks. Canal was abandoned in this way in 1914 and an attempt was made to relinquish the Stratford Canal in the same way as recently as 1958. By allowing the waterway to become impassable and by making high toll charges and awkward restrictions, an unscrupulous owner could create a lack of navigation.

During the 1939-45 war the Great Western had permitted Reading Corporation to strengthen an allegedly weak bridge in the town with girders. This effectively reduced the height for craft using the River Kennet to 4 feet 6 inches, although larger craft could pass by special arrangement. This was one example, at the very gateway of the Kennet and Avon, of the obstructions to traffic placed there to deter it and to hasten the grant of a warrant. Gould's case, and the persistent efforts of others, notably canoeists, to navigate the whole canal had frustrated these knavish tricks. As a result, the B.T.C. was forced to try another tack—to abandon the canal by special Act of Parliament.

By 1955, however, the enthusiasts' lobby, particularly the newly formed K & A Association and the older Inland Waterways Association, were feeling their muscle and Public Opinion, slowly but inexorably, was turning in their favour. The B.T.C. Bill was thrown out after great public campaigning and lobbying, and, although none of us realised it at the time, a turning point in the Canal's history was reached.

The atmosphere in those days round Newbury Lock, the headquarters of John Gould (Waterways) Limited, was that of a front line command post. Attitudes to the local canal staff were rather similar to those of front-line soldiers towards the enemy in the trenches opposite; of mutual respect, but official hostility, with the occasional foray or trench raid by either side. An outflanking move would be to form another Branch at Reading and I was duly directed to this part of the front and given the address of one Denys Hutchings of Reading.

I met Denys Hutchings (or "Hutch" as everyone knew him) soon after, and it was not long before I was involved in the campaign from the Reading end. I made my first trip over the navigable section at Easter 1956 when Captain Lionel Munk of Maid Line Cruisers Limited most generously provided a flotilla of hire cruisers. We cruised this armada up to the tail of Burghfield Lock and I had the strenuous honour of rowing a boat containing Mr Robert Aickman, the founder of I.W.A., and other notables along Burghfield Cut, then, at its top end, about ten feet wide.

Two years of small boat rallies, meetings and general campaigning passed and the river water continued to flow quietly along until the news broke that a passenger service was to be operated from Reading. In March 1958 I received an invitation from the Directors of the Kennet Carrying Company to be present on their inaugural cruise, which was to be graced by the presence of the Mayor of Reading and other dignitaries.

Excitement on Kennetside ran high. The tripper turned out to be a motor narrow boat, modified in design to seat 52 and to pass under the Bridge Street girders. She had been renamed "Enterprise" to suit her new role, while, to give moral support and carry the overflow of invited guests, a pair of narrow boats operated by the Willow Wren Canal Carrying Company were sent along to act as escorts. These two, "Grebe" and "Snipe", had earlier that week unloaded coal for Morrell's Brewery at Juxon Street Wharf, Oxford and were en route for Brentford, via the Thames, to reload. The Captain was Bill Wilson, always known as "Billy Wilson Greasy Ocker" to distinguish him from other Bill Wilsons, and his wife and two sons made up the crew. They were the first boaters that I got to

11

know on more than mere nodding terms and were as good an introduction to the breed as one might hope to find.

I became a regular crew member for "Enterprise" at weekends and on evening trips after work and began to accompany her on journeys further afield. Then, in the spring of 1961 I heard that the owner of the Kennet Carrying Company was considering ending this service. Encouraged by John Gould and Hutch, I found two friends who were prepared to have a go with me, made an offer for the Company and suddenly found it had been accepted. Although I had recently changed jobs, my spare time was limited and it seemed this must be a spare time activity. The previous owners had provisionally acquired a skipper who was willing to work for us until the end of the 1961 season but two problems arose. Firstly, the boat was lying at Aylesbury, which was only about an hour's drive by road, but by canal and river was a considerable haul. Secondly, the skipper was doubtful about the sheer hard work and unfamiliarity of navigating a large boat all that way on his own. I mentioned this problem to John Gould, who said "Old Bill Fisher'll do it for you" and he introduced me to a blonde-haired, stocky young man who I recognised as having been at "Enterprise's" inaugural run of three years before.

So it happened that in May of that year Bill and the regular skipper brought "Enterprise" round via Braunston and Oxford in time for the Whit weekend. 'Tripping' soon began in earnest. The Reading Branch had carried out temporary repairs to Burghfield Lock, thus enabling us to run to the tail of Sulhamstead Lock near Theale, some seven miles from the Thames. As we were a campaigning as much as a business venture, we initiated a once weekly run to Theale as well as several daily runs to Burghfield.

As a business venture its success was modest, but from the campaign point of view it was a valuable exercise and every run scoured the channel. We gained useful experience and the fact that a 70 foot boat could make timetabled runs encouraged a number of other boats to come up from the Thames. All in all, we had a successful season, rounded off in the Autumn by some towing work and two household removal jobs for the Thames Conservancy. Bill Fisher bought out one of the partner's shares and suggested that, as he had now completed his indentures in his job and was at a bit of a loose end, he might run the boat himself in the 1962 season and that we might start tripping at Easter rather than Whitsun.

The boat was due for renewal of its M.O.T. Tripping Certificate and this meant dry docking and a complete engine overhaul.

Thames boatyards were demanding outrageous slipping fees (there was then only one drydock on the Thames which was at Sunbury and belonged to the Conservancy), so plans were made to take "Enterprise", in February or March, to Samuel Barlow's dock at Braunston, Northamptonshire, where the Grand Union joins the Oxford Canal.

I was at this time working in Central London and had taken to riding down to Brentford during my generous lunch time to check on any developments at the Canal Basin. It was here that I first made the acquaintance of Leslie Morton. He was interested to hear of our doings on the Kennet and mentioned casually that it seemed a shame that a good motor boat should be doing nothing in winter. Bill and myself had often discussed the possibility of trading with "Enterprise" in order to put jam on the summer's bread and butter. Now Morton was offering us work, plus a commission on any traffic we could obtain on the Thames and Kennet.

This was heady wine indeed and it seemed that all we needed to do was to canvass waterside firms, obtain trade and . . . bingo! It came to pass that just after Christmas the managing clerk of the firm I worked for made an unjust accusation. We had always disliked each other and now he came out into the open. I doubt whether anyone had ever answered him back before. His eyes bulged and he went white with rage. "Get your cards!" he shouted. I said that it was my pleasure, whereupon he telephoned the Accounts Department to make up my salary for a month in lieu of notice. Having done this, he made a sneering jibe at my professional competence, at which I put the waste bin over his head, picked up my cheque and walked out of office jobs for ever.

Such was the chain of events which had brought me to Morton's office, now the die was cast. Much to my amazement he had set me on and it was for me to act on it.

In the meantime, I had to teach myself something of the inner mysteries of marine diesels, to clean up and prepare the cabin and to strip the passenger seats out of the hold. At this stage it might be appropriate to describe the boat which was to be my home and source of income, on and off, for the next four years.

"Enterprise" was in fact an ex-Fellows, Morton and Clayton carrying boat, seventy-one feet long with a beam of seven feet—the classic narrow boat dimensions. Fellows, Morton and Clayton boats were always known as "Joshers", after the late Mr Joshua Fellows. As "Enterprise" had been built at the Company's dock at Saltley,

Birmingham in 1903 she was known technically as a "Saltley Josher". A number of boats built at that time were named after places prominent in the South African War and she was given the name "Kimberley". She was of composite construction, which means that the sides were made of iron and the bottom of elm. Unlike metal boats today, her plates were riveted together. In the 1930's she was converted from a horse-boat to a motor and had a counter stern fitted at Yarwoods of Northwich. The extension to the rudder which eventually forms the tiller of such a boat had an ornate boss with Yarwoods' cast on it. In this guise she continued working on the northern canals, mainly between the Mersey and the Black Country until the B.T.C., as Fellows, Morton and Clayton's successors, sold her to Charles Ballinger of Gloucester. Charles Ballinger's boats were mostly named after girls—he had some big, old ex-Severn and Canal Carrying Company boats called "Bridget" and "Olive"—so "Kimberley" became "Susan" and worked between the Severn and the Black Country until 1957. In that year she was bought by the Kennet Carrying Company, modified by Willow Wren at Braunston, and renamed "Enterprise".

The aspect of the boat had not been improved by the fact that height above waterline had to be restricted to 4 feet 6 inches because of the Bridge Street girders. Originally she had had her own cabin sides painted in a similar style to Willow Wren—light green panels on a scarlet background lined with yellow. However, her refit in 1960 had been done by Samuel Barlow's dock and so she was now painted in Barlow style with dark green panels and grained oak background lined in yellow. Unlike most working motor boats she had two landscape panels, one each side of the stern superstructure which had been painted by George Crowshaw, who was one of the last of the traditional boatyard painters. These depicted the traditional views of lake, bridge, mountain and romantic castle. Both the cabin side doors and the engine hole doors had similar paintings, with a green vertical panel beneath sporting an upright swag of roses. The cabin top was grained and two slide hatches above the doorways painted with the usual red, Barlow club motif. There were two polished copper cowls ventilating the engine room, polished brass mushroom vents, brass portholes (three each side) and brass port and starboard light mountings on the cabin fore end. Finally, a black brass-bound chimney completed the decor. When all was clean and polished she looked a brave sight.

Having arranged with a friendly, adjoining proprietor to store the seats and unwanted gear, the hold was first cleared out. I should mention that below the false floors there were ten tons of concrete block ballast to keep the boat low down and some of this was removed. We later found that it should all have been removed, but we were still learning.

By mid-February all was ready. I arranged with Cyril Rogers, the Newbury Section Inspector, to make a run to Theale and back with some tools and plant for British Waterways. Water and diesel tanks were filled and a supply of coal laid in. I rang Morton at Brentford, to be treated to Stanley's telephone juggling, and he said, "Come down any time after next week." Bill was working a month's notice to expire at the end of February and it was agreed that he should come aboard on the first Sunday in March, ready to leave the next day. There was a stoppage at Molesey Lock which was due to come off on the Tuesday and after that the road to Brentford was clear.

So, at last, at about 10am on the first Monday in March we slipped our moorings from High Bridge and backed carefully down to the old river where some local journalists were waiting to be taken on a sight-seeing tour of the Huntley and Palmer's biscuit factory. Although we had an electric horn, we found an old army bugle was more effective and in the frosty air Bill blew a fanfaronade which echoed round the factory walls and caused many a head to pop out of the factory windows.

Kennetside has been largely demolished today. Of the old buildings round Blakes Lock only the Fisherman's Cottage now survives as a pub. There used to be some tall, grim, old slum tenements, which have been replaced by tall, grim, new tenements, and an old Kennet and Avon boatman called Dick Freeke lived in one near the lock. He waved us on our way as we slipped past gasholders and huge aluminium pipes, past the old Board School building and terraces of Newtown, under the great arches of the Southern and Great Western railways and the Horseshoe Bridge, and on to the wide expanse of the Thames. Down Dreadnought Reach, Reading slowly faded out of sight and we slipped swiftly along in flurries of snow with smoke curling up from the cabin chimney, the brass glinting and the exhaust stabbing patterns across the water.

The journey down river was unremarkable at first. It was noticeable how much more friendly the lock-keepers were than in the summer. In winter they were pleased to see some life and to exchange gossip. In later years I found out why they were grumpy in summer; they often had to work a 12½ hour day for six days (occasionally seven) without relief. This meant operating the locks

15

manually forty or fifty times daily, maintaining their log books and accounts, keeping the gardens trim and looking after the weir—all for a flat wage of £8 to £15 per week.

Towards evening we put the journalists ashore at Maidenhead. A friend who lived aboard a large river cruiser at Maidenhead Bridge saw us and declared that we looked like a tug as we forged downstream with smoke rolling from the chimney and a feather of white water spurting up the stem. We lit the navigation lights below Bray, exchanged chat with Edgar Light the keeper at Boveney Lock in the dark, and went to pull up below Windsor Bridge. The river was still running fast and pulling-up whilst heading downstream is always difficult. Here it was complicated by the fact that a long masonry spit called "the Cobbler" projected up river from the head of Romney Lock Cut, just below the Bridge dividing the channel. We intended to tie up near the steamer moorings on the Windsor side, so held over away from "the Cobbler", slipped towards the steamer moorings and went hard astern. Panic ensued when nothing happened. The engine raced but no swirl of water came from below the counter. The stern swung towards "the Cobbler" and for a moment we thought we should be grounded on it by the current. However, we managed to get a line off the fore end and pulled clear. Once tied up, we lifted the inspection plate on the gear box to find that the reverse brake band had apparently slipped. After some clever juggling with spanners we tightened it up and tested it. All seemed well enough for us to be able to repair to the nearby "Donkey House" after supper.

Next morning there was thick fog on the river. "The Cobbler" was dimly visible but beyond that, nothing. By 9.30am we felt it was no use waiting for the fog to lift if we were to get to Brentford that night, so we crept gingerly down to Romney Lock. At the lock a large sign stated that dredging was taking place in the cut below, so we very cautiously edged round the bend from the lock. I stood on the fore-end peering into the whiteness and let drive a monstrous blast on the bugle. As I did so, the black shape of a steam dredger loomed up, secured to both banks by stout wire hawsers and apparently deserted. I drew off another blast and men suddenly appeared on deck, some with bits of sandwich in their mouths. They evidently thought that a super tanker was about to interrupt their tea break. Winches clattered and we slipped over the hawsers with inches to spare. They seemed to see the funny side of the incident, particularly the bugle.

Once the dredger had disappeared into the fog astern and her crew became ghostly voices speaking from a void, we had to give a wide berth to Black Potts Railway Bridge. Happily, down Datchet Reach the sun appeared and the fog lifted suddenly to give a breathtaking view of Windsor Castle rising above the meadows.

The Conservancy stoppage duly came off that afternoon and on we went, getting cheerful waves from Captain Munk's Maid Line Base at Thames Ditton and, at about five in the evening, we came down Teddington Lock cut. It was growing dusk and once more the reverse gear failed. This time we managed to snub the boat on a T.C. mooring post, but not before the fore-end had slid under the catwalk of the Launch Lock top gates.

By now we were increasingly nervous about getting in to Brentford. Firstly, we had doubts about entering the British Waterways lock at the end of Brent Creek because it only operated for a certain time either side of High Tide. The Molesey 'stoppage meant that we would go down on a falling tide and might well lose time by having to pass through the half tide lock at Richmond. This could mean waiting in Brent Creek for the next tide and it would then be the small hours of the morning when we would get through Thames Lock into Brentford itself. Secondly, there was a lot of land water going down which, in addition to the falling tide, would increase the difficulty in manoeuvering off Brent Creek. Thirdly, it was getting dark. Fourthly, neither of us had ever been down river this far before and we had only a vague idea of how to find Brent Creek. Finally, our reverse gear had permanently failed because the brake band had broken. Despite the hazards, however, we pressed on.

So far we had had a swift run downstream aided by a fresh current. Hardly any other craft were about, so we had the locks and river to ourselves, but when we left Teddington and got into the main stream we were in for a surprise. We had a falling tide behind us and the benefit of a fresh following wind. It was as if a giant hand had grasped "Enterprise" and was pushing her through the water. Between Twickenham Ferry and Richmond we swept round a majestic bend, keeping to the inside as far as possible, and here we overtook a motorbike going along the towpath on the outside of the bend. As Richmond Bridge rushed towards us out of the gathering gloom, we gazed at each other in wild surmise, for there were the unmistakable arches of the tidal barrage with a man's figure outlined against the sky evidently setting the gates. With no reverse gear it could have been very awkward. However, the man evidently spotted us and waved us on. We sped through to his cheery encouragement. Soon after, the gaunt gasholder at Brentford came in sight. I knew we had to turn before reaching it. The point was, where?

We scanned the banks looking for a gap. The quay wall of Brentford Railway Dock appeared and ships, cranes and lighters loomed out of the darkness. Bracing ourselves, I put the tiller hard over and opened the throttle wide. "Enterprise" skidded round, still sweeping downstream but broadside on. A concrete-piled island appeared in our path, then miraculously the boat was plodding ahead through the racing water towards the dark opening of Brent Creek. Two minutes later we were threading our way through a mass of moored lighters towards Thames Lock. In the Creek it was pitch black between the concrete walls and we slowly fumbled our way to one of the double lock gates.

After negotiating the lock we crept up to and tied alongside Durham Wharf. We were still on semi-tidal water but already a new atmosphere was forming about us. No longer was there the lonely dereliction and quiet of the Kennet, nor the majestic royal progress of the Thames with its trim tidiness, but a sense of purpose and bustle, of a workaday world of black working hulls and cargo holds. The Town Lock, below which we were tied, had heavy duty fenders by it. Its gates had no frills; there were no flower beds or neat gravelled paths. There was a utilitarian control room with lamp standards surrounding it. Walking past it after supper, we could see the crouched forms of warehouses overhanging the wide basin and, underneath, the bulky lighters and the low-down shapes of waiting river barges. There was not another narrow boat in sight. We both felt suppressed excitement because at last we were where the action was. Only one lock separated us from the mysterious world of working canals about which we had both read so avidly. At the same time we were apprehensive. How would the boaters take to us? True, the ones we had met seemed pleasant enough, but what would they think of two outsiders? They might be expected to be stand-offish, if not downright hostile. With these nagging doubts in our minds, we dodged the whining trolley buses in the High Street and went into the "Magpie and Stump" as a prelude to further investigation of Brentford.

2
The Junction Cut

We awoke to a grey Brentford morning by being severely joggled as the lock was drawn. It was about 7.30am and the world was astir.

A voice said, "That facquin' Josher'll be on the bottom when the tide's aht." Above our heads came the coughing of a twin cylinder diesel. Peering out through the slide I could make out a small towpath tractor whose driver was a wizened, bottle-nosed old man in bib and brace overalls, checked muffler, donkey jacket and cloth cap. "Ah do, me ole cock sparrer," he called, "Lookin' fer Stan?" I nodded in amazement. "Opens up abaht nine, look aht fer 'is jam jar, an ole Morris 8," continued my informant, who then clutched in and roared away towards the basin.

Low tide was about 10am that day, so we were unlikely to be disturbed below the lock for a few hours. We had had our breakfast and were walking round exploring when a scrunch of tyres in the yard outside Company Head Office announced Stanley, charioted, as forecast, in a pre-war Morris 8. He greeted us affably and told us to return after he had dealt with the post.

Accordingly, about half an hour later we clanged up the ladder. Stanley was expostulating gently but firmly to the telephone. When he put it down he said, "Another one wind-bound on the Shroppie". I said that I thought those high embankments of the Shropshire Union main line would be bad with a pair of empty boats in a high wind. "Perhaps," he said, "but it's a funny thing they always get wind-bound outside a pub."

We asked what orders there were and it happened that we had arrived just at the right time. The nearest Willow Wren boats were unloading at Croxley and could not get down until Friday evening. This was Wednesday morning and a lighter-load of timber was due on the evening tide for transhipping and forwarding to Aylesbury. This, we thought, was it, a quick 'chuck-over' and away. We had reckoned without the great British Closed Shop principle.

The rest of the day was spent impatiently waiting until the tide crept up from Brent Creek and the long strings of lighters came surging up from the Pool. Outside the Creek, where we had spent such a breathless few minutes the night before, the guardian tug loosed them off and, one after another, they came bumping in, banged through the double Thames Locks, were catapulted by the capstans on the lockside into the lower pound, and were then pulled in a disreputable string up to the Town Locks by a battered old tug. Their mufflered, overcoated, trilby-hatted steerers ostentatiously read newspapers as they rolled onward, steering with the tiller between their knees. At the stern of most of them was a heavy casting in which giant rowlocks could be placed for use with 'sweeps' or gargantuan oars. The lightermen were proud of their skill with the sweeps and, as he rose in Town Lock, one of them saw Bill looking at the casting. "Not many knows what that's for mate," said he, "an' I bet you don't an' all." Bill said in his most innocent fashion he supposed it was for supporting a sunshade when the weather was too hot for delicate complexions. Fortunately, at that moment the top gates opened and the lighter began to pitch out into the Basin, for the lighterman's face was a picture.

Into the Basin from the Docks came the day's cornucopia in steady procession, shooting out of the locks, past the lighters waiting for the ebb tide and the British Waterways wharves where yet more lighters waited to load and unload. Some 'up the cut' barges nosed low through the water towards the railway bridge where our tractor-driving friend and his companions were waiting to hook on. Others dropped into the Waterways wharves and some came to our side of the Basin. Vokins, General Steam Tug and Lighterage, Tough and Henderson all paraded their names past. Then came a smart blue-trimmed hatch with Woodward Fisher's name on it. "That's your'n", called the lock keeper.

The barge bumped up to some others and tied up to them. The steerer, a likely-looking lad of about our age, nodded to us and we gazed at the towering pile of timber rising out of the hold. "When can we start?" we asked.

He looked amazed. "Tomorrer o'course mate." It was our turn to look amazed. It so happened that there was a pocket-handkerchief sized tarpaulin over the top of the load and removing this was a lighterman's job and could not be performed by non-union labour. Oh yes, he could take it off now, but he had to go home and who was to replace it when we had finished? Eventually he said that if we gave him 'two bob' and bought him a couple of pints, he would make us his subcontractors and we could put the cloth back on. We were tempted, but stood by our consciences and refused this magnanimous offer.

"Jolly good job you did," said Stanley when we went to the office, bewailing our fate. It turned out, such was the militancy amongst the river and wharf men, that had we been seen by any of the myriad eyes in the Basin removing or replacing the cloth, both Woodward Fishers' and Willow Wren's boats would have been blacked.

Having escaped being the unwitting cause of a labour dispute, we brought "Enterprise" alongside and made her ready for the next morning. As we did this, a string of empty British Waterways narrow boats began to emerge from under the railway bridge, each breasted pair appearing at roughly five minute intervals. These were the pairs which had been awaiting orders at Bulls Bridge Depot, Southall and had been notified of the arrival of the lighters by telephone from Brentford Creek.

Immediately the whole atmosphere of the Basin changed as, with staccato throbs, the motor boats came down the canal; chimney brasses gleaming, white lines scrubbed on cratches and butty tillers, smoke rolling and women and children clustered in the butty hatches while the men in berets or flat caps nonchalantly wound the pair round without slackening speed. Unlike the solemn lightermen who pleased themselves whether or not they noticed anyone else, each steerer nodded, said "Ow are ye?" and inspected us at length as he passed. One by one they pulled into Brent Meadow Wharf. The evening was loud with women's voices, children chattering and men exchanging badinage. Miraculously, Brentford Basin had become a living village. In contrast to the slumberous atmosphere of the place the previous night, it was now alive and crackling with vitality. As engines died away, up went aerials on cabin tops, dogs tore up and down the wharf, shovels grated in coal bunkers and we smelled that wonderful reek of East Midland coal smoke that is inseparable from memories of working boats.

The rear of the procession was occupied by a single motor boat, "Barnet". The steerer of this, a middle-aged man with a trilby hat, was dwarfed by a tall engine exhaust pipe. His boat was somewhat shabby and the brass rims on his chimney looked dull. One of the boatmen called, "You wants to get up in the mornin'!", but the reply was drowned by the racketing of "Barnet's" engine. "Barnet" winded and some of the waiting boaters helped the steerer to tie up. The steerer put his engine out and dropped into the cabin. Seconds later a hairy arm came out of the doors holding a handbowl which was dipped into the canal. A few minutes later I looked out of our cabin door to see this last boater, his evening toilet completed, standing in his hatches staring intently at our cabin side. He saw me and a sonorous voice boomed across the water, "Do'ee ole' boys coom from Reddin' then?" Bill and myself started. Amidst the welter of Cockney and the Midlands twang of the cut, the musical tones of West Berkshire took us straight back to the Upper Thames. I said that we did and he replied, "Oi seed yer name on yer cabin soid. Do 'ee ole boys know Abendon?"

"Not half," I assured him. He told me that was his home so, bursting with curiosity, I asked him if he would care to have a drink later on.

"You don't mean to say ye ole boys goes a-boozin'?" he asked in an amazed tone, declining the offer. It seemed that we had found an expatriate from the Abingdonian Temperance Society. We made our way to the "Northumberland Arms" while mulling over this problem. We had not been there many minutes when two vaguely familiar figures came in.

Bill nudged me, "See those two over there?" I looked in the direction he indicated. The two men were of indeterminate age wearing blue overalls, mufflers and berets and were leaning against the bar. One was round-faced and stocky, the other lean and gaunt. They kept glancing in our direction and then looking away guiltily. "I'll bet they're boaters," Bill murmured. It was my round, so I walked across to the bar near to where they were standing. I said "Evening".

Both of them replied, "Ow are ye?" Then as I was waiting for our glasses to be refilled, the stocky one asked, "That your boat tied across from us?" I said it was. "We was just arguin'. I says its Fellerses ole "Kimberley" as Willow Wrens had on Braunston slip."

"You're right too," I said. Then, realising that the ice was broken, I asked them to join us. Immediately they grasped their glasses and marched across to Bill, From then on we had no more doubts about boaters—at least the men, the women took longer to get to know. Their names were Bill Grantham (the stocky one) and Bill Ambridge—so far most canal people seemed to be called Bill—and they were bursting with polite curiosity about us. The evening flew by and we parted after closing time, having stood on Brentford Bridge chatting for a good half hour, with promises to meet for another drink another day.

7.30am the next day saw the world astir again. Cases of foodstuffs were being loaded for Birmingham. Two pairs were loading grain for Wellingborough Mills. Up came the grab to swing over the waiting narrow boat and the lighter rose fractionally in the water. The catch was released, grain spilled along the bottom of the boat, dust flying, pigeons coming in like Stukas, and the boat settled comfortably downwards. Behind, the stone tower of Brentford Church and its skeletal churchyard trees stood clear and fresh against a cloudless early morning sky, counterpointing the corrugated iron gauntness of the warehouse buildings. The contemplation of this pleasant scene was marred by the consciousness that it was both time-consuming and wasteful. The boats had to hang about at the depot until the lighters were available. Then the operation itself was both labour-intensive and slow and finally, a fair amount of grain was wasted or spoiled. Had a couple of hundred ton silos been built, the grain could have been sucked into them, stored and released into boats as required, and all with the minimum of time and grain wasted. However, such plans were repeatedly frustrated by lack of capital and obstruction from the unions, who claimed that men would lose jobs. Eventually, the whole operation became uneconomical and everyone concerned lost.

That unhappy day was then some years in the future, but the signs were already there. At Brentford I first became really aware of the background of frustration, incompetence and apathy which so nearly lost us our canal system. It was in fact a microcosm of Britain of the 1960's and 1970's. Here was an industry, hard-working in some ways and wastefully indolent in others; with one foot in the twentieth century and the other in the nineteenth; living and trading on memories of past greatness; many of its officials and leaders largely out of touch with day-to-day practicalities of the job, but full of grandiose schemes; the workforce confused and divided among themselves, held together only by traditional esprit and the comradeship of the job. Time and again I was to be forcibly made aware of this background.

For the immediate future, our concern was with transhipping by hand some twelve tons of tongue and groove boards. The lighter-man ceremoniously removed the cloth and away we went. The boards had to be carefully packed tongue to tongue or groove to groove to prevent splitting and I began to curse my lack of fore-thought in not removing the gas-pipe canopy supports. It became an exasperating exercise in wriggling long lengths of wood up and out of the lighter and into our hold. From time to time boaters across the Basin looked across and grinned.

By lunch time, the first 'Waterways' pair was loaded and being sheeted up. We had stowed about seven tons and went round to the

"Six Bells" for a pint. Our tractor driver had passed and repassed several times during the last day or so and he was downing a pint of London heavy as we came in. Over another pint he became a confidential informant.

"Them General bleeders is watchin' yer mate," he said. It turned out that the "General bleeders" were employees of the General Steam Tug and Lighterage Company and were engaged in internecine strife with their comrades employed by other lighterage firms who did not enforce a closed shop.

"An' that ain't all," he went on, "You look how them bastards is workin' 'emselves aht o' jobs, mine an' all 'll go." We asked him what he meant. He laid a dumpy finger to his red-veined nose, screwed up a rheumy eye and said, "You wait an' see cock, you'll find aht."

We reported to Stan by four o'clock that all was loaded. He walked round and looked at how "Enterprise" was sitting. "About 12 tons—all right. Jumbo'll keep an eye on you up the locks." We asked him who Jumbo was. "The tractor driver you were talking to," he explained, giving us our loading ticket. Presumably his well-developed proboscis had given him his name but on this occasion we came under the wing of another tutor.

The single motor "Barnet" had been loading cases and the steerer was now sheeting up. He saw us making similar preparations and called over to us, "When be 'ee goin' orf?" We said we were ready and he suggested that we wait until the next day, then work together. We looked at each other. The temptation to be gone was great, but this offer was difficult to refuse. A discussion then ensued about a leaving time. We suggested 6am. He suggested 8.30am. Eventually we settled for 7.30am. It was a decision never to be regretted.

Early on Friday morning we awoke to the cough and growl of a Petter PD 2 diesel. Smoke rose vertically from top and bottomless National Dried Milk tins thrust into the tops of brass-ringed chimneys and feet clanged on enginehole plating as one by one the boats started up. The tops of the cranes and warehouses were cloaked in mist and cabin lights gleamed blearily in the half light as the first boats slid away into the gloom. Dew-soaked tarpaulins hung limply over the holds. Men and women called out eerily and disappeared into the grey blanket hiding the railway bridge. Behind them the waters settled as the noise of the engine was swallowed up by the continual boom of the Great West Road.

By 7am, the fleet had gone except for "Barnet", from whose

24

chimney a thin stream of smoke proclaimed that the steerer was up and about. Soon after, our worthy mentor appeared. He waved to us, started his engine, loosed off and drew alongside. He was aware of our lack of reversing facilities. "We'll go abreast, so's I can 'old you back," he said. We untied and as the strip of dirty water between us and the lighter widened I felt that indescribable thrill that always accompanies a long journey by water. We really were off into the unknown along the whole ninety three miles of the Grand Junction Canal to its end at Braunston Stop Lock.

Our self-appointed mentor was called Wilfred. We got to know him well over the next few weeks and he was indeed a remarkable character. Although he rarely had anything complimentary to say about any other boater, he was greatly liked and respected. His background was interesting; his family name being recorded amongst Thames watermen for two centuries. His father had never taken to the boats but Wilfred went to work them with his uncle and grandfather, Alfred and Matthew, on leaving school in Abingdon aged 12. The family was one of the last boating families to work in the pre-railway manner, with their own boats and no women or young children aboard. It was the custom that the men worked the boats and the families lived ashore. In Wilfred's case his family lived in a large old Georgian house in West Saint Helens Street, Abingdon.

Most families surrendered their houses and took to the water when the railway competition drove down carrying rates and wages in the mid-nineteenth century, but Wilfred's family still kept on the house and the women never boated. His was also the last family to work long distance horseboats on the River Thames, carrying coal from the Coventry area to Benson, near Wallingford, until 1939. The coal merchant had then tried to knock Uncle Alf down 6d (2½p) per ton, so Uncle Alf had sold his boats and labour to the Grand Union Canal Carrying Company. It had been their custom for the women (two sisters of Alfred) to board the boats at St Helens Wharf, Abingdon, clean out the cabins, collect the washing and generally revictual the boats while the men had a day off. Now this ancient practice had to cease and, with it, their more sedate way of progress. "The bloody war came," said Wilfred, "an' we was at it, 'ardly 'ad time fer a crap." Uncle Alf and Wilfred worked together for the "Grand Union" and British Waterways for over twenty years until Uncle Alf, then in his seventies, was taken ill. Sister Mary Ward of Stoke Bruerne nursed him but his boating days were over. He went home to Abingdon to his ancient sisters and there he was now, in retirement, while Wilfred worked a single boat on his own. He was philosophical about it but once admitted that he got lonely sometimes with only a chimney to talk to. We later found he had little cause to be lonely for he had friends everywhere, all of whom thought the world of him.

We clattered under the Great West Road, through some of the most evil-smelling water on the entire canal system, to the first of the locks, number 99. Since, in those days, there was heavy "up the cut" barge traffic, each of the next ten locks had a lock keeper who worked the outside gates and paddles. Boat crews were supposed to work the inside (i.e. towpath side) gates and paddles. Up, and then away, under the Piccadilly Line and the hump-backed iron roving bridge to Osterley Lock with its neat little Regency lock keeper's house and on to the "Thick of Hanwell", a flight of six locks, closely spaced on a curve, with the ugly bulk of Hanwell Mental Hospital rising behind a high brick wall. By a factory just below, an old Seddon's boat from Cheshire lay mouldering away opposite a notice proclaiming the best piece of bank piling in the whole country, which had won the Sir Reginald Kerr Challenge Cup.

Wilfred had to call at Bulls Bridge depot to pick up his money. Apparently he had left without his last settlement, which explained his abstemiousness at Brentford. So we bade him a temporary adieu and set off up the Cowley Pound, running straight as a ruler towards Southall and Hayes. Brentford's great gasholder and Firestone's chimney were no longer visible as we crossed the watershed from the Brent to the Colne valley.

At Bull's Bridge, where the Paddington Arm joins the main line, were the main workshops, depot and docks of the British Transport Commission's waterways fleet. They were then operating about fifty pairs in the South Eastern Division (mainly on the Grand Union, Oxford and Coventry Canals). There were several empty pairs lying stern-on in the wide lay-by waiting for orders; washing neatly arranged fore and aft and children playing on the bank. The crews stared at us as we passed, most waved, a few seemed to take no notice. However, we soon learned that our passing had been noted by everyone. Nestle's factory ('Hayes Cocoa' to boatmen) was the next landmark, which had a grab crane by the boiler room for emptying the coal brought from Cannock Chase. I had sometimes seen Willow Wren boats when passing over the adjoining railway bridge, but the sad news was that the factory was converting to oil.

The scenery here was rather depressing that day. Chill mists clung round to Southall gasworks, reinforced by great clouds of steam from the coolers. The large factories producing jam, cocoa, porridge oats, gramophone records and corks churned inexorably in the grey light. Steam cranes dipped and chuffed in the Western Region sleeper depot on the towpath. Trains roared and clanked over the main line bridge. The leafless hawthorn hedges seemed stunted and the towpath was black mud, yet even this landscape seemed to have a glum hideous beauty of its own.

Beyond the end of the Slough Arm, we came to the first pleasure boats we had seen since leaving the Thames. There were not many in those days, and they were all tied on the outside bank. In fact, we did not meet a single pleasure boat under way until we reached Braunston. The day of the mass-produced hire cruiser and the investment boat had yet to dawn. Winding through the trees we came to the gates of Cowley Lock and here we paused, waiting for Wilfred. The sun came out, so we polished the brass and sat savouring the first really attractive canalscape since Hanwell.

The pastoral aspect of the canal bordered by overhanging trees contrasted with the functionalism of cast iron bollards, brick staircases and wing walls. The symmetry of the paddle gear and gates, with their simple contrast of black and white paint, blended easily into the backdrop of toll office and lock house with white-washed walls and low-brimmed roofs. White wooden rails led to an old pub, "The Shovel", where once boat horses were stabled whilst their masters consumed pints in the low-beamed tap room.

At about 10.30am Wilfred came clattering along, complaining that our polished brass showed him up. We breasted with him and plodded onwards, past Uxbridge gasworks and power station, where the unloading gear was being dismantled. The bold concrete-capped Grand Union piling with its 1930's date and bold injunction to "Dredge 4ft 6ins B.W.L." (below water level) was mocked by the dereliction of the industrial wharves and Fellows, Morton and Clayton's old dock which was now nearly silent. It was obvious that trade was in full flight. Wharves still busy two and a half years before were now deserted and no boats or barges enlivened the rather dreary run to Uxbridge Town Lock.

Proceeding under Western Avenue to Denham Deep Lock, the deepest on the Grand Union and surrounded by woods and streams, we continued up Denham Straight which, our mentor told us, was the longest straight on the Grand Union. As we passed the tall railway bridge Wilfred nodded towards the distant road bridge and lock, then still a tiny pinpoint in the distance.

"Yur comes the Willer Wren," he said. Sure enough a breasted pair of empty fore-ends were creeping from under the bridge. At last, here were our professional colleagues and the first pair of independent carriers we had seen so far. The boats drew near and became discernible as a 'Josher' motor, "Tern", and "Drake", a big Rickmansworth butty. A stout woman with fair hair; a pretty girl of about thirteen with large teeth, another younger girl with red hair, a mop-headed fair-haired boy of about five, a tiny toddler with fair hair, and a thin quizzical-looking man with glasses and a cloth cap, stared hard at us from the stern ends. The two boys were on the motor boat's cabin top with dad, the girls on the butty with mum. They chattered past and the conversation began as the fore-ends met, continuing until distance prevented further communication.

" 'Ow do George!"

"Whee up there Wilf. Where yer for?"

"Brummagem"

"Oom them bastards wi' ye?"

"Ole boys as is a-workin' fer Morton"

"Gor boogger. 'Ow much timber 'ave yer left us?"

Bill shouted, "We took twelve ton".

"That's all right then. You got Lock 80 ready for yer."

George's last information meant that he had met no boats since Lock 80 several miles up, so there would be no need for lockwheelers to go and get the locks ready. Above Coppermill lock came a whiff of something not very pleasant. " 'Tis th'ole Stinko", said Wilfred. Soon, amid the thinning willows, appeared a side bridge and a modern factory building overlooking a wide pool. It was in fact Maple Cross Sewage Works and lying alongside were two pairs of Willow Wrens. The captain of these was on the wharf. He waved and shouted to Wilfred, then stopped and ran to the cabin ends. Heads popped up from the hatches and cheerful shouts and gestures came to us. Then, as Wilfred said "Ole Billy Wilson Greasy Ocker," we knew who it was.

"Ow are you Billy?" called the Ocker. "Where'm you for, Aylesbury?" We nodded. "See you," he called. Now the amazing thing about this meeting was that he had only seen us once and that was four years before, yet he recognised us instantly. Of course, the boat was fairly distinctive but even so, it gave me an insight into the prodigious memories of so many boaters.

It was mid-afternoon as we approached Rickmansworth. The brief sunlight had gone but there was still enough light to appreciate the canalscape as we came through the bridge. There is a short branch

28

canal here to old wharves and yards on the River Chess which leads off into an uphill lock immediately under a side bridge, while the main canal also rises through an adjoining but deeper lock. The usual neat brick staircases were replaced by grand curving flights, worthy of a town hall, punctuated by iron strapping stumps. The classic Grand Junction motifs of low brimmed roofs and black and white paint completed the picture of purposeful orderliness and mingled with the romanticism of the canal itself.

On the lockside we made a new acquaintance. Wilfred had been busy on the telephone, first at Bulls Bridge then at Widewater Lock, Harefield. The reason for the calls was now apparent. A tall, pleasant-looking man, some years our senior, with a diffident manner and slight hesitance in his speech appeared on the towpath. "Tis ole Romeo," said Wilf, by way of introduction. "These are my two new mates."

'Romeo' looked at our boat. "Fellows and Morton's old "Kimberley"', he said. "Off the 'K and A' are you? Where are you for?" We told him. Wilfred then announced that he was tying up here, so we pulled into the side above the lock. 'Romeo' said, "See you later" and disappeared.

There are worse places to tie up than above 'Ricky' Lock. In those days everything was to hand: water, dustbins, a well-stocked shop by the bridge—where the staff were evidently used to serving boaters while they locked through—and several good pubs (including one called "The Railway" perched right on the canal bridge.) We shopped, had our supper and, as it grew dark, 'Romeo' appeared. In fact his name was Alan but Wilfred was severely practical and, considering his own erudition to be rather quaint, had given him this epithet. We later found that Wilfred had his own name for everyone—we were known as the "Kennet 'olers".

Once Alan had overcome his initial shyness, I found he knew the detailed history of the canal system. I had met several such railway enthusiasts but he had a positively encyclopaedic knowledge of boats and their lore. When he realised that neither of us was going to 'take the rise' out of him he became positively eloquent. Sitting in our cabin waiting for Wilfred to finish his supper and cleaning-up, he warmed to his theme. Suddenly he stopped, cocked an ear and said, "Bolinder!"

We listened. Faintly there came the "pomp, pomp pop, pomp, pomp" of a single cylinder diesel. Looking out of the hatch we saw the gleam of a headlight advancing steadily towards us as another empty Willow Wren pair came down the pound. They entered the lock and we walked down to see two wooden Joshers, the butty with a forecabin. They were called "Quail" and "Kingfisher".

Greetings were exchanged. The skipper, a tubby little man with a round cheerful face beneath a cloth cap, stood in the motor boat's door holes, the yellow lamplight showing up a cigarette stuck between his lips. His wife, a slim dark-haired woman, was drawing the bottom paddles. "Come from Aylesbury, six o'clock this mornin' Wilf," she said.

"Jumbo's next in turn. Met 'im in Denham Straight dinner time," Wilf replied.

She smiled at us, teeth flashing. "Fust trip is it? Ah well, we all got to learn." Clustered in the butty hatches two small girls and a boy of about thirteen stared solemnly at us their faces lit by the lamplight streaming upwards, as the boats dropped down. The motor suddenly ponked into reverse, the thumblines straining at the bottom gate handrails. The gates cracked open and the beam of the headlight shot through them, lighting up the bridge and the water beyond.

The gates swung back and Mark, the skipper, put the motor ahead. Then, with a "pop, a-ponk, a-pomp, pop, pomp, pomp, pomp", the boats slid away into the dark—shouts being exchanged with the lockside.

Wilfred, who had donned a collar, tie and his best hat, said "Where's the car Romeo?"

"Just down the road," he replied. So, having cleaned ourselves up sufficiently to lessen the contrast with our smart new friends, we now set forth on a tour of the more fashionable hostelries of the Rickmansworth area. Alan had a large old Standard Vanguard into which we piled. Wilfred sat bolt upright in front, his sharp eyes flickering from side to side at all things of interest, from likely-looking factories to nubile young women. It was then we discovered that his abstinence at Brentford had been enforced, for he proceeded to consume ale with missionary zeal.

Next day, Saturday, a fresh northerly wind with a feel of rain in it whipped the water as we resumed our journey. Below Rickmansworth the locks are fairly well spread but as the canal heads up the valleys of the Colne and Bulbourne towards Tring summit, the hills draw in, the valley narrows and steepens and the locks crowd thicker and thicker towards the top lock at Cowroast. The first pound of the day wound through meadows, following the River

Colne. This was badly polluted by the paper mills further up and we soon sampled its full bouquet.

Lock 80, with its flagpole and trim lockhouse was officially called "Lot Mead", but I never heard it referred to by boaters as anything other than Lock 80. Mark had left it ready for us the previous night but, for the time being, this was the last one prepared for us, as an empty pair had started uphill from Croxley that morning.

The sheds and chimneys of Croxley paper mills now dominated the view ahead and I went ahead to get the next lock, Common Moor, ready. Boats were lying under the gaunt iron sheds. several being British Waterways pairs whose captains grinned cheerfully and shouted something incomprehensible in the argot of the canals to Wilfred. After Cassio Bridge with its tall Metropolitan Line viaduct, we entered the very attractive section known as "The Parks".

Another pleasant canalscape followed at Hunton Bridge, a nasty turn under a handsome modern arch which led to more white walled canal houses framed by overhanging trees. Above the two locks, on Wilfred's advice, we singled out. "I'll show 'ee 'ow ter stop 'un in a lock," he assured us. As we clattered round the waterworks turn below the Change Lock we were, therefore, glad to see Alan, who was accompanying Wilf for the day, winding away at the bottom paddles to give us a "straight shoot", i.e. a lock ready with both gates open. On Wilfred's instructions we took a heavy strap from the starboard stern towing stud and laid it coiled on the slide of the stern hatches. He told us to watch him and copy. As "Barnet" entered the lock he throttled right down, entered the left-hand gate and stepped ashore at the lock tail holding his check strap. "Barnet" slowly nosed into the lock, and he trotted up the steps and checked it on a stump just beyond the bottom gate. Once his fore-end touched the sill, he transferred his strap to a stump on the lockside just slightly ahead of his stern deck, threw a hitch on it to stop it slipping and went to the balance beam of his gate to pull it to. Alan had been sent up to the top gates and was waiting, windlass poised on the top inside ground paddle. I was sent up opposite him and Bill did the same as Wilfred had done. As soon as "Enterprise" touched the top sill and Bill had made fast, Wilfred gave a shrill whistle, gestured upwards with one hand and jerked the gate with the other. We whirled the paddles, water burst up under the fore-ends and the bottom gates gently but swiftly moved together with a slight thud as they closed. We drew the gate paddles gently to avoid swamping our low-down foredecks and Wilfred expressed his

31

approval. "If we'm goin' to get ahead today, that's how we'm got to work," he said.

Looking back I can see his reasoning. The day before he was in no great hurry, so we had 'pleasure-cruised' up to 'Ricky'. Now that he had brought his fledglings through the difficult turns and awkward water in "The Parks" we were from this point to start learning something about real boating. He now had a mate and if we held him up too much he could go ahead and leave us to our own devices. However, we had a little chuckle at his expense soon after as we followed him up the straight to Five Paddle Lock, which is approached by a sharp turn under a bridge restricting the view ahead. This time Wilfred was lockwheeling on foot and had got to the lock only to find it full with both top gates open and water cascading over the gates. He was, therefore, drawing off both bottom paddles just as Alan came thundering round the bend into the bridge. We saw Alan frantically whirl the gear wheel into reverse and water go funnelling under "Barnet's" counter, so we slowed right down, but "Barnet" continued to forge under the bridge. What had happened was that the draw from the lock had created a back current in the bridge hole and lock mouth which was sucking "Barnet" forward. There came a loud crash as "Barnet" hit the gates. Alan shot down the door holes, the chimney wobbled and canted crazily, while water flew out of the water can and the mopstick fell. Wilfred watched impassively. We waited awestruck as Alan climbed back onto the stern deck and apologised feverishly. Wilfred merely said, "Tut! Tut!" and turned away.

Past the Ovaltine factory with its now silent wharves and Home Park Mill, we went up to Kings Langley Lock. Above here we slacked by the footbridge for a few moments to drink a cup of tea. While we did so a large cheery-faced man rattled by on a bicycle and stopped when he saw the top gates open. Wilfred said "Barlow's a-comin'," which brought us scurrying out of the cabin, mugs in hand.

"'Ullo Wilf"

"All right Bill?"

"Boats is close to. You got the top o' the new 'uns already. Oo's these?" he nodded at us. We told him where we were going and that we were going to his firm's yard for docking. "We'll look arter yer," he said. "Shall arra goo, they'm 'ere."

We looked up towards the bend and beheld a breath-taking apparition. A loaded pair was gliding round the turn, the wooden boats sitting majestically low as they purposefully shouldered aside the still waters. The fore ends were white with red designs, while behind were the first painted deckboards we had seen, each surmounted by a scrubbed canvas belt. Behind this, neat green side cloths enclosed the hold, which was piled full of coal.

The motor boat "Ian" had dark green cabinsides, panelled engine hole doors and grained panels, similar to our own colour scheme. The spotless and gleaming Lister engine ticked away like a giant grandfather clock in a linoleumed and carpetted engine hole. A polished brass cutter deflected the apologetic-sounding exhaust. The steerer, crouched beside the paper-wrapped chimney bands, was a woman with a weather-beaten face and muscular arms. Beside her was a cheeky-looking red-haired boy.

Behind "Ian", on a short line came the butty boat "Iona", her deck board and false cratches similarly finished, a row of running blocks taking the tow line aft to the steerer. A buxom woman in a headscarf was steering with a girl of about fifteen beside her. A painted mat hung over the gorgeous stern painting and the butty helm was set off by scrubbed, white, cotton ropework. The check strap trailed behind in the water.

This magnificent ensemble epitomised everything that was best in narrow boating. Later we were to see many more similar turnouts but, though many were as good, we never saw any better than this family. I am happy to record that the Whitlock family not only became great personal friends, but also preserved their noble standards right to the very end of regular, long-distance commercial boating in the 1970's.

The pound above Kings Langley was wide but noisome—thanks again to the paper mills—and the river outfall near the top sent up a brass-blackening stench as we ploughed through it. We dropped abreast in the bottom of the "New 'Uns" and worked steadily up past Nash Paper Mills, where the vast modern unloading apparatus stood disused and forlorn. We were told at the time that the contract for bringing coal in from the Midlands had recently expired and that the British Transport Commission could not, and would not, guarantee the availability of the number of boats required weekly. Consequently the Mills refused to renew the contract. This sad tale was but one of many and ran very much contrary to the official line that canal carrying was a dying industry. Time and again we were to hear of traffic being lost or turned away to rail or road by official obstruction. Caught between the millstones of Luddite labour relations and bureaucratic sloth, the canal was inexorably being reduced to impotence.

Up through Boxmoor and the Fishery we met more loaded boats in each pound but things were quieter by the time we reached Fishery Lock. Here, there was another small shop near the lockside from which we bought more supplies. The 'Ricky' shopkeeper had persuaded us to invest in some bottles of sterilised milk, since keeping milk on a boat was difficult, even in cold weather. No milk lover, I had swallowed my distaste at this nasty-sounding substance and bought a bottle. However, it was better than I had feared and certainly was an improvement on evaporated or condensed milk in tea or coffee. Since it was now Saturday afternoon, we needed milk for Sunday plus victuals. Wilfred came with me, saying that he too needed to stock up. When his turn came, he ordered forty Players and ten Swiss rolls. The assistant was evidently used to him and did not bat an eyelid. As he pointed out, he had twenty-five tons of dates aboard that would last him to Birmingham at a pinch!

In the next few pounds we noticed more and more evidence of detergent in the water. Through Winkwell with its picturesque old pub and swingbridge the locks kept us busy, but by the top of Winkwell locks, the evil, greasy suds were over "Barnet's" deck board and rolling along our cloths. Wilfred said that this was the fault of the 'Sewerage'. Sure enough, below Lock 58 an outfall was voiding its unpleasant tide into the cut.

All the way up from Brentford it seemed that the most useful function the official mind could conceive of for the canal was that of a drain. Quite apart from pollution, one felt this was a disgraceful waste of natural organic resources. To officialdom it was cheaper to pour the sewage into the canal than reclaim it. The environmental bandwagon had not then started to roll but I felt, and indeed wrote, at the time that a society which was content to pour away its riches into rivers and canals and to use expensive chemical fertilizers instead, was one which was all too ready to treat all its resources in a wasteful and reckless manner. Time has not proved me wrong.

Berkhamstead struck me then, and still does, as one of the most attractive towns on the canal. Both canal and railway jostle for position with the main Aylesbury to London road and the little River Bulbourne, which below Lock 55 gives the canal its last natural feed. The towpath here was very broken and muddy and I walked ahead deep in conversation with Wilfred, whilst Alan was so taken with the scenery that he missed the slight turn and went up the Bulbourne instead. Having proved to his own satisfaction that the Bulbourne was not navigable for loaded craft, we had to pull him out. Wilfred shook his head and said, "Tut! Tut!"

Two locks up, at Broadwater Number 53, a gang of urchins appeared on the lockside and were encouraged by Wilfred to push and shove the beams. When the lock filled and the urchins had pushed open the top gate, Wilfred opened his ticket drawer, took out a handful of small copper and silver coins and, with a grand gesture, threw them to the boys, who scrambled like puppies for the largesse. Then, taking off his trilby with one hand as he spun the gear wheel into neutral with the other, he raised his hat above his head at arms length, shouted "Wagons, roll!" revved up his engine and clutched in. Water poured over the bottom gates, black smoke shot skyward, "Barnet" lurched forward and the children screamed and danced in sheer delight.

On and upward we plodded: Sweeps Two, Broadwater, Gas Two, Bushes, Northchurch, Dudswell Two. Until through the gloomy murk of late afternoon, the gates of Cowroast Lock loomed up to signal the end of our long climb out of the Thames Basin. The light was on in the lock keeper's hut and for the first time our loading ticket had to be produced. Every boat passing the summit in those days was logged and her tonnage noted. The lock-keeper told us that more boats were coming up behind us to clear Marsworth that night.

Away into the gathering dark our engines echoed through the summit cutting at Tring. By the time we reached the far end a cold rain was falling and night was closing in as we began the last stage of our joint trip down the seven Marsworth Locks (or Maffers as the boaters call it). This flight is extremely tortuous and it was perhaps as well that Wilfred was with us to pilot us round the turns in the darkness. I lockwheeled to the bottom lock. The bottom pound is lengthy and, after the lock filled, silence fell—rain dripped off the leafless hedge. Then came the distant growl of "Barnet's" Petter in chorus with the popping of our own Armstrong. The sound grew louder and first the glow, then the gleam of twin headlights appeared as our boats came plodding down the pound; the twin eyes picking up garbled reflections from the rain and wind broken surface.

Just below 'Maffers' the Aylesbury Arm branches off, so it was here that we had to part company with our friends. Somehow it did not seem just two days that we had been with Wilfred. We were rapidly discovering that there is a comradeship engendered by "buttying" (working boats together) which forms a bond between men and women which is not easily broken.

Our farewells were short and sweet. The lock-keeper was hovering chain and padlock in hand, waiting to lock up and a loaded pair of uphill boats were advancing towards us. Wilfred called, "Ta ta!" and threshed out of the lock. We followed in the pouring rain, slipping round the oncoming boats. The pair coming towards us dropped abreast and both had rain sheds. This was a construction of wood and canvas which fitted over the slides in wet weather. The shed had a slit like a letter box in the front for the steerer to look through and my main impression of this occasion was of two pairs of eyes peering at us out of the slits. By the time we had passed them Wilfred had vanished into the night, so we slipped out of the main line and tied with our fore-end by the top gate of the first lock of the Aylesbury Arm.

Next morning we regarded a chilling vista of ranked black gates and white handrails which seemed to stretch for miles down the Vale of Aylesbury. There are, in fact, sixteen locks in the five miles or so of the Arm, but most of these are clustered at the Marsworth end and being narrow locks were, we found, quick to work. The morning was fine after the night's rain and the buds in the hedgerows were showing tiny signs of breaking after the chill of winter. The eighth lock has a bridge leading to the village of Wilstone, but after this the signs of habitation receded. The contrast between this rural solitude and the bustle of Berkhamstead, a few short miles away, was startling. Also, the character of the canal had changed. The main line, for all its decay, still had the feel and atmosphere of a trunk commercial route; the paddle gear, stumps, ropeworn grooves in brick and ironwork, all had a look of everyday use; the mud on the towpath had the tyre marks of lockwheelers' bicycles and the bridges had smudge marks made by spluttering exhausts and smeeching chimneys. Down the Arm everything looked as if it was hardly used. Tyre marks were absent from the towpath and in places the brown, dead sedge of winter left a mere boat's width in the centre of the canal. It was all the more welcome, therefore, to see, framed in a bridge hole, as we 'popped' our way down the lengthy pound above the twelfth lock, the green deckboard of an uphill boat rising in the lock. By the time we had come through the bridge the boat was out and the lock being emptied for the butty. We shut right down and coasted into the bank opposite the motor. It was another Willow Wren pair, "Sandpiper" and "Teal", both ex-Fellows, Morton iron boats. The boatman, known as "Phippy", was a thin figure with bib and brace, cloth cap and a dewdrop on the end of his nose. He greeted us affably and informed us that we were

36

ordered to pick up an empty motor boat in Aylesbury Basin and deliver it to Braunston. Phippy had worked it down with his pair loaded with timber but now his daughter had left him to get married, so Stanley had told him to leave it in Aylesbury for us to pick up. This transaction had been carried out over the telephone on Friday, while we were 'pleasure-cruising' with Wilfred.

Phippy proceeded to give us detailed instructions on how to start the engine. "It's a bleedin' cow," sniff, "the fritchin' rings are gone an' yer can't get compression," sniff. We asked if anything else was wrong. "Nah! Nah! Get 'er a-goin' an' she'll run like an old shoe."

The butty was now floating out through the top gates, so Phippy threw a cross-strap from its fore-end into his stern stud and motored forward. He raised a horny hand as he passed and called "Don't you young gents bend my motor," then sniffed and clattered off.

Unfortunately, it being Sunday morning, the "Red House" by the thirteenth lock was not yet open. Sadly, I was never to have another opportunity to visit this wonderfully isolated pub, as it lost its license soon after—thus another pub of character vanished from the scene. We went steadily ahead down the long straight, running nearly due West and the grim bulk of Aylesbury Gaol loomed ever nearer. After the fourteenth lock near Broughton the country became less open, youths with airguns stalked the towpath, rubbish began to bestrew the banks, pylons closed in and more trees and houses appeared.

Beyond the fifteenth lock the canal became distinctly urban. Now it became necessary to ease back at every bridge hole in order to listen for the tell-tale labouring of the engine which announced a bladeful of wire or similar rubbish slung into the canal by the locals. We were almost at our journey's end. Suddenly the canal widened out into a basin with several boats, including "Thaxted", Phippy's ex-motor which was still in British Waterways livery, coal wharves, timber wharves and pleasure craft moorings. We slipped alongside Cousin's coal yard, about an hour's drive from Reading by car. Less than a week had elapsed since leaving the Kennet, but a whole new lifetime of experience was opening up.

3

The Fields & Long 'Uns

Sunday lunches were cooking in Aylesbury when we tied up. There was a nearby pub which did sandwiches, so thither we went. In the afternoon we examined Phippy's "bleedin' cow", the motor boat "Thaxted".

She was lying beneath the overhanging roof of Richard's timber yard, where our cargo was destined for. We opened her up with the key Phippy had given us and surveyed the engine. It was a twin cylinder hand-start National and neither of us was very certain how it worked—though Bill had seen something similar in the twin Russell-Newberry engine John Gould had salvaged from "Colin".

There followed about thirty minutes fruitless cranking and dropping of compression taps. As Phippy had so rightly said, there was no fritching compression. We were both chorusing our ribald opinion of the wretched machine when a figure appeared in the engine hole doors and with a most upper crust accent asked if we were having trouble.

"I always drop lubricating oil in the top of mine when she gets like this," he said after trying his arm unsuccessfully at starting. In order to humour him, we poured some down the air intake and into the rocker case. Bill whirled the handle, I dropped the compression tap and Bill was nearly jerked off his feet. There came an encouraging bang and cough, followed by dense smoke from every aperture, which settled to a contented chugging as the engine picked up. Our helper smiled the smile of the successful prophet.

After dark we had supper and sat in the cabin making toast. As catering and supplies officer, I had traded some extra groceries with Wilfred for some bags of steam coal which had been his 'perks' on his last trip supplying the steam dredger. It was a cold frosty night and we drew up the fire well. I sat on the cabin steps with my back to the side doors toasting bread with a long piece of iron wire fashioned into a toasting fork. Bill retreated to the far end of the bed as the Pooley Hall Colliery's 'best' did its stuff. The heat was so intense that I opened the door for some fresh air, only to find to my horror that the cabin chimney was beneath the shed roof. Sparks and flames were roaring out of the chimney pipe and playing round the roof supports. We hurriedly loosed off the stern and shoved into the basin, narrowly averting a catastrophe. Fortunately for the timber yard's insurers, the woodwork of the canopy must have been wet through with the recent rain and next morning we could see no signs of charring.

We awoke the next morning to a gorgeous smell wafting in our direction from a nearby bakery. This resulted in my being sent to investigate and I was able to obtain two fresh-baked crusty loaves. I think we ate one each for breakfast.

The next few hours were what old boaters call "billy bally work", as we set to chucking out and stacking the timber. It took us four and a half hours, for which we earned the princely sum of 48/-between us. It worked out at about 10/- per hour, which was not a bad rate for those days. The carriage rate was, I think, 15/- per ton—which was about top rate for sub-contracting. On the short haul, canal carriage was still both economic and reasonably profitable, but the sum of £9 earned for some eighteen hours work for two men and a boat does not stand much comparison with current remuneration. However, putting a third of the carriage rate to the company and allowing another 4/- per ton for transhipping at Brentford, we netted nearly £8 each for half a week's work. This was almost as much as my London salary for a week. Of course, two-handed single-motor-boat working was highly extravagant and we realised that to make a regular living we needed a pair of boats. Our earnings, based on the same reckoning, for forty tons would have been £18 each which was good money indeed for the time. The sub-contract rate favoured by Willow Wren implied that the carrier must find his own boats, fuel and labour, but not tolls or cargo insurance. The majority of boaters, however, worked on a direct labour basis whereby the company provided boats, fuel and all out-goings, merely paying the boatmen a wage based on tonnage out of which he had to provide a crew.

Had timber handling been improved, as Morton had suggested in the 1930's, the waiting time would have been reduced, increasing productivity and making the canals fully competitive with road transport. However, this never occurred and one had the ludicrous comparison of an articulated lorry with timber in packed lengths being unloaded in minutes with fork lift truck, while we puffed and grunted in the traditional manner. If the money thrown away on unworkable experimental craft and, for instance, plastic hatch covers, by the B.T.C. in the 1950's and early 1960's had been invested in simple cargo handling machinery the commercial life of the canals could have been prolonged. Here again, organised labour opposition must take its full share of the blame.

During the unloading operations, the 'gasfitters glory', as Bill called our awning support, came to a sad end. Rolling back the awning to get at the load revealed its naked clumsiness. Out came the screwdrivers and crowbars and the whole thing speedily found its way ashore. The boat looked so much better without it that we decided to leave it off permanently.

By now it was lunchtime and after a quick replacement of the liquid we had lost that morning, we were away again. "Thaxted" started with little trouble and Bill refused to be parted from the new toy, so this time we went away with me leading on "Enterprise". Working two motors uphill on a narrow canal is easy when you know how, but does involve a certain amount of rushing about. To start with we had a good road (i.e. all the locks were ready) for a pleasure boat had come down on the Sunday afternoon and had cleared Phippy's locks for us.

For the benefit of any reader who should have to work in such a way, this is the technique. As the boat noses the double gate open— the boater having first ensured that the lock is empty (the position of the paddles helps here)—it is left in slow forward gear. The steerer jumps onto the lock tail, drops the bottom gate paddles on his side and charges up to the top ground paddle. When the boat's fore-end is about ten feet from the top gate sill, he whips this up and rushes back to the bottom gate. Then the surge of water down the chamber temporarily stops the boat and, while this is happening, he pulls one gate shut, being helped by the flush from the propellor. As soon as it is shut he jumps the gap to the opposite gate and pulls that. By this time the water from the top paddle has begun to lift the boat and is just beginning to run out of the gap, so the remaining gate is helped shut by the water. If this is done properly, no damage occurs to the lock because there is a minimum of water as yet moving out and the bottom gates mate together and come up snugly on the bottom sill. What one must look for are signs of fouling caused by bricks or rubbish preventing a proper mating. Next, one draws the remaining top paddle, then lights a cigarette while observing the scenery nonchalantly and checking that nothing on the boat is fouling the lock. When the fore-end rests snugly against the top gate, ahead gear is disengaged. Some desperadoes used to go as far back down

40

the lock as possible then go full ahead and charge, forcing the gate open against a head of water. This is not appreciated by maintenance foremen and others in like situations, but a few seconds are gained. However, it is just as well to wait until the levels are equalised, when it does no harm to let the fore-end gently nose the gate open in ahead gear. The throttle is then opened and the steerer lets the boat thresh its way up the lock on its own. When the stern is about two thirds of the way up, he draws half a bottom gate paddle, runs up to the top gate, pulls it shut immediately behind the boat and makes a flying leap onto the counter. Behind him the top gate swings gently to and the lock is emptying for the next boat.

All went well and we boated with considerable verve and élan back up the locks. I would look back from a few hundred yards above the lock to see Bill's figure flying about and the triangle of "Thaxted's" deck boad rising in the receding lock. I would then stare ahead, practising the 'black art' in which I had been initiated by Bill Grantham, of rolling my own cigarettes—using the approved "Ringers A1 Light". Of course, I should have known better. Pride goeth before a fall. Dusk was settling and the beckoning chimneys of Pitstone Cement Works were drawing ever nearer when I came into the fourth lock from the top. The sequence went as clockwork. I stood ready to draw the bottom paddle as Bill and "Thaxted" began to leave the lock below. "Enterprise" waddled forward a few feet and stopped. She had jammed in the top gate. I rushed forward and waggled the balance beam furiously but she would not budge. Back to the stern again and I put her in neutral (we had no reverse, remember) and more beam waggling followed. There came a great chattering from below the lock as "Thaxted's" fore-end nosed up to the vee of the bottom gates. Bill came and pushed, then we both pulled. We got a rope off the stern but nothing gave. The lock keeper, a doleful countryman, came out of his house and shook his head mournfully, then he said "You'm fast there, matey's."

After half an hour, by which time it was pitch dark, we got free by dint of running water from the next lock (fortunately the next pound was a very short one) to lift the fore-end, whilst drawing the bottom paddle to lower the stern and using the combined forces of the water rushing in and the water rushing out. The three of us heaved on a rope, "Enterprise" gave a wallow and drew free. The lock keeper took his rake and fished down behind the gate. He muttered and drew up a bent cashbox on the tines. Both of us rushed up with a light and the lock keeper snorted with disgust. The box was empty!

41

The next day began with one of those exhilarating mornings that occurs in late winter or early spring. The sun shone out of a cloudless sky, a fresh but not too cold breeze blew away the cobwebs as we locked back up onto the main line and turned northwards into deep water with neatly piled banks.

Marsworth is a village on a hill and the main line runs round two sides of it. There is an old shop on the waterside which was once a pub called "The Ship" and in there we restocked our supplies. A short way beyond are two locks called "Peter's Two" or "Two-below-Maffers" by the boaters, but Pitstone Locks by British Waterways, and below here we paused to, in boaters lingo, "'ave us breakfusses".

When travelling by waterway one becomes very conscious of changes in the landscape. The contrast between this rather open, windy part of the main line and the semi-secret, hedged Aylesbury Arm only a mile or so behind was marked. We had come from the lee of the hill on which Marsworth stands and now had the benefit of a bracing east wind blowing up from the wide levels of Bedford and Cambridge. White plumes from the cement works' stacks streamed over our heads towards Aylesbury and, occasionally, the flying steam of trains would surmount swaying coaches or banging goods wagons on the railway which joined us here after its parallel dive through Tring Cutting. Like the canal, the steam railway had an individuality particular to its area. Whilst the Oxford Canal, even in these days of diesels, is always associated in my mind with the Great Western Railway, the Grand Junction is almost inseparable from visions of mighty locomotives with squat boiler mountings and flailing connecting rods roaring across the countryside with their attendant maroon liveried coaches. They would be heralded by the expectant lift of an upper-quadrant signal silhouetted against the sky and watched by the silent lines of telegraph poles with their dipping wires. On that day, our breakfast spot below Marsworth gave us a full measure of this essence. The railway striding out of Tring Cutting on a lofty embankment gave the trains a worthy backcloth of pale, wintry sky. Today blue electrics zip their pantographs through a monstrous steel pergola and the particular savour which went with steam and semaphores has gone.

Beyond the railway we encountered another of life's little hazards, a swing bridge. Unlike Winkwell bridge this one had no nearby lock (at least on the uphill side) and, we speedily discovered, no operating winch. Fortunately "Thaxted" had gone first, so embarrassing moments with our lack of reverse were avoided. Beyond the bridge the canal ran into a more wooded section and from this point onward we were leaving the Thames Basin behind. The low watershed which divides the basins of the Thames and Ouse here is barely perceptible but, nevertheless, we were entering the Wash catchment and the atmosphere of a different type of countryside was becoming apparent. There are three locks here which take the canal over into clay country and they are known, after an erstwhile pub, as "Nags Head Three". Beyond them the country opened out again. The easterly wind came whipping up the scarp slopes of the Chilterns with few trees hindering its progress from the Urals. Far away to the east, smoke from the multitude of chimneys at the brickworks near Luton streamed in the breeze and scudding clouds sent shadows racing up the grassy mass of Ivinghoe Beacon. It was a breezy, fresh sort of country, very different from the populous, wooded valleys on the other side of the Cowroast. The boaters called it "The Fields".

A pair of loaded British Waterways boats was a welcome sight as we headed towards what the 'Waterways' call Ivinghoe Locks and the boaters "Corkers Two". The steerer of the motor held up five fingers as Bill passed. "'Ow are ye? You got Church Lock ready, 'ow many you made ready?" I saw Bill hold up five fingers, which indicated that he had a good road to the bottom lock of Marsworth flight, and then he turned his attention to me as his boats drew near to mine. "'Ow are ye? Where's ole Phippy gorn, Brampford?" I nodded and he grinned, "Ta ra mate". His wife on the butty nodded gravely as they swung under the Nag's Head bridge.

The massive spire of Leighton Buzzard church loomed nearer as we dropped down through Church Lock, with its lonely isolated chapel, and Grove Lock. We entered a landscape of willows and sandpits, where wharves gave evidence of sand still being loaded. Overhead a train of loaded sand hopper wagons rumbled across a railway bridge towards the main line. The barking exhaust of the locomotive clawing its way up the bank to the junction welcomed us to this, the first town on the main line since Berkhamstead. In fact, the canal ran between the village of Linslade, then in Buckinghamshire, and the town of Leighton Buzzard in Bedfordshire. An S-bend with a brick side-bridge on the towpath leading to a fine timber warehouse brought us to the main road bridge, beside which rose tall shop buildings. Through the bridge Bill was tied onto a ring on the towpath, so I dropped abreast and shut off my engine ready for lunch. We did not risk shutting off "Thaxted's" National, although it had started easily enough that morning and had run, as Phippy

43

forecast, like an old shoe.

After lunch we headed off through more budding pussy willows and passed our first hire boat base since leaving the Thames. It was run by the Wyvern Shipping Company, a firm just becoming established, which used reconstructed ex-working craft to accommodate passengers. There were then hardly any purpose-built steel hulls and precious few wooden ones on the canals. Such hire fleets as did exist generally used adapted river-type designs with petrol driven engines. 'Wyverns' seem to have been one of the pioneers, if not the first, in using craft whose hull, shape, build and diesel engines were eminently suited to the canals. With their smart but practical livery of black hulls and blue cabins lined in red, they were a good advertisement for the embryo hire cruising industry. They imparted an air of prosperity and progressiveness to what was then a general atmosphere of decay and apathy. The canal here ran along the foot of a wooded bluff and presented as pretty a setting for the start of a holiday as one might wish.

Leighton Lock appeared next, with its trim, whitewashed lock cottage and a large Italianate mansion behind. Below here the canal wound its way down a wooded valley past Old Linslade, and high above the railway came bursting out of Linslade Tunnels. There was a ventilation shaft on the hill from which smoke suddenly belched volcanically as an express hurled itself through the tunnel.

Round sandy hills and wooded crests the canal continued past Linslade Church. I later found that this, the longest pound since Tring Summit, was called the "Jackdaw Pound". One other curiosity was the surviving pub at Old Linslade which was an old brick and timber building called "The Globe". It probably antedated the canal and was certainly one of the last isolated hostelries left. As we went northwards further away from the large towns, we were to find abundant evidence of the way in which life was draining away from the canal. "The Globe" was almost the last of these lonely outposts we were to encounter on the way to Braunston. The decline of horseboating, as well as the more recent decline of motorised commercial traffic, had sounded the death-knell of these pubs and the pleasure craft renaissance came too late to save them.

The three-odd miles of the Jackdaw Pound ended suddenly and dramatically. Under the double arches of a road bridge appeared the top gates of a lock and on going forward to fill the locks I beheld a picturesque scene. The canal descended a miniature escarpment from its narrow, sandy valley into a broad clay vale by means of three closely-set locks. The satisfying setting of side ponds, trim lock house facing a neat pump-house, a pub, black posts and white rails on the towpath and wintry-looking gardens and lawns completed the picture. In the distance, the canal wound across the fields towards Bletchley, where clustered chimney stacks symbolised the brickmaking industry of this part of the country. This agreeable spot epitomised the canal nomenclature. The locals called it "Three Locks", British Waterways Soulbury Three and the boaters "Stoke Hammond Three."

Down the next pound and through another swingbridge we went to Stoke Hammond Lock. Here the less pleasant aspect of the canal's administration became apparent. We had already noted the lack of dredging in some of the pounds this side of the summit and some of the lock gates had been distinctly ricketty, but the contrast between here and the Three Locks just a mile or so back was startling. Presumably because the public did not frequent this lonely spot, it was allowed to subside into a state of decay which was barely compatible with safety—but there again it was only regularly used by boatpeople! Weeds sprouted from the gates, the lower handrails wobbled back and forth and the side ponds were choked with mud and rushes. It was late afternoon, rain was threatening and the atmosphere was thoroughly depressing.

Down the next pound the canal wound river-like through the fields to run parallel to the road from Leighton Buzzard to Bletchley. The day began to fade into drizzle and cheerfulness was improved neither by the sight of an old Seddons butty lying forlornly beside an empty wharf, nor by the fact that the pound badly needed dredging. With headlight gleaming from the fore-end I picked my way down through Water Eaton towards Fenny Stratford. The roofs of the houses along Watling Street rose above allotments and on the northwest side of Fenny Bridge a neon sign in the shape of the Star of David shone out above the road. Through the bridge my headlight caught the stern of "Thaxted" tied against the towpath. Of Bill there was no sign, so I gingerly slid abreast, tied up and made for the galley to cook some supper. Some minutes later, Bill returned greatly excited. He had walked to the lock and met the first loaded pair of Willow Wrens. They were two small boats called "Crane" and "Heron" captained by Ray White, a boatman we had heard much of. With a load of fifty tons or so of coal, these boats presented a remarkable sight, being loaded so as "sparrers 'ud drink off the gunnels" or "ring 'ole deep", as the vivid boating expressions went.

Ray, a slight figure invariably dressed with plimsolls on one end and a beret on the other, was an odd-man out amongst boaters. He was not born to the job and had gone boating for similar reasons to ourselves. He was an I.W.A. member, highly articulate and very well-read, especially on the subject of canals and railways. He and Stanley, the clerk, got on well and exchanged books and gossip. He was also a mine of information on the subject of bus and train time-tables and, unlike most boaters whose topographical awareness did not extend far beyond the towpath hedge, Ray had a wide knowledge of the surrounding countryside and its history. Unfortunately, he had no interest in pleasure boating which was a pity, for he would have made an excellent captain for a pair of hotel boats. He was also a teetotaller, so opportunities to socialise with him were rare. Boaters were rather in awe of him, although Margaret, his wife, was well liked by the women.

After supper we investigated the neon-lit star. It was not a syna-gogue or the Fenny Stratford Zionist Club but the trade-mark of the Northampton Brewery Company. At Fenny Bridge we crossed Wat-ling Street for the first time. We were entering the ancient Danelaw and accents began to change from the burr of "Buckenamshurr" to the distinct long 'u's' and short 'a's' of the Midlands. The beer and the pubs likewise altered. The lighter mild was very palatable to southern tongues used to Simonds bitter and black mild and the pubs became more austere yet full of character.

Ray White woke us the next morning as he stormed past. It was another crisp, blue morning. The sun made his brasswork gleam and the scrubbed plaits of rope on the rudder post stood out proudly as he swept by. Smoke curled from the chimneys and lingered in the archway of the bridge behind him. As we refilled "Enterprise's" water tank by the lock, we heard the chatter of a diesel from behind and an empty pair of 'Waterways' boats came forging round the turn. Fenny Lock is only a shallow one and the boats had hardly stopped moving before the lock was empty and they were away. We watched the bright stern of the butty slipping behind the bare towpath hedge towards Simpson and then started ourselves.

Fenny Lock was the end of our descent from Tring. The next pound was nearly twelve miles long and we would not converse again, barring accidents, until we reached the next lock some three hours later. I began to understand Wilfred's point about loneliness. That morning the pound was well up (i.e. there was plenty of water in it) and we made good time. I began to look for mile stumps and to check them against my watch. Every fifteen minutes one would pass by, indicating that we were averaging four miles per hour. After a sharp bend near Simpson signs of habitation began to fade.

46

Some three miles or so further on from Fenny we came into rolling open country beyond Peartree Bridge and we swung backwards and forwards across the landscape, our direction indicated by the winding hedge. At Linfold the canal changed its general direction from northwards to westwards as we left the valley of the Ouzel and ran up the valley of the Ouse. A lofty spire appeared on the northward horizon. It was to be almost continually in sight for hours as we moved away from the deserted lands adjoining what was then a tiny village called Milton Keynes, into warmer, more populous country.

After a slight tussle with shallow water near the Newport Pagnell railway bridge, we ran round a bare hillside to see the tall chimney of Wolverton Works smoking bravely in the brisk northerly wind. Now the canal really boxed the compass, turning south, then west and finally northwards again as our engines shouted under the long mainline railway bridge at Wolverton. By now I had a feeling of mounting excitement, for I knew we would soon be entering on the most dramatic section so far, where the engineers had been forced to negotiate the natural obstacles of the River Ouse and the North-amptonshire hills. It seemed as though we would never reach the Wolverton Aqueduct which I so much wanted to see, but eventually we turned through a bridgehole onto a long straight which narrowed perceptibly half way along. After a large timber yard on the left, the land began to fall away and soon we were riding along on the crest of a great embankment. The aqueduct itself seemed quite insignificant until we reached it and then for a moment the boats were apparently suspended in air. On the right was the railed-off towpath, on the left a sheer drop of some forty feet to the river. Then it was gone and Bill was waving to indicate the low-down deckboards of a 'Waterways' pair creeping slowly out of Cosgrove Lock towards us.

The Ouse was the actual boundary of the Danelaw of Alfred's time and was still a tangible frontier. Behind, across the valley, the red Victorian terraces of Wolverton marched neatly up the hill. Ahead, stone cottages with steep, pitched roofs—some still thatched, with eyebrow windows—or buildings of mellow dark brick, straggled up the slight hill beyond the lock, where the canal cut the main street in two. It became obvious that the South was behind us.

A fine, old, seventeenth century house nestled close to the church against a backdrop of bare elms whose topmost branches held the reddish tinge of early spring. Before the house, meadows ran gently down to the canal bank. The rush-filled and long-disused Old Stratford and Buckingham Arm joined the main line immediately above the lock. It is worth remembering that the British Transport Commission were then actively engaged in dismembering and filling in this Arm despite the I.W.A. and other objectors. Less than a decade later, the B.T.C.'s successors were supporting, unsuccessfully, a scheme to re-open it, but too much official vandalism had been allowed and planned in the interim. As a result a potentially valuable amenity for the town of Buckingham has been lost for ever.

About a mile further on, a group of cottages lay clustered round a still functioning lonely pub—"The Navigation"—which looked drear and chilly in the grey light of what had become an overcast day. The country was bleak and open here and several deserted farms only increased the atmosphere of desolation. After "The Navigation" no major roads crossed the valley and the villages turned their backs from the canal and clustered on the hill tops. The tall spire of Hanslope Church we had seen at Linford was now about two miles away across the wide, lonely valley.

Beyond Yardley Gobion Wharf, the hills began to close in and it became evident that the crossing of the watershed could not be delayed much longer. The cut twisted back and forth, avoiding the green shoulders of the outliers of the uplands.

As we neared Grafton Regis—perched on its eyrie above the valley—a blue-painted crane jib rose above the hedge and we slowed down to pass a new looking mud-hopper being unloaded by a British Waterways grab crane. Nearby was a business-like wooden tug about to set off in our direction with an empty hopper. The workmen were the first 'Waterways' gang we had met. They waved cheerfully with cigarettes spiked into their round, cheerful, red, country faces. Through Grafton Wharf bridge the cut began a long sweeping curve to the right and as I followed it round I beheld a strange phenomenon on the left hand side.

A long sloping spur ran down this side and, slightly to the left of dead ahead, a tall thin chimney was jetting steam upwards beyond the skyline of the spur. As I got further round the turn, I noticed that the cut was turning back on itself, opening up a view further into the hill country. The view was blocked by a stout-looking church tower some two miles or so away on a hill top. The chimney was now evident as belonging to a steam dredger whose jib and iron cab were coming into view. A cessation of smoke and steam allowed me to see the jib swing round. There was a visible splash as the boom fell, then the dredger lurched, steam shot skywards and up came the dripping grab. Back swung the jib over the waiting hopper, the grab yawned suddenly, vomiting its load and the steam died away. As Bill approached operations stopped and a cheery, stout man in a blue bib and brace with a cap on the side of well-brushed, dark hair and the inevitable white cigarette clamped into his red face leaned out of the cab. "Ho there, me old dook! Are ye'all right?" he called to each of us as we passed. We had not yet realised that this was the standard Northamptonshire greeting, to be answered by "Whee-oop there mairt," but our interlocutor did not seem to mind our ignorance. The boats slowly slipped along the side of the dredger pontoon to be met with a warm scent of oil, steam and coal smoke. The chimney smoked above the long, low steel roof of the boiler room and in the cab steam sizzled from pipe joints and gauge glasses twinkled. As the dredger faded away behind and the gang repositioned the hopper I heard the engine start to clatter, and steam once again snorted from the exhaust.

Bill was gesticulating and waving from in front as I turned towards him. A brownish grey smeech of smoke was rising from behind the towpath hedge where the canal bent out of sight and faintly, over the sound of my own engine, could be heard the distinctive growl of a PD2 diesel. Sure enough brass-rimmed chimneys appeared ahead as I swung round the turn, sliding towards me under the overhanging willows where the deep water lay. It was another 'Waterways' pair, so I picked up the bugle, turned round and rasped it at the dredger. One of the men looked up and I pointed towards the oncoming boats. He waved in acknowledgement and began hauling the hopper out of the way again.

The oncoming captain had seen this pantomime and raised a horny claw in greeting, "Thanks mate, 'ow are yer? You got the top o' Stoke ready." His wife on the butty smiled pleasantly—it seemed one only needed to perform some small token service to get a smile, rather than a suspicious stare, from the women.

Two long overflow weirs on the towpath led to the bottom lock of the Stoke Bruerne flight of seven locks. The hilltop tower turned out to be Stoke church; as we began our climb up into the hill country it dominated the surrounding scene. Evidently the empty pair which had passed us at Fenny Lock had gained considerably on us, for the loaded pair had set all seven locks in our favour so, with no lockwheeling to do, we went up abreast in some style. Secretly I was a little nervous at the prospect of Blisworth Tunnel looming ahead. The valley was narrowing and with the hills rising in front at the same time, we would soon have to face the prospect of one and three quarter miles of blackness and goodness knows how many oncoming loaded pairs. "Thaxted" had no headlamp, so it was agreed that I should go first and light the way. I had never been through a long tunnel without a towpath before. Accordingly, I set about more of Billy Grantham's black art and in each lock and up each pound carefully rolled, licked and put in a tin on the slide a number of cigarettes ready to smoke in the depths.

I had only seen one picture of Stoke Bruerne and that was in the Waterways Cruising Guide to the Grand Union Canal. This made it appear a most delightful and picturesque place. The village did not seem to shun the canal like the settlements further back. A double-arched bridge led into the top lock and on this chilly, grey March afternoon I caught my first sight of this place, which has become the most famous of canal villages and, incidentally, my home for longer than any other place in my lifetime.

Two figures appeared near the lock side as we rose. One was an elderly lady with white hair and a dignified mien. She wore a blueish habit and a white headdress and bustled towards us with her arms opened wide. "My dear boys, who are you working for?" We needed no introduction to gather that this was the far-famed Sister Mary Ward.

Born in Stoke Bruerne in the 1880's, she had been partially crippled as a small child and had been forced as a result to train abroad as a nurse. She had been a colleague of Edith Cavell, eventually returning to England to marry and nurse her ailing father. Sister Mary became interested in the welfare of boatpeople and virtually exhausted her small fortune in caring for and nursing them. Eventually the B.T.C. had granted her a miniscule pension and this most Christian old lady had continued to nurse and care for her chosen flock. In return, she had won the fierce and undying loyalty of boaters. Although I was to hear quaint tales of her medicinal methods later on, we never heard an ill word said against her by any boater. She was one of those straightforward characters who, with all her little foibles, could only be described as loveable. Our one and only meeting was destined to be brief. She wished to know if we were in good health and did we need any medicine. Sheepishly I asked her for some aspirin. She produced an enormous tin containing a dozen for which she refused any payment. She watched as we churned away northwards with a beatific smile on her sweet old face.

The other character that we met here was the lock keeper; a stocky old man with a hawk-like face and white hair peeping from his cloth cap. He regarded us intently with rheumy eyes and said,

"Readin' folk ain't you?" Bill bridled at this—as a good Newbury man would. Then the old man continued, "You knows my son, John". It suddenly registered that John James of "Jason", who bore so much responsibility for my subsequent career, had a lock keeping father. I told him this was indeed so and he beamed. I explained that we were en route for docking and he gravely wished us a good season to come. Since, to the best of my knowledge, there were then only five other passenger-carrying narrowboats at work in the whole country, the industry was very intimate and all were interested in one another's well being.

One other person watched our progress. A tall, thin, lugubrious-looking elderly man with a Doberman Pinscher dog stood on the bank. This, we were later to discover, was Colonel Ritchie, one time Adjutant of the South Staffordshire Regiment and Provost Marshall of West Berlin, now resident with his wife aboard the converted narrowboat "Lupin". Otherwise the canalside was deserted. The average age of the inhabitants of Stoke Bruerne seemed to be high.

I led the way now as the canal narrowed and wriggled its way up an ever-steepening defile and, as we rounded a slight turn, the entrance to Blisworth Tunnel came in sight. A simple brick face was crowned with bare trees on the rising ground behind. Just as I entered it I glimpsed a tiny oval of light. It was a day when smoke and fumes were not hanging in the air, despite the traffic of the morning, hence the far end was visible.

As I entered, the most noticeable feature was the noise. The chattering of the engine, to which I had grown accustomed, suddenly achieved shattering proportions as the dark brick-work threw its sound back and forth. "Thaxted" loomed into the entrance behind me with Bill silhouetted against the light. With great aplomb I lit one of my waiting cigarettes and promptly ran against the wall. Trying to regain my sense of direction and peering vainly for my headlight, I hit the other side then ducked as I became conscious of sooty brickwork whizzing past my left ear. Luckily "Enterprise's" low profile meant that she did not catch her cabinside. Not so with "Thaxted", which I could sense rather than see close behind. To the drumming of the engines was added a deep booming as her high-riding steel hull struck one wall or another while Bill desperately tried to find his way. I put on the engine room light and opened the stern doors to try and light the way for him, but until our eyes became accustomed to the gloom it was a desperate struggle. Suddenly the fore end was lit by a ghastly white glow as it passed beneath a dripping ventilation shaft. I glanced upwards to the distant circle of sky and got my eyes full of drips as a reward, while the glowing end of my cigarette sputtered and went out. With soggy tobacco clinging to my lips, I blew the remains over the side and reached for another. My tin, when I eventually traced it, was awash inside and all my carefully prepared roll-ups were ruined.

It occurred to me that Bill's lot might be improved if I rigged up a spotlight. We had a small one which clipped into a socket beside the engine room hatch so, after a few moments of groping to locate it, I plugged in. Immediately the tunnel sides leaped into life in a profusion of brown brick streaked with ochrous hues. Stalactitic formations glistened on the walls, some of them several inches thick, seeming to disprove the theory that stalactites take a thousand years to grow an inch—according to this theory Blisworth Tunnel would then be the work of the Belgic tribes who first settled in Northamptonshire about the time of Christ.

Slowly the waning Stoke end of the tunnel dwindled to the size of the waxing Blisworth portal, fading into a reddish tint with our joint exhaust fumes. Then, above the noise of the engine I heard the sound of approaching waterfalls and, in the wan light from another shaft, beheld a curtain of falling water. I held on until the last minute as the mini-Niagara rushed towards me along the open hold then, as it drummed on the cabin top, I abandoned the tiller and dived into the engine hole. Water thrummed above me on the skylight and splashed onto the foot board, then it was gone and I saw "Thaxted's" fore-end disappearing ghost-like in the deluge. Seconds later I heard Bill yell as icy water went down his neck.

Suddenly I realised that I could see reflections on the stove chimney bands and the separation of the dark water from the tunnel walls—my eyes were getting accustomed to the dark. Two more ventilation shafts came and went and as the tunnel end drew nearer the features of the cutting beyond became visible. I no longer needed the headlight or spotlight and switched them off. The opening grew larger and larger then abruptly, the fore-end glided out into the light. The banging of the engine changed to its accustomed popping as I emerged into a grey afternoon with cabin top glistening from the moisture of the tunnel. "Thaxted's" high fore-end cratch came towering out behind me; her fore-end shoulders streaked with red brick dust and being steered apparently by a negro. The negro blew out his cheeks and removed his waterproof hat to reveal Bill's fair hair. I smirked to myself. "Thaxted's" exhaust, like that of all working boats, rose vertically about ten feet in front of the steerer.

Phippy had removed the cutter (a small brass hoop which fits over the top to deflect the blast away from the tunnel roof) and consequently Bill had suffered a barrage of soot and brick particles from the roof.

Glancing at my watch I saw that we had taken twenty five minutes to come through. Now it was all speed to Buckby some twelve miles or so ahead—or so we hoped.

We had come through the watershed between the Ouse and the Nene valleys and were now running through a distinctly upland region. The canal twisted through another wooded defile away from the tunnel, then curved round the edge of Blisworth village and past a tall brick mill which was used as a 'Waterways' Traffic Depot. Although the countryside was pastoral, it was more rolling and significantly more prosperous-looking than the land further back. There were fewer derelict or empty farms, and silos, concreted yards and smart buildings were signs of money being reinvested—yet the spectre of agricultural depression was still there and loomed from time to time in the shape of tumble-down barns and antique, rusting machinery in the fields. On this pound we were to see, more than ever, the melancholy spectacle of de-licensed pubs (I counted nine between Blisworth Bridge and the bottom lock of Buckby), and disused, decaying wharves underlined the stagnation of the canal and its environs.

Below the Northampton branch railway at Blisworth we churned as a cluster of buildings by a hump-backed bridge rose on the skyline. This was the "Arm End" as boaters called it, Gayton Junction according to British Waterways and "Blis'orth Arm" to the locals. It was our first junction since Marsworth. Here another narrow branch led northwards to the town of Northampton. Unlike the Aylesbury Arm, it was not a dead end but led to the River Nene and was regularly used by boats carrying wheat to Wellingborough mills.

On we went, swinging back and forth, by Gayton village with its pinnacled church perched high above the Vale of Rothersthorpe; by Banbury Lane where the signal-box, crouched in the lee of a shoulder of hillside, sent up a pothering cloud of smoke from its stovepipe; over the great bank by Bugbrooke and through the shallow cutting beyond, past a poplar-fringed gasholder set incongruously in the deep countryside; by Heyford Wharf, site of a derelict ironworks, a deserted pub and a coalyard which turned its back on the canal; through the Heyford Deeps where the boats surged forward with an abandon rare on the canals; by a neat white cottage flanking narrows where there had once been a swing bridge; past houses with high pitched roofs looming over the canal at awkwardly skewed bridgeholes; by Flore village and its old, brick watermill shyly hiding across the valley; to the bridge at Stowe Hill with its water tap, Company house and the first pub still in business on the waterside since Stoke Bruerne. Dusk was descending, cars and lorries with headlights full on roared above our heads as we came under the modern concrete span of the A5.

By now "Thaxted" had regained her place in front. With darkness gathering her lack of a headlight and the fact that there was still a good three and a half miles to the bottom of Buckby Locks made us dubious about the prospect of venturing much further. However, the distance between the boats prevented anything more than simple semaphoring and we pressed on. As we drove into the sharp turns beyond Weedon Bridge the problem was solved for us as "Thaxted" picked up a bladeful of rubbish. Coughing black smoke and sparks, she slowed to a crawl and floated slowly past a deep water tying-up place close to and above the A5 and a derelict garage. We caught the boats abreast and fished a tangle of wire and rope from under the counter. Bill announced, "I've about had enough, what's for supper?"

We washed and sat eating our supper, listening to the wireless and mulling over the day's adventures. At about half past eight a throbbing noise drowned the BBC and, before we could get up the slide to look out, there was an appalling crash. The boat shook and smoke puffed out of the top of the stove. A stentorian voice called, "Bloody silly place to lay abreast!" As we were strangers and it was pitch dark we had not realised that we were lying on a sharp turn in the very place where loaded boats had to travel. Consequently, a pair of Birmingham-bound 'Waterways' boats had struck us a glancing blow. We hastily grabbed a torch, pulled up a few yards and singled out. We had two small oil lamps which we lit and mounted on the fore and aft extremities of "Thaxted" to warn any other night-owlers. Whilst we did this, I saw a light moving slowly through the trees on the other side as an empty pair, riding high, glided round the turn. It was "Ian" and "Iona" on their way back to reload. Bill Whitlock's cheerful face loomed up on the gang planks as they passed. "We'll tell 'em you're a-comin'," he called.

"I hope we're not in your way," I said, but Rose Whitlock at the tiller of the butty just laughed. Her face was lit by the golden glow from the cabin lamplight, the two children crouched either side and a primus stove roared cheerfully by her feet.

"We knows our way around," she replied. "We ain't like 'Grand Unions' you know." She implied by this remark that she knew what it was to have to pay for damage to the boats, unlike the big carriers' men who just had any necessary repairs done by the firm.

We awoke the next morning to another blue-skied, frost-rimed day. After a hurried breakfast and a quick cup of coffee, we settled to our morning ritual of starting the "bleedin' cow". By now we had got it off to a fine art and only a few minutes passed before rings of blue smoke chuffed contentedly from the exhaust stack. Loosing off, we moved round Railway Turn, a very sharp hairpin bend caused by the cut following the contours of a small re-entrant valley. The canal seemed close enough to the railway to touch passing trains. On the other side of the line, a branch line led off into the hills towards the tall mast at Dodford. A goods train was awaiting clearance onto the main line, its locomotive sending a roaring plume of steam skywards from its safety valves.

Beyond the A5 bridge, where love messages from boat children adorning the walls gave the lie to the theory that all boaters were illiterate, we ran into woodland known as Brockhall Spinneys. A droning noise began to get louder and louder, betokening the advent of the M1 motorway (then only complete in truncated form from Watford, Northamptonshire to near Watford, Hertfordshire) but before we came too near this buzzing intrusion we saw something better. Sweeping majestically round the turn towards us came a tall, painted deckboard heralding the approach of a pair of Samuel Barlows, low-loaded and going hell-for-leather. The white-painted fore-end of the motor with its red motif knifed aside the water, while behind it the butty rocketted round the turn with its steerer shoving the tiller hard over. The motor "Roger" was steered by a stoutly-built young man with brawny arms and a maroon beret pulled hard over his head. He watched us gravely as we passed and intoned in an organ-like voice, "'Ow are ye? Ooncle Bill told us yer'd be close to," as he thrashed by. The butty steerer, a wiry little man with a weather-beaten face and twinkling eyes surmounted by a trilby hat, smiled and lifted his hand in greeting. The butty "Raymond" was handsomely accoutred with all the decoration of a well turned-out boat, but the chimney bands were swathed in newspaper against the morning damp. A stout elderly lady peered up from the cabin doors and conversed with the steerer.

So it was on again, past the booming motorway and out of the spinneys, down a long straight, to where, in the distance, Buckby Bottom Lock stood ready for us. We slipped in, myself now strapping "Enterprise" in as to the manner born, and commenced our last climb to the final summit. Again we became aware of internal differences within the British Waterways system. From Fenny onwards locks and installations had been smartly painted and generally well-maintained. Now, once more, weeds sprouted from gates, handrails were rickety or red with rust, side ponds neglected and disused. Only the oil and grease on the paddles and a smart array of white painted railings by the second lock showed that the lock keeper at least cared. In view of the fact that these seven locks were among the deepest on the canal after Denham and that they drew directly off the vital summit reservoirs, it seemed incredible that leaking gates and disused side ponds should have been tolerated by the authorities. All the more so in that pumping stations had been installed to pump back lockage water to the summit from the long Blisworth Pound, yet lockage water was being wantonly wasted.

We really had entered hill country. Just beyond "Bugby" locks the Leicester section branched away to the right on its lonely plod across the wolds by Watford, Crick, Husbands Bosworth and Foxton to the River Soar and thence the Trent. This canal was completely deserted by trade. The main line ran westwards through open, rolling fields and past the feeder from Daventry Reservoir whose green, earth dam stood silhouetted against blue sky to the south.

After our experience at Blisworth, we had arranged for me to go first through Braunston Tunnel with a short line from "Thaxted's" fore-end to prevent her yawing about. I had understood that because of a double bend caused by an error in construction in the 1790's, it was not possible to see through it, so was pleasantly surprised, as I came under the tall bridge by Welton Wharf, to see a little oval of light similar to that at Blisworth.

Above the end of the tunnel was a handsome, grey house in a very derelict state. The towpath near the portal had nearly all collapsed and trees and brambles sprouted everywhere in the cutting leading up to the entrance. It was an isolated, desolate and creepy spot and I was not sorry to be swallowed up into the darkness.

This time there was no banging from astern since Bill had one of our oil lamps on the boat with him as an added precaution. He had also placed an old lock windlass over the exhaust pipe to avoid being showered with filth. Apart from a nasty moment when a brick wall appeared before us and then resolved itself into the beforementioned bend, our passage through was uneventful. Although, as L.T.C. Rolt stated in "Narrow Boat", dribbles of water came down from the roof and from air shafts, the wetness was nothing like that in Blisworth. Slowly the far end drew near and the sunlight reflecting from the water in the cutting danced on the roof and made the crystalline deposits on the bricks shimmer. Bill called out as we were about to leave and I looked back at the now indistinct south end to see the glow of a headlight about to enter behind us.

Soon after leaving the tunnel the top gates of Braunston Locks appeared and, for the last time, we caught the boats abreast and took brief stock of the new country.

That first morning I came down into Braunston was the first morning of the year with a feel of Spring to it. The sun was warming the grass on the slopes of a smiling green valley, birds were whistling, sheep bleating and buds were showing on the trees and bushes. In the distance, a rash of red council houses bestrode a ridge and a cluster of slate and thatched roofs led to the stump of a windmill and a lofty, crocketted spire. Nearby another ruined pub faced a modern-looking lock-keeper's cottage. A grey brick bridge humped itself below the top lock and the canal led down the valley under elm trees to more locks. We worked steadily down through four locks to where a long, low, brick pub crouched invitingly. A weather-beaten signboard announced that it was called "The Admiral Nelson" and painted on the facia was an announcement that "Phipps Ales and Stouts" were on sale. A cardboard sign saying "Open" was displayed in a window and above the door a black piece of wood, signwritten in white, stated that H.U. Clarke was licensed to retail beer, wines and spirits for consumption on or off the premises. It was then approximately twelve-thirty and, as we brought the boats into the lock, we were hailed from the pub door. Leslie Morton, looking prosperous in a city suit, was standing with a glass in one hand and a pipe in the other, beaming at us.

"Well done lads, that's the style. Take 'em to the yard and come up for a drink," he said. As we left the lock he stepped across and, holding the paddle spindle of the bottom gate with one hand, pipe in mouth, glass on the balance beam, he deftly released the catch and let the paddle drop. This was the one and only time I ever saw him physically touch the canal for which he did so much.

At the next lock, by a brick cottage beneath whose walls the overflow weir disappeared, a fat, balding man came out from behind the cottage and jumped aboard "Thaxted". He was Willow Wren's fitter and seemed vaguely surprised that "Thaxted" was still floating much less running. I asked where we should leave her. "Going to Barlows are you?" he asked. "Best take her down to the

'Stop'. We're a bit full up." A young man on a bicycle came clattering down the towpath.

"Boats comin' down," he called. We would not be thanked for holding them up, so we agreed that perhaps it would be as well to get out of harm's way.

The next lock was the last of our present journey. It was an interesting place. On the towpath a row of nineteenth century cottages and a larger house faced across the lock to a long enclosed dry dock, from which emitted the sound of hammering and oaths. Below the lock was another grey, brick bridge with some brick sheds and a tall, brick chimney on the towpath side. Opposite were sheds and brick buildings with the legend "Willow Wren Canal Carrying Co. Tel. Braunston 324" and beyond this was a modern sideways slip on which a steel hull was resting surrounded by the hiss, snap and blue glare of welding torches. On the water boats in all states of canal-worthiness lay jostling one another with a narrow passage through the middle. Some had chimneys and cans on the top of the cabins showing that crews were in residence. Shafts reared in the air from the bottom of butty holds and displayed long lines of washing, children shouted and cried, dogs barked and women leaned on hatches and gossiped. A loaded pair, the "Flamingo" and "Smew", (both immaculately painted and neatly sheeted in green tarpaulin) were taking on diesel oil under the supervision of a stout, jolly-looking, bespectacled man in blue overalls and maroon beret. Smoke drifted from chimneys and tillers inverted in rams' heads swung lazily to and fro in the swill from the lock. In the distance a new footbridge on the towpath seemed to collide with the end of the mass of boats.

Singling-out, we moved slowly through this tangle, greeted by friendly smiles and nods. Bill said he thought our destination lay beyond the neat brick bridge on the towpath side, so we steadily made our way in that direction. Beyond the bridge was yet another towpath bridge, this time an elegant, iron one. As the view opened out we saw the yard for which we were bound at the end of a short arm. We headed in and tied up on a vacant mooring just through the bridge. A few feet away the Grand Junction Canal ended, ninety three miles and six furlongs and one hundred and one locks from Thames Lock, Brentford. The first stage of our voyage was over. We silenced both engines and walked up to the office.

4

Spring
at Braunston

Although the yard was still called Barlow's Yard and boats were still trading in Samuel Barlow colours, the dockyard was not in fact operated by that firm any more, for they had ceased their canal trading activities a few weeks before. They had sold out to the firm called Blue Line Boats Ltd and it was to this company's office Bill and I now addressed our steps.

After the general air of decline and decrepitude so evident since Brentford, the yard was a pleasant surprise. Buildings were being modernised, gravel and white paint gave a neat effect and the place had a cared-for air. However, the new business had its feet in both camps, for it ran a hire fleet of pleasure craft as well as a fleet of four pairs of working boats and a single motor boat.

In the office, a slim secretary regarded us severely through her spectacles. I felt the same guilty feeling as when I once came under suspicion of putting a grass snake in the form mistress's desk. It was evident that she did not approve of riotous young men who turned up with strange motor boats at lunchtime. Nevertheless, with considerable hauteur, she announced our presence and we were shown into the manager's office.

The manager was another maker of canal history, Michael Streat. He was one of that great generation of people inspired by L.T.C. Rolt's "Narrow Boat", which included Robert Aickman, John James and John Gould, to whom so much is due from those who love our waterway system. He had operated a successful hotel-boat business for some years, branched out into hire cruisers and now had acquired the yard. He was a donnish-looking individual, which belied his shrewd business mind and mordant wit. His boatmen called him "Mester Streaks". It was agreed that we should meet the following morning to discuss fully the work we wanted doing, so we went in search of Mr. Morton.

The bar of the "Nelson" was empty save for Leslie Morton; a wizened ancient wearing a trilby and scarf and the landlord—a fat,

59

balding, middle-aged man who glared at us grumpily. Our opening the door set an electric bell ringing and the landlord said brusquely, "Boock oop and shoot that bloody door!"

Morton bought us a pint each, placing his change in a pile on the bar, and I looked round to take stock. There were two rooms knocked into one, the bar occupying the smaller part. The larger room had a door at the far end leading into a games room and the door by which we had entered on the canal side. On a wall adjoining the games room was the dartboard and, opposite the entrance door, stood an upright piano. Another door led out to the Gents and Ladies. Along the canalside wall ran a cushioned bench and there were several iron-framed tables and stools. These continued into the smaller part, down one side of which ran the bar. Behind it were the usual stock shelves which also contained chocolate, sweets, nuts, Ringer's A1 Light, Old Holborn, Rizla cigarette papers, Woodbines and Park Drive packets. Beside the hand pulls for beer stood a wooden firkin from which the landlord would occasionally draw himself a half pint. A clock ticked on the wall at the end of the bar above an iron grate. The landlord had the racing page of the "Daily Mirror" before him and was trying to persuade the others to back a horse that had taken his fancy.

After he had pulled our beer, he took a copious pinch of snuff from a tin, sniffed loudly and marched out. Morton said, "Bad news on the cut I'm afraid lads, 'Jam Hole' finishes next month". This was a reference to the contract held by Barlows for the supply of coal to Kearley and Tonge's jam factory at Southall. Actually, Michael Streat succeeded in renewing it until the factory closed eight years later, but this news was typical of the gloom and pessimism which surrounded canal carrying at that time. What we did not know— nor did he enlighten us—was that the crafty old rascal was trying to obtain the contract for Willow Wren. Barlows had been general coal factors, dealing with the coal on a wholesale basis and using boats as such factors would today use lorries. In some cases, such as Banbury Dairy, they had subcontracted to small, independent carriers known as 'Number Ones'. Barlows were now getting rid of their boats altogether and Morton was angling for their subcontract. He had, in fact, obtained the Banbury contract before Blue Line took over, which meant that Streat had a single motor going begging, but he never prised the 'Jam Hole' traffic away from Barlows boating successors.

That lunch time, with a captive audience, Morton was in his element. We listened eagerly as he related fascinating snippets of gossip and information. From time to time he referred to 'B-J' and plans for the future. 'B-J' was Captain Vivian Bulkeley-Johnson, the power behind the throne in Willow Wren.

Bulkeley-Johnson was, like Morton, a survivor of a generation which was virtually destroyed in Western Europe by the 1914-18 War. From an impeccable social background, he had been a Guards subaltern in that appalling conflict and was said to have been one of a relief party who found a badly-wounded Harold Macmillan sitting in a shell-hole reading a book of Greek plays. 'B-J' had risen in banking circles and had a large landed estate in Oxfordshire. After joining the I.W.A. in its early days during the late 1940's, he became its Honorary Treasurer. He and his wife were interested in ornithology, particularly water birds, and cruised the canal system in a small motor boat cruiser called "Willow Wren".

Typically of his generation, 'B-J' believed that wealth should be used for the patronage of worthwhile causes rather than be squandered upon extravagant excesses, whether private or state. To this end, he believed that the best thing he could do for the canal system and its unique culture would be to use his wealth and influence as a patron. It must be recalled that, even in the early 1960's, the idea of using canals for pleasure and amenity was greeted with widespread derision and in the 1940's and 1950's there had been no hope whatsoever of saving the waterways for pleasure use. I believe that what finally clinched the matter for 'B-J' was the widespread publicity given to the management's decision to paint out the decorative work on the nationalised narrow-boat fleet. This final straw made him resolve to put his own fleet on the canals; a fleet painted in traditional style and worked by skilled boaters whose culture and way of life would be thus retained. Above all, he wished to inject that vital ingredient, 'traffic', which the canals needed so badly. The early 1950's were a critical time, when narrow boat carrying nearly died. Had it done so, the bulk of our narrow canals would have gone with it—as very nearly happened to the Oxford Canal in 1954-5 and as had happened to most of the Kennet and Avon. At that time, the I.W.A. was still too weak to do very much to stop the trend. It was 'B-J' who held the line for a decade at enormous personal expense until a more favourable attitude began to develop amongst the authorities. He belongs, very properly, high in the Pantheon of largely ignored figures who have left their mark upon the Waterways system as surely as Brindley and Telford, and whose contributions have immeasurably enriched our whole national life.

Leslie Morton, depending on which side of the canal fence one sat, was either 'B-J's' hatchet-and-fugleman, or his trusty and resourceful adjutant. Both views had one thing in common, that Morton was absolutely loyal and devoted to his leader. This was an attitude understood and respected by boaters, if not by some of the enthusiasts and 'know-alls' who talked to them.

The ancient in the bar corner listened attentively to Morton's discourse, being consulted from time to time in such asides as, "That's so, isn't it Bill?" or, "Don't you reckon, Bill?" to which Bill would nod sagely and spread his gummy old mouth in a wide smile. At one point Morton, gesticulating as he lit a cigarette, swept his whisky glass (fortunately empty) onto the polished floor, where it shattered. We were retrieving the fragments when the landlord reappeared. Morton said, "I've folded up one of your glasses Hubert. It was taking up too much room."

Hubert scowled and grunted, "No bloody profit in this business. That's the second boogger today."

"You'll survive," said Morton cheerfully and Hubert snorted derisively.

Bill, the ancient, whistling through his gums, told us "He'd a bin round the Oxford River a time or two when he were a Josherin'," also that he had been "...up the Ippey Cut a flyin' with his dad." This meant that, when working for Fellows, Morton and Clayton, he had navigated the Thames and that, when a boy, he and his father had worked flyboats on the Wilts and Berks Canal. I had only met one boatman hitherto who had worked this long-defunct route to the West of England. He was Bill Chivers of Reading, who had died in February 1960. Although Wilf had said his Uncle Alf carried the last load to Wantage Wharf, this old chap must have been one of the last people to work right through from Abingdon to Bath in the early years of the century. He told us that one of the flyboats had survived to work on the Grand Junction until the 1930's but he did not know where it had ended up.

It was a symbolic gathering in that quiet, sunny, little bar parlour as the clock ticked its brass pendulum back and forth. Five men, four generations, each committed to the canals in different ways. We ourselves were in our early twenties, but the old one was of a generation which was our age when the century changed. Morton, most of whose youthful companions had been lost in the 1914-18 War, was the eternal survivor and Hubert came between him and us. Anywhere else the old one's tale would have been ignored. In this company it was listened to with rapt attention because it meant something to all of us.

Morton sighed when the old man finished. He carefully poured water into his new glass and saying, "You young lads, if only I were your age," strode to the window and gazed at the full lock and the rising green fields beyond the towpath hedge. "You've got the youth still in you. You could really do something with the cut." He turned round and faced us, "Now you know what it's about, Old Bill there, Hubert, those families you've met, that's what we're fighting for. It's a way of life lads. You work hard and play hard. It's pretty rough, especially on the women, but it's a dam sight better life than many folks have because there's more to it than just money." He stopped, sipped and resumed his place by the bar. "I'm getting too bloody serious. Anyway, I hope if you two booggers live to ninety five like him there, you won't be able to tell folks you worked the last boats on the Grand Union."

I asked him, frankly, how long the boats would last? He put down his glass, gathered up his change, counted it absently and put it into his pocket. "If the Government bring in licensing without delay (we've paid eighteen thousand pounds in tolls in eight years); if they put someone in charge who really cares about it; if they stop closing warehouses and wharves; if they ease up with restrictive practices in the docks; and if they stop the railway deliberately undercutting, we could survive until the year 2000. And that doesn't mean spending millions on maintenance and new schemes, but a political change. It's policies rather than commerce that's killing us. But be sure of one thing, if they don't do what I've said, you can give it two years, ten at the outside. And you know what, then? They'll have proved to their own satisfaction that narrow boating doesn't pay and that you, me, old Bill and all the rest are bloody fools," he answered.

We grinned, rather sheepishly, as he continued, "What we've got to do is to hold the fort. I know narrow boats are doomed eventually, we only built them for the Grand Union as a stopgap. It's hundred and fifty tonners, self-propelled, you want—or even bigger. But I believe the only way to get them is to hang on and make the best you can, and the most publicity, out of narrow boats until one day some Government Official gets it into his noddle that canals are a good idea. Then he'll push the idea through and get the credit, like an OBE, you know— 'Other Boogger's Efforts'—but at least our poor, old country will get the cheap transport it needs."

Hubert began gathering glasses. "About time you lot booggered off," he muttered. "I'm supposed to be shut."

He took a prodigious dose of snuff and Morton said, "Come on Bill, I'll give you a lift home." The old man creaked to his feet and hobbled out to Morton's car. I never saw him again and so never got the opportunity to find out more about boating the 'Ippey Cut'.

Outside Bill said "I'm not sure that I like Morton." I asked why. "I dunno really. I think it's because I hope he's wrong but know he's right." However, we both agreed that the landlord was rude and surly.

There was much to do over the next few days in the way of cleaning, tidying and catching up on correspondence, which was ever a problem in the confines of a boat cabin. Shopping had to be done and the remainder of the ballast put ashore. Not least, there was the boatyard and its people to get to know.

Unlike the carrying industry and the canals themselves, the boatyards generally—at least those which had survived—were beginning to feel a distinct new breath of life from the pleasure-boat revival. As yet no new boats were being built, but there was plenty of evidence that the docking facilities were by no means a thing of the past. We would have to wait our turn for the dry-dock. In fact we had to wait until paintwork and other drydocking work had been completed on another boat. This took ten days, whilst the Board of Trade Inspector was not available for a fortnight, but we had a lot to do, there was much to see and time did not hang heavy on our hands. Accordingly, when the next morning we met Michael Streat and his foreman boatbuilder, Aubrey, we were not unduly dismayed. We began, idly, wondering whether we could do some boating for someone else while we waited, and Streat said that although he did not have anything available himself, having just lost the Banbury job (which would have suited us down to the ground), we should try Morton. Hitherto we had not really considered that we should work any other boats, but as we mulled it over the idea seemed to get better and better. Unfortunately Morton had gone and would not be visiting his far-flung Imperial outpost until the following Wednesday, so, keeping it in mind, we turned our attention to the job in hand.

Aubrey was a lean, alert-looking man with a soft Devon burr. He had originally worked in West Country shipyards with fishing and inshore craft and there was no doubting his competence. He was one of the gang that had built the last wooden boat for Barlows in 1958, the "Raymond", which we had met pelting through Brockhall Spinneys the day before. His practised eye roved over our cabin work, appraising itself of the required work and then he and Streat retired, promising to give us a full estimate by Monday morning—including fitting a new brake band to our reverse gear.

Braunston overlooks a deep valley running up into the scarp slope of the Northamptonshire Wolds. To the west the land levels out towards the Vale of Avon and the plateau of Birmingham. This Midland plain is a land of low watersheds and few large rivers and, not surprisingly, is the hub of the canal system. Two routes to the Thames Valley from the Midlands pass through Braunston; the Grand Junction up which we had come, and the older, narrow route through Banbury and Oxford. Both routes pierce the watershed within fifteen miles of each other and both join up to other waterway systems. Moreover, from Braunston there are three alternative routes to the North so, insofar as the South Midlands is concerned, Braunston is the focal point. The actual village lies along the top of a ridge jutting out into the plain. It was an ancient settlement long before the canal came up the valley bottom and one could, with care, make out where the long, thin mediaeval fields had once swept down from the backs of the houses on top of the hill and over to the other side of the valley. In several places the hedgerow ended on the canal side, to be continued on the opposite bank by a row in line with it, in some parts traces of ridge and furrow ploughland showed a similar trend.

Another ancient survival was the large number of tracks and footpaths criss-crossing the fields between the village and the canal. These, often fitted with kissing gates, formed a useful and convenient network. One of these led upwards from Butchers Bridge and we followed this until near the top of the hill, where it became a lane, running between cottages. Near the end of this land a fragrant aroma from the village bakery in the High Street filled the morning air.

We went inside to find that the shelves were piled high with crusty tin loaves and cottage loaves. In front of the counter a number of air-tight, glass-topped biscuit tins displayed a tempting variety of cream biscuits. The proprietor invited us to sample one and its mouth watering crispiness induced us forthwith to buy a half pound.

Further up the street were the other village shops. The grocer's was an old-fashioned country shop crammed to bursting with merchandise, and no nonsense about self-service either. The grocer himself stood behind the counter in his brown coat of office. Behind him rose shelf upon shelf of tins, the bacon slicer stood ready to hand and overhead dangled mops, bowls, washing-up cloths and similar domestic paraphernalia. I told him we had a large order, so he rummaged for a box and started to assemble our requirements, repeating our requests in a sort of verbal shorthand.

"Half a pound of sugar please "—"half of shug"

"Half a pound of streaky bacon"—"half streak"

"Two tins baked beans"—"two whistleberries"

"A dozen eggs"—"one doz cackleberries"

He assembled the growing pile on the counter without apparently leaving his position. An arm would shoot out and the article would appear as if by magic. I asked for a tin of peaches which was on the topmost shelf and he knocked the base of the cabinet, stretched out his hand and the tin fell into it. In the meantime, he kept up a running patter with ourselves and the other customers.

At the butchers a dark-haired young man in white shirt and blue-striped apron earnestly desired us to try the beef sausages, which were homemade. Once again there was that personal service which was dying out so fast, even in small towns. It was not a matter of nosing about in a freezer, picking up various timber-like pieces of red meat and gristle, but a discussion on the weather, how long we would be in Braunston, what was to be done to the boat, who was doing it, and the liver which was cheaper this week.

We wandered back down the path to the canal as an empty Barlows pair "Kent" and "Hazel" came down from the locks abreast. We learned that this was the usual procedure when arriving at Braunston empty, provided they could get through the Willow Wren tangle without singling out. They would go to the 'Stop', which was the point outside the yard where officially the Oxford Canal joined the Grand Junction, and then back in to the arm for refuelling.

Diesel oil was delivered by a semi-rotary hand pump with gauge glasses such as roadside garages used for retailing petrol in the days before electricity was available in the countryside. Responsible for this tedious chore was an elderly ex-boater called David Hambridge. David and his wife lived in a caravan in the yard and he made himself busy as general factotum about the place. He greeted us from across the water in a voice which had the timbre of a tipper-lorry emptying pea gravel onto corrugated iron sheets. "Mester Streaks says you can tie over this side termorrer," he grated, "and there's some letters up the office for you."

We put our stores in the cabin and went to pick up our mail. "Kent's" skipper was in the office, a wiry man with a sharp face and wearing a maroon beret. He nodded affably, told us his name was

Jim and that we must have missed him while we were down the Aylesbury Arm. We walked down to the oil pump with him and spoke to his family; a neat-looking, youngish woman, a pretty daughter of about fifteen—about whom I had to speak to Bill sternly—and a younger, lively boy. Like all the Barlows families we had met, there was an air of gentility and prosperity about them and they all retained this characteristic under the flag of Blue Line until the final demise of regular, long-distance carrying in 1970.

When David had finished refuelling the pair and stowed away the delivery pipe, the boats singled out and motored off towards Coventry and the coalfields. In conversation we found out that David was an ex-'Number-One', or owner boatman. Until the 1930's most of the coal traffic on the Grand Junction and Oxford Canals was handled by such men on a subcontracting basis, either from a large consignee, such as the Oxford Co-operative Society or John Dickensons Ltd of Croxley, Nash and Apsley Mills, or for factors such as Barlows. Many of them acquired motor craft in the 1920's in place of horse boats, as David had done, and many of their boats had been built at this yard at Braunston, then run by the famous Nurser Brothers. The 'Number Ones' had had a period of great prosperity, particularly as their traffic was frequently to factories producing consumer goods or to merchants supplying prosperous areas. However, their prosperity came to an end when, after the formation of the Grand Union Canal Carrying Company in 1929, that company set about building-up and controlling its own traffic. The heavy, southwards coal traffic to the London area would balance the increasing northwards traffic in steel, copper, grain and other imports then being carried by the Grand Union's subsidiary companies. Their traffic manager was instructed to negotiate new contracts with the mills and other consignees at lower all-in rates, the boats and crews to be provided by the Grand Union. The traffic manager concerned was none other than Leslie Morton, and even though he had left the Grand Union in 1936 under a cloud, many ex-'Number Ones' still regarded him as a villain and the author of their woes. For, as a result, most of the 'Number Ones' were forced to sell their boats and labour to the bigger carrying companies.

By the time of the Second World War there were very few 'Number Ones' left but some survived the War into Nationalisation days. Among these was David, whose home port was Banbury on the Oxford Canal, but who continued subcontracting on the Grand Junction and elsewhere. He had, however, sold out to Barlows in the end for very much less than the cost of his boats. His last butty

"Fair Trader" had been laid-up on the arm behind the stores at Braunston and had eventually sunk. He now had the melancholy task of burying it with ashes and rubbish from the yard. Barlows had given him a light job round the yard and Blue Line had taken him on. His wit was pungent and, as he told us his story he would intersperse the tale with picturesque simile and vivid incident. In particular he relished his parting shot to Barlows' manager when the sale of his boats took place, "I says to 'un, best change 'er name, cos "Fair Trader's" the one thing you ain't."

We were rapidly approaching the end of our second week afloat and it was becoming evident that our wardrobes needed replenishing. There were now two drawers full of discarded clothing and the weather was wet and dull, preventing large-scale laundry activities. The vest and pants situation was nearly as bad as that of the shirts, so Bill suggested a foray to Rugby where there ought to be a launderette. Accordingly the next day, a Saturday, saw us weighed down with bulging duffle bags, catching the Midland Red bus to Rugby, some six or seven miles away. The noise and whirl of traffic seemed shattering and, although we had travelled some hundred and sixty miles, this was our first journey by wheeled transport since leaving Reading. Although Rugby is not exactly a metropolis, nor is it by any means the largest town in the Midlands, I found myself wandering about and gawping at the sights like any yokel from the outback.

On our return there were some new arrivals at Bottom Lock. "Quail" and "Kingfisher" were tied up empty by the Willow Wren yard and, opposite, by the British Waterways oil stores, being oiled up Tom James the second lock-keeper, lay "Barnet" deep loaded with coal.

Wilfred appeared from the stores, and in his poshest voice said, "Ho there my old fruit, h'are you h'admiring my Bentley?" Before we could reply he said "I sees your 'sports model' a-lyin' at Barlows Yard." There then ensued much chaffing and discussion of adventures, cut short by Wilfred announcing that he must do his shopping before the shops shut. So we parted, agreeing to meet in "The Nelson" that evening. I played a ukulele banjo at that time which Wilfred had seen hanging in our cabin the week before and he suggested I bring it with me to liven things up.

When we arrived at about eight o'clock the bar of "The Nelson" was full. There were several familiar faces besides Wilfred's. The couple we had met at Rickmansworth were there and at the end of the bar on a stool, dressed in collar and tie sat the fitter from Willow

Wren who, we found, was none other than the Landlord's son, Dennis. Behind the bar a little woman was drawing pints alongside Hubert, who paused in the act of drawing up snuff to say '"Ow do, me dooks." Darts flew perilously close as we entered the door, crashes and shouts came from the games room where a game of skittles was in progress and a tremendous reek of hand-rolled cigarettes filled the air.

Wilfred was in animated discourse with Mark from the "Quail" and his dark, attractive wife, called Dolly. Dolly motioned us over to a seat beside them and wanted to know why we had not gone for a drink with them at 'Ricky'. Once more I was struck by the direct friendliness of boaters, we had only met once in the rainy darkness beside Batchworth Lock, yet they both remembered us and made us welcome. Mark said, when we told him of our proposal to work for Willow Wren, that he thought there might be a spare pair of boats and it would be well worth asking the 'Gaffer' when he came up the following Wednesday.

By about 9.30pm several pints had been lowered, the pub was filled to bursting and someone suggested I give them a tune on 'that there banjee'. My musical ability has always been strictly limited. Beyond strumming from three main chords, I fear little can be said for it. Nevertheless, I obliged and, after a few false starts, had them singing "Daisy Bell", "Paper Roses" and similar tunes. Bill attended to the choral work and after two or three numbers we paused for breath. Instantly two full pint glasses appeared before us and voices cried "Come on, gie us some more." Towards closing time and several pints later, something prompted me to sing solo a rustic ditty with a mildly lewd flavour—a Berkshire version of "Seven nights drunk". This innocuous song brought roars of delight. As it approached its denouement where the cuckolded hero sees off his unfaithful wife and her lover with a shot gun, Hubert, his collar wide open, a mighty pinch of snuff hastening up his nasal passage, tears streaming down his cheeks, gave an ear-splitting guffaw, Wilfred banged his glass on the table and most of the company roared out the final chorus. Never had I seen an audience so appreciative. More beer appeared and shouts chorused for an encore. Hubert called 'Last Orders' so we sang a suitable song and I laid the instrument down.

When the singing died away, people began to leave but we were still talking to Dennis, Mark, Dolly and Wilfred and did not notice for some minutes that the towels were over the beer pumps and the pub was emptying. The lights went off in the games room and the main room, but the chat went on. The landlady drew a heavy maroon velour curtain across between the two rooms enclosing the bar. There was a handful of people left and I prepared to leave, but Hubert went to his firkin on the bar and said "Coom on, you two, get this down you and give us another." Sunday was well advanced by the time we left.

Sunday saw the arrival of large numbers of visitors to the yard; a number of whom found our cabin interior a source of great fascination—sticking their heads in the slide hole or peering inquisitively through port holes. Anyone who has stayed on a boat in a popular spot will be familiar with this annoying habit of the British public. Many otherwise patient and law-abiding boaters can be driven to violent acts by inconsiderate nosey-parkers. Incidentally the books on canals, quoting Rudolph De Salis I suspect, nearly always say that boaters call such people 'Gongoozlers'. This is repeated even by such people as knowledgeable in the ways of the cut as L.T.C. Rolt. All I can say is that I have never heard boaters use this word. The expression I heard used by many 'old ones' was 'Rodneys', a word current in the 1870's according to George Smith of Coalville. The younger ones called them 'Towneys'. Anyway these unwelcome attentions resulted in us pushing across the arm to a mooring indicated previously by Michael Streat, which was beside the fitters shop just up from the diesel pump.

This vantage point was destined to be our home for the next ten days and from it, framed in the arch of the side bridge, we could watch the passing pageant of boats. We discovered that about fifty five or sixty pairs of boats were still working in the South Eastern Division of British Waterways. This was mainly the Grand Union system, including the Northampton and Aylesbury Arms and the Leicester Section—the Coventry, Oxford and Ashby Canals—though there had been little or no commercial traffic over the Leicester Section, the Oxford south of Banbury or the Ashby Canal in the previous two years. From all over the system came grim rumours. The 'Runcorn Gas' (ie coal traffic from South Lancashire to Runcorn Gasworks) was "a'finishing" because the unloading gear was worn out; the number of coal boats loading at Anglesey Basin near Cannock was being cut back; Pooley Hall Colliery beside the Coventry Canal was threatened with closure; no more cocoa crumb was being boated to Cadburys at Bournville; British Waterways were to cut down to forty pairs; Apsley, Croxley and 'Jam Hole' were finishing; British Waterways were going to pack in completely next October; and so on and drearily on.

Yet the traffic, although it was a pale shadow of only a few years before, continued to move against all odds. Four pairs of Barlows, twelve Willow Wrens and at least forty British Waterways boats churned back and forth, each fleet with its own style and character. Had we but known it, the latter, which was the biggest, most imposing and in some ways the best run, had only twelve months to live.

The 'Waterways' fleet had been formed by amalgamation of the Grand Union Canal Carrying Company and Fellows Morton and Clayton fleets following the take-over by the Government in 1948. In the early days of Nationalisation the canal and the subsidiary fleets were run by the Docks and Inland Waterways Executive. After the re-organisation of the British Transport Commission they were operated under the name of British Transport Waterways, but were known for convenience as British Waterways. By 1962 the 'Waterways' fleet had no Fellows Morton boats left in trade, because their age and small size made them easy victims to cutbacks in fleet size. In 1948 the fleet had numbered approximately one hundred and seventy pairs in trading condition. In the late 1950's and early 1960's there were curious tales of mass sinkings in Harefield Flashes between Uxbridge and Rickmansworth, whilst many boats were sold out of service. Wilfred once said of Willow Wren, "Course they'm only workin' wi' our cast-offs."

Of course, as the number of boats in commission fell, the number of administrative staff rose. As Morton had said, the authorities could prove entirely to their own satisfaction that narrow boats did not pay! Like their colleagues in British Railways, the 'Waterways' officials struggled on, hampered by antiquated equipment, financial stringency and overmanning. The picture we had first seen in perspective at Brentford was even clearer now and the saddest part was the plight of all ranks in the narrowboat industry. The officials, many of whom had had honourable careers with the Grand Union or Fellows Morton, were frequently anxious to help and advise but were hamstrung by circumstances. They were frustrated men who had the will and ability to push their ancient industry forward and yet were prevented by bureaucracy. On top of this the Transport Commission had become a sort of dumping-ground for ex-officers and Civil Servants from elsewhere. Worthy as they may have been, they had little interest in or understanding of the task. Some indeed were downright hostile to canals. Many had no sympathy or rapport with the boaters, who soldiered on stoically, knowing in their hearts that their jobs were finishing. Yet the boats generally looked smart and were always well-appointed. Docking was still done regularly, engine maintenance was of a good standard and the best rates of pay possible were paid. With all its faults, there was much that was good in the British Waterways fleet and its operators.

By the Spring of 1962 the fleet had been re-equipped with Petter PD2 diesels, which were air-cooled and thus required the installation of trunking and duct-vents for air, in place of the water pipes of Nationals and Bolinders. They made a growling clatter and gave an impression of great power although they were only twin cylinder engines. They were all right for a well-maintained fleet with full dockyard resources but for smaller concerns they were not as good, because, as modifications of stationary engines they tended to develop crankshaft trouble, possibly due to torque forces in the drive shaft or more likely as a result of the thrashing they got! When this occurred, the only way of getting at the crank shaft was to unbolt the engine room and lift the whole engine out with a crane.

The livery of the boats was dark blue, lined in gold, with yellow lettering bearing the legend "British Waterways". Between and below the two words was a device resembling a white, quartered lifebelt with the words "British Transport Waterways" on it. The fleet and registration numbers completed the picture. Cabin doors and the inside panel had transfers of rose and castle designs by Frank Jones of Leighton Buzzard. Top cloths were heavy, black tarpaulin with white, stencilled lettering.

During our sojourn at Braunston we came to know many of the crews as they passed and repassed—empties for the coalfields via the Oxford and Coventry canals; copper, groceries, steel and timber for Birmingham; coal for the paper mills and cocoa waste going south. Blue Line were one-way coal carriers, whilst Willow Wren carried much the same as 'Waterways' but had their own special traffics: coal for Banbury and Aylesbury, roadstone from Mancetter on the Coventry Canal to West Drayton. Night after night the mutter of engines could be heard round the fields behind Braunston Church or away towards Napton. Headlights would creep along the lip of Braunston Puddle Bank and under the Castle Bridge, and we would feel a sudden jerk as water was sucked out of the arm and another as it surged back in. The moored boats would rock back and forth and through the arch the silhouettes of the boats would go by.

Another lively scene was enacted at the Bottom Lock when empties were coming back towards mid-week and were attempting to reload coal before the collieries shut down at the weekend. The

Waterways Traffic Control Officer at Hawkesbury Junction in the coalfields some twenty two miles away, distributed loading orders on a first come, first served basis, this was called 'the Turn'. All the carriers had refuelling bases at Braunston, so that when, as frequently happened, boats from all three companies followed one another down the locks, all hell broke loose.

A panting lockwheeler would storm into the Willow Wren yard. Another would hammer the door for Tom James. A third, perhaps Bill Whitlock or Maurice Peasland, would rocket crazily on a bike along the towpath to the new side bridge, shoulder the bike, charge up and over like the Royal Navy doing gun drill at the Royal Tournament, remount and pedal under Butchers Bridge, up and over the side bridge, brake, turn, skid and shoot underneath up to Blue Line's office to get David Hambridge out. Meanwhile cantilever arms would swing out on either side at Bottom Lock as the respective pairs headed in, the Barlows would pother past pretending indifference until safely tucked into the yard. Then poor old David's arm would be encouraged to waggle back and forth at the pumps, before throttles were cracked wide open again and the empty pairs set forth on a neck-and-neck race for Hawkesbury Junction.

Our first set-back occurred on the Monday and was a most unfortunate mishap—not typical of Blue Lines's workforce, I might add. The fitter arrived, a cheerful little Irishman called Kevin, to remove the gear box casing. For some obscure reason the box refused to move and Kevin introduced a crowbar and lump hammer by way of persuasion.

"Bejasus, me ould son, ye'll be comin' when I tell yez," said he and applied what he called the 'Kerry Screwdriver'—a sharp blow with the hammer! After several such blows the box disengaged itself—split down the middle.

A Council of War then had to be called with Michael Streat, who looked pained. It seemed that there would be at least a three week delay before a replacement could be delivered ex-works, for the Blue Line stores contained no such parts. Meanwhile we were completely immobilised and charging our batteries was becoming a problem. Streat suggested trying Willow Wren to see whether they had such a part and the three week delay made us think even harder about taking on a pair. We waited impatiently, therefore, for the arrival of the 'Gaffer' on Wednesday and in the meantime settled down to life in the Yard.

We were tied outside Kevin's fitting shop, from whence he would make forays to different parts of the Yard for various parts and jobs. Despite his hamfistedness with our gearbox, he was a delight to listen to. Everyone from Michael Streat downwards was addressed as "Me ould son" and, as he worked away in his shop or toiled in some dark engine hole we would, when time allowed, pass him tools and assist generally. He came from Athlone and his voice had the soft lilt of the Irish countryman. He had also served in the Republic's air force and gave us frightening visions of Ireland's aerial might. "We had five Spitfires in t'e squadron," he told us, "and one day we had all t'e booggers in t'e air at once. I don't know if t'ey frightened t'e Rooshions, but bejasus, t'ey frightened me!"

The making of fenders, ropework, side cloths and allied crafts were entrusted to David Hambridge and another remarkable old ex-boatman, Isaac—or Ike—Merchant, who had served his time in the steamers which Fellows Morton and Clayton had once operated from the yard. He had the boatman's gift of vivid, figurative speech and intoned away in a sort of plainsong as he worked. As I so often came to experience with boat people, the years rolled away. When Ike talked about "the War" he meant the 1914-18 conflict; the Thames, to him, was cursed with flash locks; the nearby railway line, about to be closed, was the "noo North Western line". His gnarled, old fingers would snake round ropework or sailmakers' needle as he talked.

In the small drydock lay the hotel boat "Nelson" on which the boatbuilders were working and, inimitably adding his touches to the upper works was the painter Ron Hough. Ron had learned his craft from the master painter, Frank Nurser, who had previously run the yard. He was a lively-faced young man with a ready wit. He was working partially in the building trade with a bricklayer mate called Fred, who had a knack of appearing in the yard with news of disasters or business opportunities at inopportune moments. Ron would be about to shade a length of signwriting when the door would burst open.

"OOFFY!"

"Whadda ya want Fred?"

"They're sellin' up Barby Camp"

"So what?"

"Wull, there's thirty lavatory pans an' cisterns goin' cheap!"

"Ang on, I'll come."

Or else

"OOFFY!"

"Whadda ya want Fred?"

74

"Ole Mother so and so's chimley pot's blowed orf, gi'us 'and to put the boogger back."

The carpenter, a quiet, mild, older man would sigh at the vagaries of youth and the building trade and fall-to again, whistling tunelessly through his teeth as his saw sung through a piece of wood across his knee, or his plane swished his shavings upwards. He and Bill, who had served his time as a cabinet-maker, established a great rapport.

At tea breaks, local gossip and badinage was exchanged as the men sat round a roaring Salamander oil space heater in one of the drydocks. The chances of Northampton Town or Coventry City and, of course, the favourites in the day's racing vied with the state of Braunston's young ladies as the most absorbing topic. We learned that currently seven unmarried village maidens were pregnant. (Ron Hough called them "The Magnificent Seven".) There was no hooter or clocking-in or out, beyond the occasional reproachful glance from Aubrey if work was late in restarting, but work was done well and promptly. As work restarted and the hammering and banging rose again so did the singing and whistling of cheerful, contented men.

One morning Tom James appeared with a thin, rather hesitant youth. He introduced this young 'shaver' to us as someone very interested in boats and the cut. We eyed him with lofty disdain, as yet another canal enthusiast, but it soon transpired that he really did know something about canals—in fact, though we could not of course admit to it, he knew considerably more than we did. He had done some boating with a Willow Wren captain called Alec Purcell, whom I had met before, and had been at school with my brother. His name was Nicholas Hill and what is left of narrow boat transport today owes as much to him as to anyone in recent years.

On Wednesday night we made our way to the "Nelson" to confer with Morton about gear boxes and boats. We noticed that several Willow Wren pairs new to us had arrived. "Flamingo" and "Smew" were back empty and Billy Wilson Greasy Ocker's two pairs had been released from their long stay at Maple Cross Sewage Works near Rickmansworth, where the unloading plant had broken down and kept them waiting for several smelly weeks. We walked up the locks with Billy and his mate, a small, elderly man with a broad North Warwickshire brogue and a nose that in profile ran in steps—rather like one side of the Great Pyramid. His name was Jim and he was known variously as "Jimpy" or "Jinty". He looked vaguely familiar to me and I recalled having a pint with him some

75

years before in, of all unlikely places, a pub in Caversham Road, Reading. He was mate to Jack Monk then and they were carrying timber up the Thames to Oxford.

We were joined by the portly, bespectacled captain of "Flamingo", whose Black Country brogue was slightly more comprehensible now that we had been dwelling in the Midlands for a week. However, he did not say very much and I put Charlie down for a quiet, shy individual—which just goes to show how wrong first impressions can be.

Up at the "Nelson", the Gaffer was holding court in almost feudal style. Problems were being aired, disputes settled and a boatman engaged, over pints and, for Morton, a whisky. This Wednesday night ceremony was a characteristic part of the Willow Wren atmosphere and went far to ensure good labour relations. Boaters, being straightforward people, appreciated that Morton was approachable, could be reasoned with and could make a decision quickly. The correctness or otherwise of that decision might have been questionable but, once again, whatever faults Morton may have possessed, inflexibility of mind was not one of them. He was always disarmingly ready to admit when he had made a mistake.

When we eventually buttonholed him he arranged forthwith for the repair of the gearbox to be sent with a job lot of expert welding to a firm in Northampton. About the boats he was less forthcoming. We would have to work several trips to make it worthwhile commissioning a spare pair but he certainly needed extra boats for the roadstone traffic from Mancetter.

The next day, after a discussion with Michael Streat, we reluctantly abandoned our plan to work for Willow Wren when he suggested that we would be better employed doing some of the work on the boat ourselves to cut down on our docking bill. In the circumstances we could do no less than take his advice.

I saw Morton in his office at Bottom Lock that morning and he did not take it amiss. Instead he promised that, if we really wanted it, he would provide us with a butty and set us on the following winter. This was an offer we had scarcely hoped for and we mulled it over in the ensuing weeks.

The great day dawned when we were to go on the dock. It was to be the large double dock in an enclosed shed where in Fellows Morton days steamers had been transhipped. It had a clerestory roof vent to let out smoke, which meant that we could keep our cabin fire going, and mains electricity so we could charge our flagging battery and have a proper light in the cabin. Before we could get in, the rest of the ballast had to be removed along with the 'gasfitters glory' which had been stored in the hold. Then we carefully pulled "Enterprise" in and manoeuvred her above the bostocks—sunken piers on which a boat rests when the water is let out so that work can take place underneath.

The stop planks at the end of the dock were positioned and lowered in from each end. When the final one was in a paddle at the far end was drawn releasing the water into an underground culvert. The top plank was wedged and any leaks between the planks stopped with the aid of ashes and a pole with a flat iron piece called a podger. When all but a tiny trickle had stopped "Enterprise" lay like a stranded whale ready for work and we got stuck in with the rest of the gang. Our days of leisure were now most definitely over.

Bill decided he would construct an awning-support frame out of wood, which could also support a gang plank to enable the crew to go forward without disturbing passengers and which would be readily detachable for cargo-carrying and, with the carpenter's assistance, he produced a much better-looking job than the bent pipe we carried before. We rubbed down the paintwork and put on undercoats and topcoats. Then came the day when Ron Hough arrived to put on our lettering and repaint the roses.

Whilst there was very much more to boating than roses and castles, there was something very significant in this delightful and colourful craft. Whatever its origins the florid decoration of the boats symbolised a way of life where such things mattered. They were, like the polished brasses, the scrubbed ropework, the spotless cabins and the gleaming, tidy engine rooms, the emblem of the boaters' pride in their craft and skill—a quietly defiant gesture against the drabness of life. They irresistibly reminded me of the colours of a doomed regiment proudly borne high by its survivors as they stood back-to-back in a last desperate stand, or of the White Ensign nailed to the mast of a stricken warship as she went down, guns firing, before overwhelming odds. The heartbreak of the dying canal system was manfully concealed by such symbols and we determined to have them, not merely to attract custom but to identify ourselves with our new-found friends.

Ron was refreshingly down-to-earth about his craft and had no objection to us watching how it was done. He swiftly and deftly lettered the sides in white Gill Sans letters, merely striking a chalk line to give the tops and bottoms of the characters and then filling the corners of the panels and the centre beneath the curving arch of the Company's name with bunches of roses. The centre contained six roses, two white, two yellow, two red. The basic technique was to paint discs of ground colour for these in pink, shaded red; orange, shaded brown; and brown, shaded umber, then to apply the petals with swift brush strokes. The unadorned discs looked somewhat odd and Ron was not flattered by Bill's description of them as "apples, oranges and turnips". The transformation as the petals went on and the leaves were veined was marvellous to watch. It was completed by the swift, deft, shading back of the letters which made them appear to leap from the cabin side. It was good to think that at least the pleasure craft renaissance would continue to make it worthwhile for Ron and others to practise the art.

The days passed and "Enterprise" began to come alive and glow with new work and colour. Once the Board of Trade inspector had surveyed the hull and pronounced it fit, we blacked it round with bitumastic. A new skylight was fitted over the engine room, we reproofed the awning, repainted the inside of the hold and the electrics were overhauled. The last coats of varnish were applied and Ike and David fussed about the fitting of a new stern fender which had been made for us.

One Monday morning the paddle at the end of the dock was closed, all tools and kit cleared out of the way, the wedges knocked out and the top plank lifted. The water thundered over the planks filling up the dock, rose round the hull and gradually stirred the fore-end, which began to lift. The noise of the water slowly subsided as the levels equalised and one by one the bottom planks bobbed to the surface. "Enterprise", back in her natural element, glided out of the shed into the open air and we tied her up on the opposite bank to await the return of the gearbox.

The ballast was loaded back the next day and the awning re-rigged, fitted and stowed away, ready for the journey back. The gearbox arrived late the following evening.

By now we had begun to make our farewells as boats passed and we knew that we should not meet again for a while. A pair had gone to Banbury with coal for the dairy and their captain had earnestly invited us to have a drink in the "Struggler" with him if we got away soon enough. Mark and Dolly had bidden farewell in style, so much so that Mark had to tie up at the top of Buckby the next day with an aching head. Before parting they had both pressed us to come back next winter, "We'll look arter yer," Mark had said.

The final Wednesday night epitomised everything we had come to associate with Braunston. The 'Gaffer' was at his most expansive. Hubert beamed, guffawed and snorted copious draughts of snuff and Thirza, his wife, tut-tutted and pretended to look shocked at some of the more outrageous ditties. The rest of the company had faces brimming with merriment and good companionship. It was not just the canal way of life, it was the fact that its environment encouraged a way of life and attitude of mind which did not belong to the industrialised, urbanised, mechanised society which we have with us increasingly today. It was a rougher, simpler, more structured, less neurotic society and with it went a rugged individualism in which people were still people, with foibles and nicknames but respected nonetheless. Above all there was room for kindliness and sheer, unadulterated fun.

On the Thursday afternoon the reassembly of our gearbox was completed and so, on a sunlit evening in April, we left Braunston. "Enterprise" slipped quietly away, past the toll house onto the Oxford Canal, under the humped iron bridges of the Turn, across the puddle banks and into the eye of the westering sun. Behind us in the late evening light, Braunston's spire and sail-less windmill looked down on the rolling herringbone pattern of our wash rebounding from the puddle banks. Summer was coming and we were going. In six, short weeks I had entered and fallen in love with a completely new world.

5
Brummagem
Road

It was Autumn when next we came to Braunston, after a summer congenially spent carrying passengers aboard "Enterprise" on and about the Kennet. Leslie Morton had promised us a pair of boats but first we had to deliver a motley cargo of machinery to Braunston and timber to Tyseley.

In the intervening months Wilfred had been "a-finished" by British Waterways and we had snatched a day off to accompany him on his last loaded trip. "Barnet" had been loaded with over 30 tons—a splendid swansong for Wilfred who had had to get 'Waterways' to drag him through nearly every bridgehole on the Coventry Canal, to his huge delight! Later we went to visit him 'ashore' in his old home port of Abingdon. He was as philosophical as ever, working in a malthouse—where he was given a free bucket of beer twice daily—and living with his ancient mother. He wished us well with our forthcoming winter on Willow Wren boats and gave us valuable advice and tips. We returned, rather moodily, to the declining pleasure-tripping of late Summer; counting the days to our release.

To be frank, the season had been a financial disappointment—largely due to the dreadful weather of Spring and early Summer. By the time the weather brightened in July and August the lucrative charter work was almost finished because the clubs and societies who wanted this sort of service had nearly all disbanded for the holiday period. We had put in a tremendous effort on the Kennet, had numerous memorable experiences and made many new friends, but the English climate had beaten us. True we had not made a loss, but the profit was very meagre and financial problems were looming unless we could earn some money before next April.

Then one day in September my mother said to me: "What a charming man your Mr Morton is!" The old warhorse was a notorious charmer with ladies, but why should he have got in touch? Mother said she should have mentioned it before but he had rung asking for me. Within seconds I was on the line to Brentford and Stanley was giving me the telephone-juggling treatment.

Morton's voice came on the line. "Was there," he asked, "much land water coming down river?" I assured him that all was quiet. It seemed he had six pairs due to load timber for Birmingham and the British Waterways engineers had thoughtfully arranged consecutive stoppages at Braunston and Stoke Bruerne, which would mean no through traffic for three weeks on the Grand Union, so he was going to send them up the Thames and through the Oxford Canal to Napton.

I told Bill the news and the next day we were on the train to Brentford to find out more. Morton, expansive as ever, puffed at a pipe and put us in the picture. He also told us that there would be a pair available for us in October. Outside in the basin several 'Waterways' pairs were loading for Birmingham. Morton said, "They'll never beat the stoppage." I asked why they did not go round the Thames as well. He laughed and replied, "Bloody good idea, let's see."

He picked up the telephone, dialled Bulls Bridge and asked for a certain official. There was a delay, then the telephone crackled and he held it so we could hear.

"Major General ———— here," said a military voice.

"Commodore Morton here, I think I outrank you."

"Oh hello, Leslie, what can I do for you?"

Morton explained that he was sending boats round the Oxford Canal to avoid the stoppages and that he would instruct his captains to assist any 'Waterways' pairs which might go that way. There was a pause, then the voice said, "But how on earth do you get to the Oxford Canal from Brentford if the Grand Union's closed?"

Morton, rolling his eyes heavenwards, told him that there was a river known as the Thames.

"Yes, yes, but surely our boats can't use it?" came the reply.

Morton assured him they could and the voice continued, "So you want to form a bandobast with us?" Then, after some consideration went on, "Well, thank you, but I don't really think we could do it," as if declining an invitation for tennis rather than the earnings of six families for three weeks, and rang off.

Morton asked, "What the hell's a bandobast?" I said I thought it was a Hindu word meaning 'organisation' and he chuckled, "He ought to be back on the bloody Ganges."

We heard later that the six 'Waterways' pairs concerned duly

81

took three and a half weeks to make the five day journey, that six lots of 'laying money' for twenty one days each had been paid to the captains in lieu of real earnings and that the consignees had run dangerously low on stocks. As Robert Aickman was wont to say in those days, "The insolvency of British Waterways was strictly self-induced."

A few days later we returned to Brentford to see the cream, red and green of Willow Wren boats in the basin as we rattled over the railway bridge into the station. Some had already gone, Ray White and Mark and Dolly, but four pairs were left: Jack Monk, Ken, big smiling Charlie on "Flamingo" and "Smew" and the owl-like George, whom we had met briefly in Denham Straight with "Tern" and "Drake". They evidently knew all about us. George patted "Tern's" tiller and boomed in a rich Gloucestershire voice, "You'm 'avin' this bastard next."

We looked at "Tern" with renewed interest. She was rather faded but in a workaday, rather than down-at-heel fashion. We asked George what she was like. "An 'eavy arsed bugger, like all Joshers," was his main comment. For some reason her propeller blades were prone to fouling. "'Er'd pick up a tea leaf," he asserted.

Some days later, when the stoppages had cleared we left the Summer and the Kennet behind and brought "Enterprise" and "Southam", a redundant butty bound for Lapworth, up the Grand Union, retracing our voyage of the Spring. It was early on a Sunday afternoon as we locked down into Braunston to be greeted by Jinty, sporting a most magnificent pair of tweed check trousers. He was now a watchman and general factotum at the Willow Wren yard and was resident aboard the butty "Snipe".

Some machinery which we had brought with us—an extinct Bolinder engine and a defunct towpath tractor from Brentford—was unloaded next morning then we set forth again with our lightened load down the now-familiar Braunston Pound to Napton Junction, or in boater's parlance, 'Wigrams Turn'. After a wide sweep under the Grand Union's concrete arch, which had replaced the narrow, old, brick stop lock bridge in the 1930's, we were once again on unknown waters.

When the Grand Union Canal Company was formed in 1929, it was a 'grand union' of several smaller, independent companies. The two largest and richest were the Grand Junction and the Regents companies. Two other smaller companies lay between 'Wigram's' and the goal of Birmingham, both of which were in financial straits when they were taken over.

To reach 'Wigrams', boats had to pass over some five miles of the Oxford Canal from Braunston and relations. generally, were rarely cordial between the Oxford and Grand Junction Companies. However, the Grand Union obtained what railwaymen would call "running powers" over the Oxford for this distance and were allowed, at their own cost, to bring this section up to the standards they wanted to impose on their new acquisitions. Of course the late 1920's and early 1930's were a time of industrial slump and depression, but eventually the Government made sums of money available for various capital works of public benefit in order to help reduce unemployment. The Grand Union, therefore, planned to modernise its whole route to the Midlands and to rebuild all the locks between Braunston and Birmingham as a start. The Government guaranteed the interest on a debenture loan and work commenced; the final objective being to run hundred-ton motor barges from the Port of London into the heart of Birmingham. Widening the locks was to be the first stage. This was done, without great interference to traffic, between 1931 and 1937, but the scheme was not completed as far as widening the bed of the canal and certain bridges when War came in 1939. The Grand Union therefore, remained a narrow-boat canal albeit with wide locks, until Nationalisation in 1947 and the subsequent decline, dashed any hopes of efficient, modern, water transport to Birmingham.

The prospect of fifty one locks in the next forty or so miles was a daunting one, but we were pleasantly surprised when reaching 'Wigrams Three' to find how quick and easy they were to work. Boaters told us later that in Grand Union days they were even easier, for the gates were so finely balanced that when the water made a level, they automatically fell open and it only needed a slight draw of water for them to close of their own accord. By now, though, many had steel beams which were not well balanced, although the gates still moved smoothly. The paddles were all-enclosed, worm-geared, iron constructions mounted on the lockside, feeding the water in and out of the chambers by means of large culverts which entered the chambers at several points. When they were drawn, the lock filled or emptied in a very short time. They must remain the most efficient hand-worked locks anywhere.

Below the last lock the cut curved away and headed down the upper reaches of the Leam valley. Set in clay country, oaks and more luxuriant vegetation appeared at the canal side, whilst away in front and to the left rose signs of industrial activity.

The Rugby Portland Cement Company, whose works with their

tall, white-plumed chimney were visible across the fields, had a short and very narrow arm, twisting its way across the fields from above the final lock of the Stockton Flight. The company still made regular use of the canal between here and Birmingham. It was a 'Waterways' contract, inherited from the 'Grand Union'. The boats on it had to keep their holds dry and consequently used to run with the hold clothed up even when empty. This is the most common way in which the few remaining narrow boats in trading condition run about today, but it never really looks right and is a menace in windy weather.

Below Itchington came the Bascote Pound, a long, lonely stretch where high towpath hedges shield a pleasant view across pleasant, rolling countryside.

Past lonely Welsh Road, once the main road for cattle-drovers from Wales but now deserted, we headed. Beside the towpath there were electricity poles, some with stern injunctions to boatmen about tying-up to them. These carried the wires for a 'back-pumping' system installed by the Grand Union to return the lockage water. By 1962 this was almost unusable for most of the pump outlets were choked with mud.

Down Wood Lock and the Fosse Three the bushes on the outside were loaded with blackberries—whilst lockwheeling I picked large quantities. There were more smart Company cottages against Fosse Way bridge, and another delicensed pub. The Fosse Way had once been the frontier mark of Rome's first province of Britannia. This section was still used by motor traffic but long lengths of it from Devon to Lincolnshire had become, like disused canals, forgotten green tracks through deep countryside. The locks beyond here began to space out and we were very glad of our bicycle, taking turns at bumping over the towpath towards the bottom lock at Radford.

Several canal writers, one as early as Hollingshead in 1858, have commented unfavourably on the canalside aspect of Leamington Spa. We certainly found little to dispute this in general but some differences were already apparent from earlier descriptions, such as the purple and puce doorways and window frames of terraced houses which proclaimed the occupancy of immigrants.

Under a narrow and cramped bridgehole between high buildings the colourful sterns and polished brasses of a 'Claytons' pair caught the evening sunlight. They were "Umea" and "Orwell" and their captain was a piratical looking man with a brood of children. They were about to load gas tar at Leamington Gas Works wharf which they would carry up to Oldbury.

Opposite Leamington Station we entered a cutting with a housing estate at the top. The canal and the cutting sides were liberally sprinkled with old bicycles, prams, filthy mattresses and other debris. The contrast between the urban squalor of Leamington and the pleasant, rolling country of the Fosse, a mere three or so miles back, emphasised forcibly the foulness of industrial urbanisation. The humbler inhabitants of the rural communities are doubtless just as poor, deprived and disadvantaged as their urban cousins many years of rural life and work have left me with few illusions about the countryside. But in the poorest and meanest quarters of rural habitation I have never seen the filth and general untidiness of some of our big, planned estates.

Approaching Warwick, the surroundings became more bourgeois with neat villas hiding away behind hedges. We curved sharply under the main road, crossed the railway on an aqueduct and headed towards the crossing of the Avon valley, where the canal went over on a large, stone arch. The arch was wide with paths on both sides and a sturdy parapet but was not as imposing as the iron trough at Wolverton with its narrow lip. Below, the Avon ran sluggishly on towards the Castle; its rubbish-strewn banks knee deep in nettles and sorrel. Between the river and the canal, on the opposite bank, stood a fine example of the corrugated-iron school of architecture, housing a power station. This was "Warwick Light" to the boaters, sited by thrifty businessmen and councillors to take advantage of canal transport. Now that the State had taken control of the electricity supply as well as canal transport, rusting telphers and derelict wharves told their own story.

The canal skirted Warwick and ran through open, green fields (now long covered with houses) beyond the Kenilworth Road Bridge. We came to a curious little pocket of industry round a pub called the "Cape of Good Hope" where two adjacent locks heralded the climb up to the Birmingham plateau. Our route led a short distance beyond to the padlocked bottom gates of Hatton Locks. Here we stopped at dusk, in the lock tail. Early the next morning, the padlock came off, we started and moved into the lock, hearing as we did so the dull, echoing 'ponking' of a single cylinder Bolinder behind us. It was the 'Claytons' we had seen at Leamington coming throttle open for Hatton. A furious yell came from "Umea" as the captain saw us rising in the lock ahead of him. The ensuing locks were against us, so I set off on the bicycle, seeing clouds of exhaust smoke rise from below the bottom gate as Bill forged out. Behind, a fist was vigorously shaken in our direction.

There are twenty one locks at Hatton, but they are well-spaced at the bottom and only begin to close up about a third of the way up the flight. Beside the eleventh lock a wide concrete arch, legacy of the Grand Union modernisations, spans the flight. Here there was a wide basin where once coal boats unloaded for the nearby mental hospital—whose frowning bulk dominated the lower part of the flight. I wondered if there was any deep significance in the proximity of mental hospitals to lock flights but there was little time to dally for the pursuing 'ponk, ponk, pop, pop, ponk' of the Bolinder was in our ears.

Beyond here the "thick" rose in all its ghastliness. Tier upon tier of black and white gates, paddles and handrails mounted the hill. After about five locks I looked back to see, with some satisfaction, that the 'Claytons' were by the Hospital Basin. Beyond the 'Waterways' maintenance yard, four locks from the top, the flight curved and we lost sight of them. We thoughtfully dropped paddles for them, but when we reached the top lock they were still not in sight.

Soon the hills rose up ahead and after rounding a slight turn Shrewley Tunnel was in front of us. Although one can see right through the tunnel it is longer than it seems. It is also very wet and at the far end, where the canal ran out between stone cliffs, dripping water had caused luxuriant vegetation to grow. Ferns and mosses sprouted, brambles dropped round the mouth and an intriguing little tunnel at a higher level took the boat-horse path over the hill. Open country, with traces of the ancient forest of Arden and no signs of habitation near the canal was followed by a deep cutting and led towards the attractive village of Rowington. The water was deep and our boats swam along happily to Lapworth Junction.

Canal junctions can be misleadingly insignificant places. When one thinks that intersections of water trunk highways are not all that common, one tends to think they would appear more imposing than they frequently are. Bulls Bridge, where the Paddington Arm branches off at right angles to the main line under a towpath bridge looks, at first sight, like just another factory arm. Lapworth is similarly unassuming from the main line. There is merely a brick bridge with a cut beneath at right angles, no toll house, pub, stop place, wide hole or similar paraphernalia. Little suggests that here is a link to the Avon and the Severn or another direct route to the Black Country and the north until one goes beneath the railway to the first, narrow lock. "Southam" was loosed off and Bill swung her round the turn while I brought "Enterprise" into the towpath bank. He 'shoved' her along the short, linking arm between the Grand Union and Stratford Canals, having been asked to deliver her to a Mr Hutchings. The Southern Stratford Canal had been neglected for many years and was now the subject of a restoration bid led by a dynamic young Coventry architect called David Hutchings. Bill went up the steps to the office and, before he could speak, was pounced upon as a volunteer. Only with difficulty did he make the enthusiastic David Hutchings understand that he did not wish to be issued with a shovel and transported to Wilmcote, Preston Bagot or some similar Gulag settlement!

From Lapworth to Knowle the lush pastureland drowsed in the morning warmth of the October sun. On each side a wooded landscape dotted with brick and timber farms and cottages bespoke the wealth of nearby Birmingham. I sensed a similarity between this area and parts of Sussex, both were 'Stockbroker Belt' areas and the scenery was akin to parts of the Weald. The canal, concrete walled and broad, ran boldly onwards ending with a left hand turn into the great water terraces of Knowle.

By means of clever engineering and juggling the Grand Union reduced the Knowle flight of six narrow locks to one of five wide ones, it being the last section to be so treated. Of all the lock flights between here and Braunston it seemed the most impressive. I think this is due to the sharp escarpment which the canal comes upon suddenly through a cutting and descends, as well as to the wide, spacious pounds and side-ponds which offer a very satisfying view—especially from above.

Similar country followed until the double bends at Catherine de Barnes—called by boaters 'Kate Deebarns'—after which a change became apparent. A succession of tree-lined cuttings, whose vegetation had begun to turn into autumnal tints, led us into the suburbs of Solihull. There were unmistakeable signs that we were approaching a city. Rubbish began to festoon cutting sides, shoals of bricks and old iron would appear near bridge holes, slogans and obscenities were written on bridges, but still we ran through tree-lined deeps.

As we came round a slight turn into a long straight a bridge-hole framed a distant scene of sheds and walls and the cream and red sterns of Willow Wren boats. We slipped through Acocks Green Bridge, the trees and cutting fell away and we came out into an industrial scene. To our right the walls and stacks of a factory, to our left Tyseley Wharf—a modern-looking place with two travelling electric cranes, a weighbridge, corrugated iron warehouse and spacious open stacking ground.

Charlie and George were standing on the wharf, hands in overall pockets, gravely watching our arrival, their families clustering in the hatches and looking on with solemn curiosity as we tied up at our journey's end. Both captains had emptied one boat each and paused for refreshment. The method used was similar to that employed at Aylesbury—man-handling. Each tediously loaded plank was landed onto stillages on the wharf and a pile of planks steadily grew with one end flush. When about ten tons had been landed (gauged by the amount the boat had risen in the water) the cranes would rumble up on their rails, coiling or uncoiling their umbilical cables on large revolving drums. Then slings would be placed and the stack moved away to a pile whence a fork-lift would place it on a flat lorry. Today such timber arrives in packaged bundles, coming by lorry and ferryship without transhipment. Had the Grand Union's plans been developed the timber could have come by water all the way at a fraction of the cost in road maintenance, vehicle charges and fuel.

We ate a late and hurried lunch and were entertaining three of George's children in the cabin when we felt a slight jerk. George called out, "Clayton's a-comin'" and we peered out to see a pair of loaded fore-ends nosing under Acocks Green Bridge. At this point, faintly borne on the air, we heard the captain begin to give his considered opinion of boats that went up Hatton 'afore' him. The noble sight of loaded gas-boats nosing aside the water and swimming past us with beating Bolinder was somewhat marred by the captain's angry face.

"Next time you does that, I'll slip in a-twixt yer and jom 'em," he roared. Bill said he wanted to be careful lest the fore-end fell off his old wooden motor. This caused him to become nearly apoplectic and he carried on his tirade until "Umea" bore him out of sight through the next bridgehole. George and Charlie were highly amused and I could not help chuckling at the way the captain broke his angry flow to say "'Ow do George, 'ow do Charlie" and, after a brief conversation with both captains and their families resumed his tirade. Years later I made my peace with him, he had neither forgotten me nor the incident. But to this day I cannot really see it was any fault of ours, like Wilfred he "should a' got up in the mornin'".

There came another jerk. Marion, George's wife, said, "Mr Monk's a-comin'" and under the far bridgehole from the direction of Birmingham came "Avocet" and "Dabchick" riding empty. The motor boat's Seffel engine beat time more loudly and regularly than

"Umea's" stuttering Bolinder. Jack and Ken, who was close behind, had delivered their timber to Tipton in the Black Country and were hastening back to Brentford for another load. This long and wasteful empty run was apparently necessary because neither Sampson Road Depot, just a few, short miles on from here, nor Tyseley could find a return load for Brentford at twenty four hours' notice. The boats rode past, lit by the westering sun. News was exchanged, messages passed on and then they vanished, brasses glittering, underneath Acocks Green Bridge.

Late that afternoon, George approached us furtively, "You ole boys want to earn a quid?" he asked. This was a useful sum in the days when beer was a little over a shilling a pint, so we asked what was on his mind. "I wants to get back to Braunston, 'cos you'm 'avin' this bastard next," he replied, indicating "Tern", "and I wants to get fixed up wi' my new motor. So, one on yous can help me chuck out an' the other 'un'll 'elp my 'ooman stack."

So, that evening, I helped Marion stack the planks into a pile ready for the crane and we set to diligently emptying the motor boat. Charlie looked on quizzically and kept silent. As we were stacking and chucking, we saw a horse come from under Acocks Green Bridge. Behind it a towline ran to a Joey boat we had seen earlier that day at Solihull. This was boating Brummagem style. The boatman was driving the horse on the towpath, the towline was taken to an upright shaft in place of a mast and the boat was nosing its way down the walled towpath on its own. The horse, a little brown mare, stepped along swiftly, harness creaking, hooves clopping as the boatman called out greetings. On the stern a red background similar to Claytons bore the legend "City of Birmingham Salvage Department". It was an everyday sight then in the Birmingham area, an old, wooden day boat and a horse moving quietly in the low sunlight of an autumn evening. I am glad to say we paused to watch.

Soon after the horse's hooves had echoed hollowly in the far bridgehole we found that "Tern" was empty. George swept out the hold and we helped him replace his stands and planks, roll up the side cloths and stow the top cloths. The next time they would be used we would be in charge. We looked eagerly at the way in which all these little odd jobs were done.

Charlie wanted us to go for a drink with him, so later that evening we strolled up the wharf to Acocks Green Bridge. Only then did we realise how close to 'civilisation' we had come. Across the bridge a wide suburban road along which traffic streamed in never-ending procession led up to a nearby pub—a huge drinking emporium set amid acres of car parking and designed to pour alcohol into the maximum number of people in the shortest possible time. It was considerably less inviting than a railway waiting-room and its only concession to non-drinking activities was a tatty dartboard. Nothing emphasised the gulf between the amusements of the industrialised, urban, working class and those of the rural workers than the contrast between this joyless boozing hall and the "Admiral Nelson". Many years later I met two Irish car-workers in a similar place near Shirley. They both came from Western Ireland and had a very low opinion of England and its people, which was evidently based on their experience of such pubs. I was forced to agree with them as one after another the patrons left to vomit; sometimes in the lavatories, occasionally across the floor. From time to time arguments would lead to fisticuffs or outbursts of vile language and the bar staff threw the refilled glasses across the bar, serving new customers with indifferent contempt.

The noise of a motor starting and coming past us at tick-over woke us early. When we eventually surfaced at about eight o'clock George had gone, having turned his boats the evening before. Charlie was not gratified. It seemed that he had had his eye on a rams head adorning the stern of "Curlew", which was laid up at Braunston and no longer being crewed, and it looked as if George was going to beat him to it. He muttered darkly for most of the morning.

While we set to and unloaded our timber we were accosted by an official-looking gentleman on the wharf. He produced a card identifying himself as an employee of the Birmingham City Public Health Committee and asked for our registration papers. These papers had to be carried by all working boats and the number prominently painted on the outside of the boat to comply with George Smith's Canal Boats Act of 1877 and 1878, as amended by the Public Health Act of 1936. "Enterprise" had been rebuilt from her original working condition and the papers lost. However, the official was not too put out. He came aboard, measured up and expressed himself satisfied, so we paid him four shillings and he promised us a new registration certificate. I think this may have been the last working boat ever to be registered in Birmingham.

By midday the timber had been unloaded and the consignment note signed, so we prepared to depart. Charlie informed us he would be back-loading for Brentford, but we wanted to return to Braunston where our pair was ready for us, so we decided to leave

90

without waiting for another load. A debate then followed about which route to take; whether to travel via the Birmingham and Fazeley, Coventry and Oxford Canals or to go back the way we had come. The former course, some 50 miles, had 43 narrow locks, the latter was 10 miles shorter but had 51 broad locks. Since narrow locks were no trouble two-handed on single boats and as we were both looking forward to exploring new waters the first course was chosen. So bidding Charlie adieu, we set off towards the delights of the Birmingham Canal Navigations.

In contrast with the sylvan approach from Knowle our route onward from Tyseley was increasingly industrial. Sadly though, the concrete-lined banks were mocked by the general air of disuse and there was, more than ever, a poignant atmosphere of hopes unfulfilled and opportunities lost. The grim, brick buildings of the BSA works with a blocked-off arm leading into their disused wharves, stood mute witness to the decay which was beginning to grip British Industry as the booming years of the 1950's receded. Even more depressing was the sight of the British Waterways depot at Sampson Road, Bordesley—'Camp Hill' to boaters. This modern depot at the very end of the widened section had been built by the Grand Union as an inland port in the 1930's. An act of faith which should have been well-rewarded. But one of the loading bays had already been walled off and the depot seemed to be more road-orientated than interested in canal traffic. However, dead ahead, the top gates of Camp Hill Locks had appeared to divert attention from such gloomy thoughts. These were "Enterprise's" first narrow locks since leaving the Oxford Canal in April and marked the true beginning of the narrow canal system of the Midlands.

The water was fouler than anything we had yet seen. There was still some horse-traffic about, revealed not only by the boat we had seen the night before but by smoking horse-dung on the towpath, bright rope marks on guard-irons and stonework and well-polished grooves in strapping stumps. Under the tangled mass of girders and bricks which formed a complicated railway and road crossing, the locks curved down, spouting and bubbling ever filthier water until we reached the sixth, and bottom lock, sandwiched between high factory walls. Here at Bordesley Junction the canal branched, one line going left towards Warwick Bar and Fellows Morton's old Fazeley Street depot, the other diving under a grey iron towpath bridge towards Saltley. Opposite the junction, against a factory, lay two Birmingham Salvage Department boats loading factory rubbish.

91

We swung under the bridge towards the next flight of locks, down one of the last narrow canals to be built, the Birmingham and Warwick Junction Canal and the last outpost of the Grand Union system. It had been built in the 1840's to provide a link with the Cannock coalfields to the south and to supply a sort of canal by-pass to central Birmingham. The canal lay ahead, straight as a ruler for three parts of a mile, terminating in a distant view of a top gate. The autumn sunlight shafted down onto a succession of similar brick arches marching in ever-diminishing progression to that remote top gate. Through this lengthy vista we chugged, blowing smoke rings towards the rows of brick walls, broken windows and grimy houses which bordered the cut.

While Camp Hill commemorates, so I understand, a camp made by Prince Rupert in the Civil War, so the name 'Garrison' for this part of Birmingham recalls the practice of stationing troops in the area from Napoleonic times up until the establishment of a civilian police force in the 1830's. Whatever the provenance of their name the ensuing flight of five locks was the filthiest piece of canal I had yet encountered, bar none. Grease oozed blackly from the lock chambers as we dropped. A sort of foul, black patina settled on brass and paintwork. In the far distance the outlines of the empty gasholders at Saltley and the fuming stacks and coolers of Neachells Power Station beckoned us on. To our left lay railway yards with their rakes of clangorously buffering wagons, snorting tank engines and mournfully hooting shunters. Further down lay the reeking steam sheds, the residence of grimy, forlorn steam locomotives.

"Enterprise" was now passing her birthplace, the erstwhile Saltley yard of Fellows Morton and Clayton where she had first been launched in 1903. Now there was just a shell of the yard left. Much of the valuable iron shaping and other dockyard plant had been sold for scrap—Wilfred had carried away some of the last in "Barnet". Now doors banged echoingly back and forth in the deserted buildings and rats scurried above the oily water level.

It was a relief to drop down beneath Saltley station and emerge from beneath the railway into a wider vista. The canal curved round a reservoir from which, as at Braunston, pumps took lockage water back to the top of the flight. Across the towpath was the River Rea and beyond it stood the magnificence of Saltley Gas Works. The giant holders telescoped up within a fretted lacework of grey, iron girders and fine, blackened stacks and retort houses were shielded by a lofty wall. Further in the distance stood the generator houses, stacks and coolers of Neachells Power Station with its ganglion of wires, pylons and transformers. Behind this pulsating heart of industry Gravelly Hill rose with its tiers of terraced houses and serried rows of chimneys. Just as in the centre of a hurricane one finds an eye of peace, so it seemed the canal had found a little oasis of calm surrounded by the roaring storm of industry. We crossed the rivers Rea and Tame on brick aqueducts, locked down the last, shallow lock, which was really more of a regulating lock than anything else, and nosed under a towpath bridge onto the Birmingham and Fazeley Canal.

Until recently regular coal traffic had come this way onto the Grand Union from the Cannock Chase collieries, some going through to Nestlés at Hayes. The course as far as Camp Hill followed the locks in the boatman's jingle:-

"Moshes, two the Ganzies seven,
The New Thirteen and the lousy 'leven."

Discounting the shallow stop lock through which we had just come, this gave the apt title of the "lousy 'leven" to Camp Hill and Garrison Locks. The other names referred to Daw End, Rushall and Perry Barr Locks respectively, on the road from Cannock. Behind us more melancholy dereliction overhung the gantries and basins of Neachells Power Station. In front a half-sunk Joey boat lay forlornly against the coal yard of T. and S. Element, one of the last great Black Country boating firms in business.

The Birmingham and Fazeley was an early canal, sometimes called by Grand Union boaters 'The Bottom Road'. Its different character was soon made apparent by the sight of an old, grimy, brick bridge, amid pylons and wastelands bearing the cast iron legend "Trout Pool Bridge". Looking down at the now turgid waters of the Tame I wondered when the last trout rose there and tried to visualise the time when the limpid Tame ran through willowy meadows beneath the bluff of Gravelly Hill. Such meditations were soon interrupted by our approach to a large, modern factory building which straddled the canal, towpath and all. On the outside, steel doors in the concrete walls led into boiler rooms, whilst mooring rings and scattered pea coal suggested that boat traffic still came to the factory. For how much longer a boatman's muscle and shovel would compete with the tipper or tanker-lorry was in doubt.

In seeming contrast, at "The Tyburn" pub we came upon a modern factory on the canalside with landscaped gardens and modern overhead unloading apparatus. I remembered how, not long before, the magazine "Waterways" had announced triumphantly that trade was returning to Birmingham's canals in the shape of specially built Joey boats and pusher tugs shuttling castings between this factory and a foundry some miles back. It was a brave idea but it faded away.—another example of too little, too late.

Dusk began to fall at the top lock of the Minworth flight, which was guarded by a typical BCN lock house with cast iron number plate and spiky tooth chimney pots. Here we had to clear quantities of floating timber and other detritus away before entering the chamber. A massive pile at the lock mouth indicated that the lock-keeper had been similarly employed earlier.

Once past the three locks we plodded slowly by a scrap yard, a sewage works and down long straights into the gathering darkness. At length the bright lights of a shop near a bridgehole induced us to stop for provisions; a busy little general shop attached to the pub was still doing a roaring trade. Since the sides were appallingly shallow and there was unlikely to be any commercial traffic—for Barlows coal trade into Birmingham had ceased and the 'Bottom Road' only saw empties bound for the Warwickshire coalfields—we tied our stern in the deep water by the bridgehole in strict defiance of British Waterways byelaws. "If they don't like it," said Bill sleepily, "they can bloody-well clean the mooring places out." Around us trees and hedges rose up towards the autumn night sky. It was as peaceful a tie-up as you could hope to find, as well as being handy for the inn, so there we remained.

The next morning we were greeted at the bottom of Curdworth locks by an elderly couple who had only recently stopped working a boat. They were living in a 'Waterways' house nearby and seemed pathetically anxious to know whether any boats were close to. The disappointment on the old man's face when we told him there were none to come for some days was heart-rending. I learnt later that they had been compulsorily retired and put in this cottage, which was three miles from any shop, nearly five miles from a Post Office where pensions could be drawn (the old man was too proud to ask for any help and walked), and had only very basic facilities. Their only contact with the outside world was a passing boat. Eventually Leslie Morton found them a pair of boats which they worked until a more appropriate home could be found for them.

Fazeley Junction, with its bay-windowed toll house, its overshadowing four-square mill and nearby workers cottages provided a pleasing glimpse of an early industrial canalscape. It also marked, for several long years, the furthest north in my journeys over the canals. Fazeley is very nearly the centre of England, providing a series of links to the Severn, the Thames, the Trent and the Mersey and there were elements of a mixture of regions in its atmosphere. The mill and its cottages suggested the hosiery trade of the East Midlands, the canal brought to mind the West Midlands, and the distant collieries were reminders of the North Warwickshire coalfields. We turned eastwards across the Tame aqueduct into Warwickshire where the river was broader and not as full of rubbish as in Birmingham. However, its black, detergent-flecked waters still looked singularly uninviting. An uneventful run through undistinguished countryside brought us under the Midland railway line to the bottom of Glascote Two, our first Coventry Canal locks. These locks had double bottom gates and side ponds—the first we had seen since the Grand Union. The top gate of the bottom lock leaked abominably and had partly drained the short pound above it, leaving rusty bicycles, bedsteads, car parts and other nasty objects stranded. We soon found that the Coventry Canal Company evidently had a great liking for small ground paddles, for the lock took ages to fill and once this was done water had to be run down from the top lock to refill the pound, a procedure which wasted both time and water.

For the next few miles the canal ran through scenery scarred by years of mining for coal. Mysterious heaps and scarps alternated with hollows and flashes where land water had filled up subsidence. The buildings hereabouts were of smoke-blackened brick and the grimy bulk of Tamworth church away to the left did little to lighten the atmosphere. Grim rows of colliers cottages with gardens coming down to the canal bank told us we were again nearing an industrial area. The West Coast main railway line, from which we had parted at Buckby, ran parallel to the canal again and stayed near until the last lap of our journey.

In places the boat would appear to leap forward as the propellor bit into deep water near some subsidence. As we wound our way up the Anker valley in a series of leaps and halts a tall, steel chimney plumed with smoke and steam appeared between the spoil heaps. At length, creeping under a low tramway bridge over which a snorting saddle-tank engine was drawing black trucks marked with white crosses, we came upon the last waterside colliery in the South Eastern Division, Pooley Hall. A lay-by formed an island between the colliery and the canal and the pithead gear with its winding-house rose directly above the water, wheels spinning in opposite directions and steam jetting from the winding-house exhaust.

Shortly beyond, just as Rolt had described in 1939, the crumbling remains of Pooley Hall, on a leafy bluff above the canal, added poignant contrast.

Beyond Polesworth lay a short section of sandy country with ferns and bracken by an occupation swing bridge; a notoriously "bad playze" for loaded boats. Then through pleasant fields and wooded hedgerows, past a small loading place which seemed almost too silted to load anything, we progressed to the Atherstone Flight. By the second lock we met the lock-keeper who lived in a nearby Company House. Lock-keepers were counted as 'traffic' staff and not, as now, 'engineering' and he gaped in amazement. "I thought all single motors was a-finished," he commented. We explained who we were and asked for news of traffic. Mark and Dolly had come from Tipton after emptying their timber and had re-loaded the day before at Baddesley Basin, and a loaded pair from Pooley Hall were an hour or so in front of us. We could leave the locks full and top gates open as empties were due down from Coventry later on. Although traffic here was a shadow of its former self, we began to feel that we were coming back into a more hopeful world than we had been in since Birmingham. At least some trade was about and there was some form of control still working.

As we rose in the fifth lock, with its little brick cottage set snugly close to the lockside, a blur of smoke could be seen from further ahead, indicating a loaded pair of boats in front. By the time we had reached the second lock their butty was rising in the top lock so we waited there for them to clear. Drawing-off the top lock, I saw that the pair, a British Waterways one, had pulled in on the towpath side while the captain, a neat, dark, well-built young man, and his wife scrubbed the cloths thoroughly and mopped down the paintwork. His tiller was upturned in the ramshead, a sign that he was going no further that day.

The boatman and his wife waved to us cheerfully as we nosed under the bridge, our exhaust echoing, and passed a factory which was devoted to hat-making. Whiffs of steam gurgled out of pipes, saucy girls shouted and laughed from windows at us and looking into a store we saw piles of trilbies, porkpies and, incongrously, several stacks of red fezzes!

At Mancetter, where Willow Wren loaded roadstone for West Drayton, the colour of the water began to change from its usual murky, greasy grey to a dull red, thickening as we progressed until it became the colour and consistency of tomato soup. Some turns were well-piled and dredged and we swam round them with little

96

trouble. Others were full of the red, sticky goo and "Enterprise's" blades thrashed noisily through them. Marching alongside the towpath and bending remorselessly with it were many-barred telegraph poles giving the canal an air of trunk line importance, like a railway or a main road. The oncoming fore-ends of two British Waterways pairs going down to Baddesley, smoke rolling briskly from the cabin chimneys, added to the impression of being on a busy canal once again.

The elegant clock-tower and buildings of Hartshill maintenance yard appeared, making an attractive picture which was spoiled by the villainous stench arising from the canal. As we entered a belt of fir trees on the canal side I saw in front a line of bubbles stretching out from the towpath, and soon my worst fears were justified. On the towpath side a sewer outfall was voiding its filthy black contents into the canal which here changed to a darker red. Just beyond, a large diameter pipe spewed out red sludge, the washing from a roadstone quarry. Where it fell into the canal we could see a pile of red mud rising to the surface. As with the Grand Union below Berkhamstead, this was the best and most profitable use the B.T.C. could put the canal to. They allowed these discharges to be made in return for a payment, supposedly to cover dredging costs, but these had risen and the payments were quite inadequate. In the meantime, this user interfered with the legitimate use of the canal as a transport route and it was this particular section which in the end broke the resolution of the long distance carriers to continue. In Autumn 1962 it was bad but by the end of the 1960's even pleasure boats were having difficulty in passing!

Signs of town life began to appear on the outskirts of Nuneaton. Rubbish strewed the banks and allotments, back gardens and playing fields came down to the canal. We passed a deep red brick mill with a clock on a tower. The section from Hartshill was called "between the clocks" and should take about fifty five minutes empty and an hour and a quarter loaded. It was dusk by now so I retired below for my supper while Bill steered round Griff Hollows and Arbury Turns. As we glided past Marston Junction in the gloom, I caught a glimpse of the Ashby Canal running tantalisingly away eastward.

We came to Hawkesbury in the dark. I was ready for the worst as we swung "Enterprise" through the tight ninety degree turn. Our headlight lit up the windows of a row of terraced cottages, one of them being a pub called "The Greyhound" as we spun round. There was just room for a single boat above the shallow stop lock and we dropped into this and tied up. Chimneys smoked in the dark, brasses picked up stray beams of light, cabin doors were closed with aerials a-hoist and wirelesses and televisions playing inside. Across the elder bushes the great power station boomed and fumed, stray dogs barked, couplings jangled on buffering rail wagons - all else was still.

At the "Greyhound" a bevy of children clustered round the door which opened onto a long, flagged passage. The familiar reek of Old Holborn and A1 Light came rolling out into the night. Inside, the passage led to a room containing settles, benches, scrubbed-top tables and an old wooden carved chair. There was no bar, the centrepiece being a fireplace in which blazed a fire banked far up the chimney and hot enough to smelt iron. A dartboard at the far end completed the picture. The room was occupied by about twenty men wearing bib and brace overalls and cloth caps. Some were playing darts, some dominoes. As we came in one man on the settle near the passage waved us down beside him. He was a complete stranger but had such a look of welcoming curiosity that I had difficulty in preventing myself from grinning.

"Wheer are ye loadin' for?" he questioned. As we explained our business the domino players turned to have a look at us. We recognised several and they nodded back. A plump, pleasant woman of about forty appeared beside us with a tray.

"Yes please?" she said.

Our new companion smiled. "Give her yer orders, that's what she wants." We ordered mild, which seemed to be the most popular drink. Bill went to sit on the carved chair near the fire and our companion said "Everyone as sits in that chair dies." Bill leaped up before realising that the statement was true of everybody, and the company chuckled. This we learned was a favourite trick played on newcomers.

On the other side of the fire sat an elderly couple. The man was tall and thin-faced with close-set blue eyes, rosy cheeks, a white moustache and white hair crammed under a battered trilby. He wore an old jacket, waistcoat and striped, collarless shirt with a neckscarf and when he stood up I saw he wore corduroy trousers of the flap-front variety and boots. The woman had a pleasant, if rather whiskery, face and her hair was topped by a maroon beret. She wore a black coat and an ancient skirt and jumper. They were, despite their age, a remarkably handsome couple. The old man leaned across to me and said in a rather high-pitched Oxfordshire brogue, "Did I hear you say as you was from Readin'?" I told him

98

that I was, but that Bill was from Newbury. "I suppose you knows Mr. 'Utchings then," he replied.

I realised then who he was, for 'Hutch' had often spoken of Joe Skinner, the last of the Oxford Canal 'Number Ones'. Joe in turn naturally assumed that everyone from Reading would know Denys Hutchings, whom he had met holidaying on the Oxford Canal with his old rowing gig. When I confirmed that I knew him, Joe continued, "Well I'm blowed. D'you 'ear that Rose, 'e knows Mester 'Utchings."

Rose said "Ar, an' we knows Mester 'Utchings an' all, don't we Joe?"

This effectively broke the ice and from that time on, until their deaths many years later, Joe and Rose became very dear and valued friends with whom I was destined to make some remarkable journeys.

All too quickly the evening passed. Mrs Nelson, the landlady, bustled to and fro with trays full of beer until time was called. At this, everyone drank up and slowly made their way to the door. Outside we stood chatting long after the lights went out and then Joe and Rose crossed to their boat "Friendship" which lay just on the Coventry side of the junction, having given us pressing invitations to visit them the next day.

Early the next morning the throbbing of engines announced the departure of the loaded boats for the south, but the empties would not get their loading orders until the boat control office opened at nine o'clock. From about nine fifteen a steady procession of empties worked through the stop lock, some heading south in the Coventry direction for the Keresley Colliery loading bay at Longford; others turning north for Newdigate Colliery Basin at Bedworth, Baddesley or Pooley Hall. Before leaving we walked round to "Friendship" where Joe was raking the cut for driftwood. "Friendship" was a small, wooden boat which had been built at Sephtons yard, opposite its present moorings, in 1923. It had been hauled by a mule, Dolly, which the Skinners had acquired as Great War surplus. Until 1958 they carried coal to Banbury Dairy and the New World Gas Cooker factory in Birmingham. The towpath on the Oxford Summit grew steadily worse as years went by and in spite of the Skinners' protests and letters from Rose, who was, as she proudly informed us, "a scholard", nothing was done. Unfortunately, Dolly fell into the cut one night at Griffins Bridge, Wormleighton, on the way back from Banbury. Joe got her out with a nearby farmer's assistance and put her under cover. She recovered sufficiently to pull to the bottom of Napton, but Joe was forced to send her from there to Coventry in a horsebox while he and Rose bow-hauled to Braunston. From there an empty pair towed them to Hawkesbury. After a rest they worked Dolly to Birmingham but the terrible effort of drawing the loaded boat through the shallows of the Bottom Road brought her down with pneumonia. Joe had had to put her out of her misery, after a lifetime's work, in the stables of the pub at Curdworth. They had then tried buttying to a motor worked by a friend but Joe could not get on with motor boats and, as he was of retirement age, had given it up. British Waterways allowed the old couple to keep their boat free of charge at Hawkesbury, where they had a cottage near the "Greyhound". However, they rarely lived ashore, preferring the familiar cosiness of "Friendship's" cabin. Although I did on one occasion find them eating Sunday lunch in the cottage parlour, Joe seemed to use the cottage purely as a store for old bicycles and similar valuables in which he dealt.

"Friendship" had been docked by Herbert Tooley of Banbury not long before the Skinners retired and, when Joe lifted up the canvas covering the cabin side, the faded richness of her paint shone out. The cabin side had three panels, two small ones and a large one between. The rear panel had a Tooley Castle painted on. The middle was a rich deep red with a grained surround, lined yellow and edged with delicate brown scallops—known to boaters as Vandyking. The name, sign-written in florid, bold capitals set out in a graceful curve, said "Josh Skinner". In the corners or spandrels above the name and in the space below were bunches of roses. The front, small panel was green with another bunch of roses. Along the top plank of the hull running forward for half the cabin's length were large diamonds with a stylised four-leaf clover design in brown quartering each one vertically. Joe let the canvas fall and the glories of the paintwork were covered once more.

"We don't go out now, we don't," said Rose. "Only with our mates from Coventry, don't we Joe?"

Joe nodded vigorously, "Oh Cri-ar mate! Only wi' old Bert." This, we discovered, referred to the trips they made in summer with a schoolmaster friend who owned a motor boat. They did in fact make several expeditions by car and were about to make another one soon to Banbury Fair, a favourite boaters' rendezvous. Joe walked back to "Enterprise" with us, shook us firmly by the hand and urged us to call on him soon.

We were both silent as we resumed our journey back to Braunston, for there was a quaint but nonetheless potent impressiveness about Joe. He had not then been 'discovered' by the enthusiasts world, although he had been both mentioned and depicted in books as far back as "Narrow Boat". In later years people were to exalt this straightforward, uncomplicated old man into almost mystic heights. In fact Joe and Rose were unspoiled but mystified by this adulation. Yet I can understand it because like 'B-J', Morton, David Hambridge and so many others in the canal world, they were survivors of a different ethos. They were born and grew up into a harder social environment than Welfare State Britain and had survived wars and hardships bruised but not broken. Their nineteenth century world still admired and respected individualism both in initiative and responsibility and, for all their lack of wealth and position, they were people of spirit and character. I think for this reason Joe became a living symbol of such a spirit to the many hundreds who came to know him in later years.

Realising that our journey was drawing to an end and knowing that there were no locks until Hillmorton, I took the opportunity of catching up with accounts, correspondence and general office work after passing through Ansty. I scribbled and typed away emerging briefly to observe our progress over Brinklow Bank where, I realised, I had first seen working boats at the tender age of three from one of the trains that ran so close to the canal here. Away to the south west the spires and stacks of Coventry lay along the horizon.

I did not finish the paper work until we had passed through Newbold Tunnel with its generous size and twin towpaths. Then I took over, in Wilfred's words, as "navigating officer". We were crossing two small aqueducts with elegant iron railings on the northern outskirts of Rugby, after which the way wound through willows and rolling country, across the Avon once more and under the great, steel viaduct which carried the Great Central line over the main West Coast Line. We travelled past Clifton Road Wharf where we met "Malta" and "Grace" hastening to Hawkesbury for the weekend. Jim, their captain, informed us that Hillmorton was ready for us. The weather had become overcast with lowering skies. The Indian Summer we had had since leaving Reading was over and grey autumn was arriving.

Up the duplicated locks of Hillmorton we went and along the straight at Barby with its motorway bridge which seemed endless, as did the muddy turns in the fields beyond. At long last came Willoughby Bridge and the first sight of Braunston spire, but the tantalising bends and curves seemed to last forever. A grey drizzle set in, dulling our newly polished brasses, as we came round Braunston turn five days and a hundred miles after we had left for the Brummagem Road. Whilst not in the "Golden Hind" class, we felt, as we tied up at Bottom Lock, that we had made a worthwhile circumnavigation. In the ten days since leaving Brentford we had travelled over two hundred and fifty miles and disposed of no less than four contracts. Despite the weather there was some cause to feel optimistic and we swaggered up to the "Nelson" to boast of our achievements to anyone who would care to listen.

Above: *Enterprise* in our early days on the Kennet. Though this scene was within the Borough boundary of Reading the waterside cottage had no mains electricity, sewerage or running water!
Below: En route to Brentford, March 1962, at Marsh Lock, Henley-on-Thames.
(Reading Museum & Art Gallery)

Above: British Waterways narrowboats transhipping steel at Brentford. The 'white' building, centre background, was Leslie Morton's office. *(BWB)*
Opposite upper: Fishery Inn, Boxmoor. *(Edward Paget-Tomlinson)*
Opposite lower: Stoke Bruerne top lock as kept by Jack James. The boat on the left is *Thaxted* as featured in chapter 3, Book 1. *(Barnaby's)*

"Sparrows 'ud drink of the gunnels!" — *Crane* and *Wagtail* tied near Blisworth. *(Edward Paget-Tomlinson)*

Arthur and Ernie with a pair of Barlows entering the Nelson Lock at Braunston. *(Mike Webb)*

Top left: "George" *(H. McKnight)*
Top right: "Ray" *(H. McKnight)*
Left: "Wilfred" *(A. Brown)*
Above: "The Gaffer" *(H. McKnight)*

Top left: "Suff" *(BWB)*
Top right: Teddy Cook *(L. Cook)*
Left: Joe Skinner *(The author)*
Above: "Mark & Dolly" *(Mike Webb)*

Above: "It was Autumn when next we came to Braunston." *Enterprise* buttying *Southam* past Willow Wren's yard. Bill Fisher, in overalls, and Nicholas Hill, coiling stern rope — see chapter 5, Book 1. *(Mike Webb)*
Below: Pooley Hall Colliery loading wharf. *(the author)*

'Proud Titania' — an immaculately turned-out British Waterways pair heading South along the North Oxford Canal near Rugby. *(Edward Paget-Tomlinson)*

Above: "Charlie" on the butty *Wagtail* at Hawkesbury Junction. *(Mike Webb).*
Opposite: "Now even the clumsy lighters were dwarfed"—Limehouse Dock in 1962.
(BWB).

"Mark...was at Boxmoor"—Mark & Dolly and the two girls with *Quail* and *Kingfisher* frozen-in during the great frost of January 1963. Mark has partially insulated his engine hole by covering it with a canvas sheet. Both boats were loaded with timber for Birmingham. *(A. Brown).*

BOOK 2 ❧
Getting 'em Ahead

1
Setting
On

On Wednesday morning fog shrouded Braunston, cloaking Butchers Bridge with a damp veil. Towards midday came the beating of a National diesel. "One of our'n," said someone and we waited to see who it was, for several pairs had gone to load. Through the fog came a tremendous boom. "COLIN! Get back on that BLOODY BOAT!" We chuckled. It could only be George, late resident of "Tern", addressing his son and heir.

George, when he arrived and tied up, was not pleased that we had not yet boarded "Tern". "What's wrong wi'er?" he demanded. "Ain't I cleaned her up enough for yer?"

We explained that we were awaiting the 'Gaffer' before moving on, which mollified him somewhat, and that very morning we received confirmation that we could consider ourselves 'set on' for official purposes from the following day. Leslie Morton made one, very important concession to us, which was, I think, unique. He agreed to stamp both our Insurance Cards, deducting the employees' portion from our joint settlements at the end of each trip. Usually the firm merely employed a captain. His mates, including wives and children, had no National Insurance contributions against their names whatsoever. This rule applied to all the carriers, even British Waterways, and was indicative of the low profit margins by then obtaining in the industry. This meant that although I was nominally the captain, we were in practice of equal status within the Company heirarchy. This status was at the very bottom of the 'pecking order' when it came to boats, gear, orders or other perks. Nevertheless, as from 18th October 1962 we were employees of the Willow Wren Canal Carrying Company, entitled to rent free accommodation aboard the Company's craft, twenty two shillings and sixpence per day if unavoidably detained by causes beyond our control, and such other carriage rates and extras as the Company might determine. In return we were to be entrusted with a fully equipped motor boat and butty in full working order to go whither the Company might reasonably order us.

Thursday and Friday were spent getting our kit aboard the pair and cleaning out "Enterprise". It was always customary among boaters to scrub out a cabin when entering and leaving a boat. Our butty was reputed to have been Fellows Morton's "Minnie" but was now called "Teal". The motor "Tern" had originally been called "Emu"; being one of the first motors to join the Willow Wren fleet on its formation in 1954. She was fitted with a modern twin-cylinder Bolinder with electric starting and closed-circuit water cooling. This was a Willow Wren idea intended to obtain the advantages of a water-cooled engine (cooler and quieter running) without the disadvantages of blocking-up with mud, freezing or running dry. The outlet pipe passed under the counter, round the stern and back into the other side. It was topped-up by a header tank in the engine room, beneath which we installed our Elsan from "Enterprise". This surprised some visitors because the ensemble resembled what house agents coyly call "a low-down suite", but closer inspection revealed no chain or flushing handle.

Across the front bulkhead was a very large fuel tank, above which was a small five gallon tank fed by a semi-rotary pump, with a gauge-glass beside it. This was the standard Fellows Morton installation dating from single Bolinder days. It did away with the need for a lift pump in the supply line to the injection pumps and thus simplified the installation. It was, however, necessary to spend a minute or so each morning pumping up the top tank. The gauge enabled one to see at a glance how much fuel oil remained in the top or "day" tank; if it was dangerously low, a few strokes on the semi-rotary would replenish it.

Each boat had a boatman's cabin quite different from that on "Enterprise". Like most working boats, entrance was from both ends, the main one being via double doors with a slide overhead, leading from the stern deck. These doors could be closed behind the steersman, whose head and shoulders only needed to be exposed to the elements as he stood on the footboard at the top of the cabin steps, his lower half being inside the cabin. On either side of the steps were enclosed shelves known as soap holes in which one kept windlasses, brasso, rubbing rags and similar gear. To the left— handy for the steersman—was a small drawer called the ticket- drawer in which one kept loading advices, toll tickets, packets of cigarettes, matches, whipping string, pens, screwdrivers, pliers and similar small but vital emergency gear, and adjacent to this was a small wall cupboard and shelves.

On the motor-boat there was a "Guidwife" coal range on which Bill unsucessfully attempted to cook. The trouble was that the smoke channels round the oven were thoroughly bunged-up with soot and to clear it would mean complete dismantling, for which we never seemed to have time. The butty had a small, slow-combustion stove, of a very efficient type, which roared away happily on a handful of pea coal. This was known as a 'bostin stove' and ensured that the lower half of the steersman was red hot. There was space next to this for the Calor Gas cooker from "Enterprise", and when clean and polished this looked quite imposing residing beside the enamelled 'bostin stove'. The gas cylinder stowed away beneath the range, which is quite safe as long as one turns the gas off at the bottle as well as at the appliance. I purloined "Enterprise's" brass-rimmed chimney to go on the cabin top above the range. On the right a low bench with lockers beneath, one containing the lighting battery, ran forward. Opposite was the circular-topped 'table-cupboard'; being a flap which let down to form a table and revealing a nest of shelves where one could keep crockery and some food. There was a small drawer beneath for knives and other eating irons, then a tiny cupboard at floor level. Next came the cross-bed which folded up during the day, above it was a 'bed hole cupboard' in which clothes could be kept, below on both sides were large drawers—again at floor level and rather prone to damp. In order to give us more seating space, George had proudly presented us with a short plank which fitted across the bed-hole by day. It had been made, he informed us, by his eldest daughter Janet—"our big wench" as he called her. Its proper name was a seat board. We always called it: "Our wench's board"!

On the motor, right at the stern, was a semi-circular space beneath the counter which made a useful storage space, on the butty a similar space—triangular in plan—lay beneath the stern deck. This proved to be an excellent store for potatoes. A large, wooden coal-box provided a step down and closed this last space off. Beyond the cross-bed a door in the cabin front—perversely called 'the back door'—led into the engine hole on the motor and into the holds on the butty. The whole of this living space occupied an area some eight foot long by seven feet wide. It was lit by a side porthole and a rooftop bullseye by day and by a 12 volt D.C. electric bulb by night. This was the space in which whole families were conceived, born, reared and died. It was decorated in varnished scratch graining with landscape panels on the doors, hatchway and table cupboard. The walls and cupboard doors were adorned with roses.

Ahead of the cabinwork lay the holds; that of the motor being somewhat shorter in length. Each one had two tapering stands extending from the kelson to about three feet six inches above the gunwales. These were to be the supports for the gang planks when loaded and were slotted into stout cross beams which, when empty, alone supported the planks. A third cross beam held a stout, square towing mast of the same height as the stands, this was hollow and contained a sliding oak extension sheathed in iron called the 'top mast', at the top of which was a sprung iron peg, shaped to accept the bight of a rope. This part was called the 'loobey'. Beyond was a tarpaulin with a wooden shelf beneath. This construction was called a 'cratch' (a word connected with the French 'creche'—a manager) which was a useful store for ropes, tarpaulins and similar gear. In the extreme fore-end, just like "Enterprise", a deck with a hinged lid provided yet more storage space for gear. The hold had an oak gunwale on either side, on the top of which were rolled-up tarpaulins known as 'side cloths'. These had ropes spliced to eyelets on one side, and these ropes could be passed over the top planks when laid on the stands to similar eyelets on the other side cloths. The side cloths then formed a partial covering for the hold, which could be completed by draping and securing 'top cloths' over the top plank. These stretched to the gunwales on each side and made a complete watertight covering to the hold. The part over the top plank was protected by narrow strips of tarpaulin known as 'tippets'. Willow Wren always used green duck tarpaulins for top and side cloths and tippets. The top cloths were stencilled with the firm's initials in black, whereas British Waterways used heavy black cloths, stencilled in white with their initials and the boat's operating number. The cloths were held down by eyelet ropes and by 'top strings' which passed over the cloths to iron rings stapled into recesses in the gunwales. It was a simple and workmanlike arrangement.

The cabin sides were light green, lined yellow, panelled scarlet with a circular device in cream which had a red centre. This heraldic device was, I believe, another product of Leslie Morton's fertile brain. A sable bird, supposedly a Willow Wren, rested on a target gules (ie. on the red circle there was a black bird); on the cream part was the company's name, while the Brentford address and telephone number filled up the vacant green cabin side. The stern cabin ends were cream with a red ogee reaching its apex at the top centre of the doors.

The top cloths had to be drawn from the store and the working tackle, in the shape of ropework, put aboard. The inventory of ropework alone for a fully-rigged pair of boats was enormous; involving the supplying of sufficient lines for us to splice and whip a long towline (coir) in six inch circumference rope, a short snatcher, uphill and downhill runners, holding back straps and cross straps in four inch manilla or hemp, a hundred foot cotton bowhauling line, two sets of front and back strings for tying-up and two mastlines in cotton, plus miles of sisal breeching strings, girders and tarpaulin ropes for securing planks and cloths.

The false floors had been lifted up on both sides to allow air to circulate freely and to discourage rot. These had to be relaid before going to load and some broken or rotten boards and bearers replaced.

By Saturday morning, however, we were ready to go. "Enterprise" was closed up, the engine snugged down and batteries disconnected before shafting her into the storage reservoir. She looked very forlorn with all her fittings stripped-off; for the first time for nearly a year there was nobody living aboard. We turned our new pair in the reservoir entrance, collected £5 starting money, which was to last us until final settlement at the end of the first trip, and set off just before two o'clock for 'Suttons Stop'.

We proudly threaded through Butchers Bridge, past the Stop and round the turn. "Tern's" exhaust throbbed urgently, with a more powerful and deeper note than "Enterprise's" Armstrong Siddeley. Our wash plopped off the piling, the butty swinging obediently behind on its cross-straps and needing just a touch on the tiller to follow the motor's course.

Pride had a quick fall. As we forged majestically through the second main road bridge, an imperious horn rang out. Thundering in from Braunston fields came the two Ted Barretts, father and son, with two pairs of Waterways boats loaded for Croxley Mills. Bill slacked "Tern" down to let them pass and we promptly went 'berry-collecting' in the overhanging bushes. As we wrestled with chimneys, mop sticks, cabin shafts and watercans entangling themselves in the branches, Bill failed to notice that "Tern's" towing studs, or 'dollies', had a slight rake sternwards Consequently when "Teal" rode forward she playfully slipped her overhanging cross-straps. The merriment of the Barrett family at our bush-bound state changed to hysteria as Bill went hard ahead and thrashed out into the channel leaving "Teal' behind with myself roaring frantically after him. Young Ted's wife laughed so loud that she in turn crashed into the piling through the bridge and was duly sworn at by Ted. Neither Bill nor I spoke until we had passed Willoughby Bridge, by which time I had made the important discovery that provided the butty's cross straps are tight, one can lash the tiller and perform little chores as one goes along.

Beyond the muddy turns below Barby Hill, the masts of Hillmorton Radio Station, weaving their fantastic, petrified giant's dance, were already decking themselves with red warning lights in the thin, chilly October afternoon. We managed to negotiate the double narrow locks at Hillmorton with little incident, but found that one had one's hands full with a boat apiece. As the butty dropped downhill, I unrolled the new cotton mast-line, took it from the 'loobey', round the bottom gate rails to the mouth of the motor's lock. As the motor came out, Bill would pick this up, take a turn on his 'dollies' and go steadily ahead. By now the butty's lock was ready, I had just enough time to 'leg' one gate open, push the other and run to the stern before the butty began to move out of the lock on a long towline. Twice we did this, but below the bottom the motor had to reverse into the butty's lock mouth to pick up the cross straps.

As we moved through the golf courses near Clifton Road Wharf and headed towards the gaunt steel outline of the Great Central Viaduct, dusk began to fall. I put the tiller strings on and prepared supper, which I took forward to Bill—balancing acrobatically along the planks with a mug in one hand and plates in the other. We wound round Cathirons, through the gloomy boskiness of Hall Oaks and Brinklow cutting into the more open country beyond Stretton Stop. Away to the south west the myriad lights of Coventry twinkled and sent up a glare into the night sky; both cabin chimneys sent rolling clouds of smoke into the blackness and the engine throbbed its deep song, our headlight catching the reflections off the narrow, wind-ruffled surface. Our spirits rose again as, just beyond the Farmhouse Turn at Ansty, Bill shouted and pointed ahead. Outlined against the lurid Coventry night sky rose the fuming stacks of Hawkesbury Power Station flanked by the Longford Gasworks. It was a sight as welcome to the canal boater as the Bishops Rock light to the Trans Atlantic mariner.

Darkness became daylight as we slipped past the gantries of the power station into the sharp curve leading to Hawkesbury Stop Lock. The orange glare of sodium vapour floodlights reflected off gobbetting clouds of steam, transformers hummed and high voltage current crackled bluely overhead. Then, abruptly, we left the twentieth century and glided in the quiet blackness towards our destination. Our light picked up the blue and gold of Waterways cabin ends moored two abreast with a narrow channel between them. At the very end, on the left, red, green and white paint bespoke a pair of Barlows lying empty, so we breasted up, moved in behind and tied up.

We woke the next day to a grey, brisk Sunday. Distantly, church bells clanged. Bill Whitlock came biking under the iron bridge by the lock, newspapers under his arm. He pulled up, propped the bicycle against a post and sauntered along to us. He grinned knowingly, "Just got up are ye?"

"Up for hours," we lied.

He nodded sagely. "I thought you'd bin busy, you ain't 'ad time ter clean yer brasses yet!" Then he settled himself down in the butty hatches and proceeded to read the "News of the World" and "Sunday Pictorial" to an audience of several families clustering in their sterns. The women listened poker-faced as Bill delivered account after account of errant vicars and scout masters. Nobody was much interested in football or racing, nor in such political comment as these journals carried, but the Pictorial's 'Rat of the Week' column received much appreciation and close comment.

Later that morning I strolled down to the open ground near where the Skinners were moored. A little knot of women and children and one or two embarrassed-looking men were gathered near the Salvation Army hut. Two Salvationists, Brigadier Fielding and his wife, were holding one of their last outdoor services before the weather drove them indoors. This couple, together with the Reverend Chapman at Brentford—representing the London and City Mission—were the only evidence I saw of organised religion on the cut. Although Sister Mary Ward, a Catholic, had gone by now, the Reverend Chapman and the Fieldings showed a truly ecumenical approach, but as an Anglican I was saddened to see that most incumbents ignored the canals in their parishes. Although few boaters professed a regular faith, there were those to whom the Church did not minister in vain, whilst at christenings and funerals they would nearly all diligently seek the Church's blessing. In marriage though, the people I knew generally went to the Registry Office. I was moved by the little congregation outside the green wooden hut. I felt that He who took His followers from among fishermen and humble folk was not in spirit far from the hearts of those few. While not a Salvationist, my heart went out to those good people who stoutly refused to abandon their dwindling flock.

Back at our boats Mrs Whitlock came to our stern ends to

demand of us what we were having for Sunday lunch. I was cooking a large steak and kidney pie with peas and potatoes which I would grill first then roast in bacon fat under the grill. She was somewhat surprised that we should be living so lavishly and then asked what we had for pudding. I replied that I would probably open a tin of pears. She nodded sagely and shuffled off and I carried on with my domestic chores. A minute or so later there was a bang on the cabin. I looked out to see Joan, her daughter, with a very tempting apple pie in a dish. She held it out, saying "Mam says you're to put this in your oven and let her have the dish back." I thanked her and took it in wonderment. Another minute or two passed, there came another bang and this time it was Bill Whitlock. He had finished his newspaper-reading and had brought us the "News of the World" and "Pictorial". He wanted the "Pictorial" back when we had finished it because it was good for firelighting, but we could keep the "News of the World".

The growl of P.D.2 engines at some ghastly hour heralded the early departure on Monday morning of the 'Waterways' pairs who had spent the weekend at the Stop. We were up and breakfasted by eight, but then had to wait until eight thirty when the control officer's car squeezed over the towpath bridge and stopped outside the red brick traffic office, into which he disappeared. Another half hour went by. We hung around, filling watercans and pumping up the day tank, until the control officer—a middle-aged, balding little man—sent his lady assistant to open the office door.

The Whitlocks and some British Waterways pairs received orders for Longford, the next pair was for Newdigate, then he caught sight of Bill and myself. "Who the hell are you?" he asked and I explained. "Oh ah," he rummaged among papers "Willow Wren's "Tern" and "Teal". Ah! Here we are. Just notified. Trainees eh? Soon see about that." He broke off to remonstrate with a boater's wife who was complaining to Miss Edwards his assistant about the state of the 'Waterways' laundrette, to which he had the keys. Then the telephone rang and he talked rapidly into it, put it down, rang another number and talked swiftly and mysteriously about "Allocations", "peas and beans", "North Warwick", "factors" and "turning tonnages". At length he replaced the receiver, pulled a pad towards him, scribbled on it, tore a top leaf off and handed it to me. "There you are, North Warwick tomorrow morning for Croxley Mills, best make haste if you're going to get there today. Who's next?"

Outside I stood stupidly turning the paper, with mysterious printed information on it, over and over. "But what does it MEAN?" I asked.

Bill gazed back at me: "Pooley Hall Colliery is 'North Warwickshire'. It's our loading order."

2
Mill
Boating

I would not recommend a pit head to anyone requiring a quiet night's sleep. Little happened until, in the early hours, the early-turn men went on duty. Then bells clanged, the winding engine snorted, pent steam roared from safety valves, trucks banged and a shunting engine trundled to and from the screens. Men called out in the drifting wrack and coal rattled in hoppers and shoots. Pooley Hall was a lively place at 3.30am and for the next few hours clanging bells preceded the rattle of cages rising and falling in the shaft. At about seven the crash and rattle of dropping coal heralded the loading of a 'Waterways' pair.

I had by now developed a morning routine which involved: (a) lighting the gas beneath the kettle (filled the previous night), which could be done without getting out of bed and meant that the air temperature would rise rapidly, (b) riddling the stove and opening the draught and damper when it was warm enough to get up, (c) lighting a cigarette and blearily contemplating the two stoves, (d) shaving and washing in the first warm water from the kettle, (e) rousing Bill if he was not already stirring and (f) making a cup of tea with the remaining water in the kettle. Accordingly I went through the drill and found that by the time I had thrown back the slide to greet the world, the motor in front was loaded and the butty nearly so.

By seven thirty the British Waterways boats had pulled away from the shoot and were busily clothing-up. This last was obligatory for boats going to Croxley Mills where the conveyor belts could clog up if wet coal was transported on them. For this, one was paid an extra two shillings per pair. Full of expectation we pulled the motor up to the shoot and climbed the steps to the loading cabin, order paper in hand. The loading foreman laughed, "Steady on nah, me pigeon, tek it easy!" It transpired that boats were not loaded on a 'conveyor-belt' system but that a ponderous ritual had to be undergone. Loading was out of railway trucks with end doors, four or five going to a pair. First the empty trucks had to be removed and taken to the screening sidings, then the four or five designated to us had to be found, collected, have their weight checked and be positioned. All this took time, in fact it was not until mid-morning that our chance came.

Tubs of coal came up the shaft and passed through the screens, their contents going into standard gauge railway trucks holding some 10 or 12 tons. The trucks were either superannuated main line ones, with diagonal white crosses painted on their sides, or British Railways standard steel wagons. The latter were taken to exchange sidings adjoining the nearby main line; the others being put in storage roads on the opposite side of the canal, behind which rose an enormous spoil mound fed by more ancient trucks. All this movement was performed by a small saddle tank locomotive which snorted importantly around the colliery with the air of a fussy butler.

At last a rake of four black wagons was propelled over the canal bridge by the saddle tank. Two were uncoupled and shoved into a siding, then with great chuffings two loaded wagons were butted up the slope to the loading bay. Between the rails a pit led to the loading shoot some feet below. The procedure was to pin the wagon brakes down with the hand lever, attach the coupling to a hoist at the end of the loading bay and release the end door catch. When the hoist was put in gear the wagon did a handstand and its contents shot down the hole.

Meanwhile "Tern" had been positioned by the black hole below. The first two wagons had ten tons in each so we clung to iron rings, feet on gunwales, holding her so that just forward of the mast coincided with the shoot, and hoped to get all twenty tons in. The foreman shouted above our heads and a preliminary shower of small coal fell as the end door catch released. Then, as the hoist began to lift the wagon, there came a swelling roar and a black river swept down the shoot with a dark spume of dust rolling above it. The boat rolled slightly, then began to settle slowly down; the pea coal running like liquid into the fore-end and rising to gunwale height. Clinging grimly to our rings we walked her forward as the black tide ran back behind the mast. Water lapped over the paintwork of the foredeck and the stern rose until the propellor appeared. The flow of coal slackened and stopped. The dust cloud thinned. We licked coal-grimed lips and then fell to with shovels to level the load while the wagon was being lowered, removed and the next one positioned. Another warning shout preceded a further black cascade. The

126

engine hole's back end came slowly nearer and nearer, the fore-end rose slightly as the stern settled and I began to fear that there would not be enough space for all the coal. Coal was rising up the back end boards by the time the flow slackened. It stopped and "Tern" was loaded. Now we had to shove her out of the way temporarily and prepare the butty by removing the top planks and positioning her to receive the contents of the remaining trucks.

We finished this and clumped up the brick steps to the loading bay. The locomotive had drawn away the first two trucks. It collected the next two and then treated us to another pyrotechnic display as they were trundled slowly up the slope. The loader was lurking in the doorway of a nearby hut and he took a swig of cold tea from a bottle before calling, "Aye oop, me pigeons, 'ave yer snap!" The engine driver climbed down from his cab, and his grizzled, greasy-capped, blue-overalled figure came crunching up the cinder ballast carrying a 'snap tin' and tea bottle. His grimy, wrinkled face with white, puckered crows feet round the eyes cracked into a grin and we were ushered into the black hut in which an iron stove roared. Sandwiches came out of greasy webbing ex-army haversacks and, with the direct courtesy and friendliness of working men who do hard and dirty jobs, we were made welcome on the rough, wooden benches. Cigarettes were exchanged and a pleasant fifteen minutes ensued. Although it was obvious that they could not make us out—our Southern speech was not of the boats—they were incurious. It was not for them to probe as to our antecedents; not for the first time I realised that inquisitiveness about people's personal circumstances is more of a middle-class tendency.

Tea break over, we returned to the boats. I should perhaps explain that, whenever possible, boats are loaded slightly by the head. This means that they tend to nose their way along the channel so that if they should run onto an obstruction they will usually ride over it. Forty-nine tons on two ex-Joshers is a fair load, but the boats certainly looked impressive as they sat there, waiting for planking and clothing up after being trimmed and mopped down.

In order partly to make running about easier and partly to emulate Wilfred, Bill removed the motor boat's stands and rigged a stylish-looking switchback of planks running back from the mast in a slope, with the middle plank flat and the stern plank running up to the engine hole cabin end. I rigged "Teal" somewhat differently. The sidecloths were unrolled carefully, bearing in mind Ray White's cautionary tale of finding a wasp's nest in a rolled-up set on an exchanged boat. The top cloths were unfolded and draped—with

127

a fine balancing act along the gunwales to secure these to the iron rings set in them. At length all was secured. The heavy, long snubber was fished out of the butty's fore deck, the loading ticket collected and we were ready to leave. It was by now early afternoon.

"Tern's" engine was started, the empty trucks rattled away, the locomotive whistled farewell and the loader waved. Bill clutched in and slowly edged into the main channel. The snubber uncoiled off the butty's foredeck, tightened, and with a slight jerk we were under way with a haul of a hundred miles or so before us—destination Croxley Mills, Watford, Hertfordshire.

We had planned to get up Atherstone Locks—our first narrow flight with a loaded pair—before dark, but lost time trying to pass a 'Waterways' tug with two laden mud hoppers at Polesworth. The tug had negotiated our motor and come abreast of the butty but then everything had come to a stop. Muddy water boiled under the tug, "Teal's" tiller swung back and forth helplessly, black smoke poured out of "Tern's" exhaust and the loaded hoppers wallowed uncertainly. However, nothing moved either way. Engines slacked down to let the water settle, curses filled the air and then we tried again. The tug gained about two yards. This was repeated, we shoved with shafts, the 'Waterways' gang did likewise and we gained another two yards. A cheerful company's man, nicknamed 'Happy' by us, got a line onto the bank from the motor and gained a bit more ground. At the end of an hour the first hopper was past and we made a pot of tea. Then 'Happy' fell in the cut! All in all we were nearly two hours passing the tug. I hope they got overtime, for it was long past their finishing time before they got free. After this baptism of fire, little untoward occurred until we came to Atherstone Locks.

Working a pair of boats uphill on a narrow flight is no sinecure. The method we found the simplest was as follows: the butty was worked in the locks by a long cotton line off the mast, so when the motor went into the lock its steerer cast the line off and then stopped with the fore-end resting on the sill. He then bounded up onto the cabin top, jumped onto the lockside, pulled the gates shut, tore up to the top and drew the paddles. Meanwhile, the butty steerer ran along the planks and pulled in yards of soggy line, coiled it and put it ready on the cratch. The butty would hopefully nose into the vee of the gates while he did this. When the motor's stern had risen far enough the line was thrown up to the motor steerer who dropped the noose over his towing 'dolly'. Back along the planks the butty steerer would rush to pull the tiller out and lay it on the cabin top. He would then leap ashore with the windlass and stand by the bottom gates as the motor began to shove herself forward, paying out the line over her counter. There was just enough line to close the top gate behind the motor, then the butty would be drawn tight against the bottom gates and the lower paddles drawn. The towline now ran the length of the lock. When the lock was empty the motor, still churning away in ahead gear, began to draw the butty through the bottom gates into the lock. At this point the butty steerer would leap across the widening chasm of the gates and drop the paddles, then rush to the head of the lock. When the fore-end was about ten feet from the sill the motor was signalled to stop pulling, a top paddle would then be drawn to stop the boat and the steerer would go down the lock side to close the gates and back up the other side to draw the opposite paddle. When he saw the first bottom gate being shut, the motor steerer would go ahead, thus keeping the tension on the line and pulling the butty ahead in the lock. As the lock slowly filled the butty would begin to move slightly ahead, the top gate would creak ponderously open and we would be ready for the next lock. For this performance we were paid an additional sum of sixpence per lock.

That night we tied up in darkness at about seven o'clock beside the sixth lock. Early the next morning we began the slow toil up the remaining five, inexorably heading for the hat factory chimney stark ahead of us. Below the second lock was a brand new Dinkum Digger, like one we had seen at Braunston in the Spring. It was positioned legs down just clear of the entrance. The motor passed by easily but the butty stuck solid. She had jammed herself onto the shoe-plate of the dredger's legs and was immovable. We tried 'snatching' with the motor (ie. backing-up until the line is slack, then going hard ahead), flushing the lock, pulling, shafting and eventually gave up baffled. About an hour and a half later the dredger's crew arrived, unlocked it and started the engine. They withdrew the hydraulic leg, "Teal" shuddered and floated free. Consequently, it was mid-morning before we came out of the top lock, to more saucy words from the hat factory girls.

We rounded the 'mucky' turns by Mancetter without too much trouble, but I learned a lot about steering loaded butties! Between Mancetter and Hartshill it stuck fast on something in a little wooded cutting below a sail-less windpump. The motor was on a bend, making it difficult to 'snatch'. I attempted to shove her with the long shaft but the bottom and sides were foul black mud from the Hartshill sewage works and it was hard to gain a purchase. In the stillness between 'snatches' yellow leaves pattered down and smoke from the butty's chimney curled upwards in the still, autumn air. We spent over an hour here but on getting free negotiated most of the remaining turns, including the one at the granite quarry by the "Anchor" inn, without mishap. After Nuneaton the water improved. "Tern" ploughed along with a pleasing flurry of water visible under her counter; a sign that the blades were biting well. Bill shouted back to me, "Good cut this!"

At Hawkesbury we tied up in daylight for once; requiring supplies from the little shop nearby and both feeling in need of our first pint of beer for three days. By now the "Greyhound" was getting used to us. It should have been a quiet night, but Charlie had arrived with "Flamingo" and "Smew" ready to load at Longford the following day. He and George had met at Stoke Hammond and settled the matter of the "Curlew's" ramshead with hard words and blows. For the time being, therefore, George's name was anathema. However, the frustration and sheer toil of the last few days faded away in jovial reminiscences and hearty laughter. For myself, the laughter would have been heartier had there not been the greater part of the journey, with all its incumbent perils, to face.

We were off next day by eight-thirty; a late start for boating but there were no other boats, as yet, going our way. "Teal's" electrics were playing up, necessitating a stop at Braunston, so there was no point in hurrying. On a long pound such as the 'Morton pound' from Hawkesbury to Hillmorton, life is rather lonely on a two-handed, loaded pair; communication between boats is limited to yells and gestures. As chief tea-maker I found the best way of serving up was to juggle with the kettle and tea pot on a straight bit of cut; reaching down from the tiller to do so. Then, when ready, I would signal a "T", Bill would slack down, hauling in yards of wet rope and the butty's fore-end would ride up to the stern of the motor. This was the opportunity to pass over cups, pork pies, biscuits or similar sustenance, to exchange gossip and views formulated over the previous two hours or so since the last stop and to attend to urgent calls of nature.

For the rest of the time, life acquired a new dimension. Time as such ceased to exist. Our days were prescribed by the opening or closing times of locks, boatyards or wharves and only in the sense of place and of distance covered did time mean anything to us. We quickly became aware of this new dimension. "Five hours round the 'Morton pound' last trip", other boaters would say, or "'ad ten minutes in the Punchbowl Bridge" or "One hour and forty minutes we wuz between the clocks" or "Yer wants ter be in the bottom lock o'Morton by ar'pass-two if yer wants ter go ter the top o'Bugby (any later would mean getting to Braunston after locking-up time).

Although on a long pound one had little to do but steer, life was never dull. It was frequently uncomfortable, especially when the weather turned wintry. The dullest time was after nightfall, when the ever changing panorama of the landscape was hidden, but even then the problem of keeping moving remained absorbing. In daylight, however, one could switch off the outer level of consciousness, leaving the steering and navigation to a sort of reflex. The mind began to range over a thousand topics and philosophical considerations. From this time on, I began to discover myself and seriously to ponder important questions. For several hours one was completely alone, with the landscape of the Midlands as a backdrop and the essential business of life lay in the achievement of the day's boating. As Emma Smith wrote in "Maiden's Trip": "The life was absorbing and we were absorbed by it."

A late hire-cruiser from Brinklow fruitlessly tried to pass us through Hall Oaks. Unless the boats slow right down, overtaking loaded boats on narrow canals is impossible, for too much water is drawn away from the overtaker by the butty. We eventually slowed down along Cathirons straight, the hire boat forged past and drove on in a tearing hurry, a rolling stern wave following. We were not amused to find it tied up at Newbold about an hour later.

Beyond Clifton Road Bridge we met an empty 'Waterways' pair thundering round a sharp outside turn. The butty was a 'dustbin', one of the all-steel boats fitted with plastic hatch covers which were then only a couple of years old. The boatman was a young, keen tearaway who evidently regarded slowing-down as a threat to his virility. In order to avoid the clumsy dustbin we had to cut the corner. The butty became unsteerable on the mud, duffed the bank behind the dustbin, stopped dead and broke the snubber. The empty pair roared off without speaking—providing the only instance of uncalled for crass rudeness from a boater that I ever encountered.

Dusk was falling as we tied outside the yard at Braunston. It was our best day's run so far, but we had to do better if we were going to keep up with the regulars. The feel of deep water under us as we came round Braunston turn was an encouragement. No wonder many captains sighed with relief when they left the Oxford and came back onto the Grand Union. It was Thursday so there were not many boats at Braunston; only Abel going north empty was at Bottom Lock waiting to oil-up in the morning. When we walked up to the "Nelson" about half-past eight we stepped into an almost deserted bar. Hubert said, "Hey oop me dooks, I thought you'd got lost."

"So did I!" came Leslie Morton's voice from the doorway leading into the private part of the house. He was apparently staying an extra night for some business reason. Later on, Tom James and Abel came in and we sat round in the cosy, curtained bar, a glowing fire crackling in the stove. The time passed swiftly in the unhurried manner of the cut. Somehow Leslie Morton began talking of the sea.

Leslie Morton was an authority on many subjects and was always worth listening to. Now, in the quiet, firelit, Northamptonshire bar room I heard, spellbound, what it was like to be a boy aboard a sailing ship bound round Cape Horn, tales of high adventure and low companions in Callao, Singapore, Liverpool, Rotterdam and Hong Kong, and an unvarnished, matter-of-fact version of the sinking of the "Lusitania"—from which Morton had emerged with a medal for courageously saving life. Some measure of his character might be gained from the fact that I did not learn about the medal for several years, and then it was from the lips of another.

It was very late when we made our way back, up Dark Lane and down the field to Bottom Lock. Abel gravely bade us adieu as we put him on the gang plank leading to his cabin. His wife's voice called quaveringly, "That you, Abel?"

"Yes, my love!" came in response as he wobbled up the plank. Back flew the hatch, the doors opened to reveal Mrs Abel in curlers and all the majesty of an aggrieved spouse. The security light on the store lit up the domestic scene. We fled, blood-curdling threats ringing in our ears. Over the bridge we ran, down by the 'Waterways' oil store. The moored boats cast a shadow about waist-height on the oil store doors past which we had to go. Above, all was bathed in the glare of the security light. We started past the oil store, but Mrs Abel spotted us.

"I'll give you young booggers bringing my Abel home like this!" she roared. A lump of DS coal cracked against the door. She had the range and opened up rapid fire. Remembering military instructions about dead-ground and keeping a low profile, I ducked below the shadow and Bill followed suit. We silently slid behind our cratches and went, bent double, swiftly to our cabins. The noise of opening slides once more drew her fire, a lump of coal clanged off the water can as I shot down into the cabin. It was the end of a perfect evening.

We did not make an appearance next morning until Abel had oiled-up and motored away northwards. Through a crack in the doors I watched his tall, mournful figure go by, crouched somewhat blearily over the tiller. His wife steered the butty with an air of grim satisfaction, looking neither to left nor right.

The electrical problem in the butty's headlight took some tracing, but we eventually discovered that a loose connection and the perishing of some of the insulation had caused a short circuit. Consequently, the bulb and the fuse had blown. Setting this right took until after lunch, during which time Charlie came up loaded. At length we followed him up the locks, passing Caleb Lane and his pretty daughter with "Tadworth" and "Bedworth"—one of the smartest 'Waterways' pairs on the cut—before entering the tunnel.

As the butty followed "Tern" into the tunnel I swiftly began to learn more lessons. The tunnel seemed much loftier when one's feet were below water level, as mine were in "Teal's" hatches. The headlight, although newly rigged, seemed quite inadequate at first and the motor's wash rebounding off the walls threw the butty all over the place. In the dark I could faintly discern the glow from the fore-end and could just make out the silhouette of the mast 'loobey' in the dimness. I could not tell what the wretched boat would do next and it seemed that none of my ministrations to the tiller had the slightest effect. One minute "Teal" would scrape one side and I would graze my knuckles on the brickwork as I frantically pumped away, only to crash into the other side.

Eventually the far end became more distinct. Framed in the distant arch of Welton Wharf bridge I could just see the sun glinting on the bright stern of Charlie's butty, while our motor began to take on a more definite shape. I had just got the hang of tunnel steering when I ran into the wall by the 'S' bend. Recovering from this, I promptly hit the second part of the 'S'.

As we breasted-up above the top lock of Buckby, Charlie's smoke was just going out of the bottom. I saw the bottom gates bump to behind and noticed that the top ground paddle was up. Charlie's bulky shape was swinging a leg over the cross-bar of a bicycle, having started the lock filling for us while his wife and daughter took the boats down. We pressed on hard behind, 'thumb-lining' the gates open and 'strapping-in' at each lock.

These were of course new techniques. A butty has no brakes and must be stopped in a lock by a heavy check strap either off the answerpin on the top strake at the rear or from the fore-end stud. The Grand Union locks had large strapping stumps above the gates or near the downhill end for this purpose. Strapping meant learning another skill. Too tight and you break the strap or stop the boat before she gets in the lock; too slack and you wallop the bottom gate. The wash from the motor usually starts the motor's gate, the motor steerer draws his bottom paddle, in sweeps the butty if the strapping is done right, the strap flicks over the top gate and the butty steerer gives the handrails a slight push as he passes. The current takes the gate and it bumps shut, the boats ride forward with the surge and 'thumblines' are quickly rigged as they do so. These lines run from the mast of each boat, through the gap in the centre of the bottom gate hand rails, along to the next upright rail where they are secured with a jamming hitch. When pulled back the hitch tightens, when pulled forward it releases. This prevents the boats from riding back onto the sill of the lock, but again one must judge the length correctly or else it will not work.

Meanwhile, the butty steerer takes a light line with an eye splice in one end and drops the splice over a little projecting pin just by the top gate. The other end goes round the 'T' stud at the stern of the boat. The object of this is to prevent the butty riding out and jamming the motor in the empty lock. Both steerers must now be at their posts because in deep locks, such as Buckby, it is dangerous to drop down onto cabin tops from the lockside when the lock is empty. As soon as the lock is empty, the motor goes astern, and the 'thumbline' tightens and pulls the motor's gate open. As the motor goes ahead, its wash sends the butty back against the sill, pulling the butty's gate open. The holding-back line is pulled taut and the butty held against the sill. As the motor goes out through the gates the tension comes off the 'thumbline', the jamming-hitch releases and the line falls off the handrail onto the motor. The short snubber is grabbed and dropped over the dolly, the butty steerer flicks off the holding-back line and the boats are away.

All this takes time to perfect as well as learn and we made several 'goofs' down Buckby, not the least being when I forgot the holding-back line and both boats tried to go out of the top lock at once and jammed. Still, I think Wilfred probably had a more embarrassing mishap one day when his thumbline broke leaving him alone, imprisoned in the lock until the lock-keeper came and opened the bottom gate.

In such fashion, and with Charlie's unseen but welcome assistance, we came down in style. Charlie's boats were vanishing into the dusk towards Brockhall Spinney as we came into the last pound. Suddenly the motor began coughing black smoke and losing way. Charlie had long vanished when we managed to make the blades disgorge an outer tyre and sundry pieces of steel wire. It was pitch dark by this time so, not thinking any more of Charlie, we tied up below, had supper and went to bed.

We were off bright and early, before first light in fact, and saw a misty autumn sun come up through the golden leaves of Brockhall Spinney. The Blisworth Pound was well up as we swung round it in the frosty sunlight. By now some of the trees were bare and the leaves were changing colour on the rest. It was plain that winter was drawing nearer. A chilly wind with a hint of rain whipped the surface of the water. We both banked the fires and crouched in the door holes.

Blisworth tunnel was clear and empty of boats, but I had similar problems to those in Braunston the day before. I was glad to emerge into the leafy waters of the cutting beyond. In the narrows after the cutting Bill called out and gesticulated ahead. A pair of 'Willow Wren' sterns appeared and standing back on the towpath, regarding them gloomily, with hands in pockets, was Charlie. He had broken down in, of all places, the middle of the tunnel the night before, declining a tow out from a pair of northbound boats loaded for Wellingborough because he thought we were following. After an hour he had given us up and shafted the loaded pair out, then bowhauled to where he was now tied. We both felt terrible at letting him down, but Charlie stuck his thumbs in his bib and brace overalls and grinned cheerfully. Violet, his daughter, walked down with him to the lock and helped us through.

Fishermen sat glumly under umbrellas below Stoke locks. The hollow punting of a football and the shouts of players in the distance could be heard by Yardley Gobion, bonfire smoke rose in the gardens at Cosgrove; in all the Saturday afternoon world we seemed to be the only ones at work. Football editions were being hawked by Wolverton Station and people were sitting down to tea and sporting results in the back rooms of New Bradwell. It was pitch dark when we came to Linford Wharf but we clattered on, determined to make up for lost time. Bill peered into the gloom, which the pathetic little electric lanthorn on the fore-end barely penetrated. I made myself a cup of tea and some toast, then hunched against the cold, spattering rain, bawling out revivalist hymns to the silent fields and dark hedgerows.

We had reasonable hopes for a pleasant Saturday night at what we understood to be a convivial hostelry at Fenny, so plunged on into the night. We passed the derelict swingbridge that marked the half way point of the Fenny pound and met a loaded pair whose skipper shouted greetings in the dark and told me that we had 'Talbots' ready. I told him in return that the bottom of the 'thick' was ready. The Pear Tree bridge went by, then, with less than an hour to go, disaster struck. The motor's exhaust faltered, picked up, faltered again, then stopped. Silently we glided round an outside turn into an inside turn, stopping the boats in deep water against some concrete piling on the towpath. Bill emerged from the engine hole baffled. The dim light made searching for the cause of our stop impossible so we decided to try in daylight. Supper was a gloomy affair in the middle of nowhere. Much later I found we had been within three hundred yards of a pub at Woughton-on-the-Green, but at the time we might as well have been in the Australian outback for all the signs of civilisation that there were.

Bill set his alarm for seven and we woke to a showery morning. I prepared some breakfast while he made further investigations. The kettle had just boiled when I heard the engine start and he clambered onto the butty grinning contentedly. A piece of scale had blocked the intake to the fuel line and providentially he discovered this straight away. I thought we had caused it by letting the top tank get too low so we kept it well filled afterwards and had no further trouble.

We made good time thereafter up through Fenny, Leighton and the Fields, but after Grove Lock we had a bad road—from a pleasure boat we later discovered. This meant bringing the boats abreast below each lock, emptying it, then tediously flogging through. At Pauls and Neils Locks water was cascading over the lower gates which, we ought to have guessed, was a bad sign, but at the time we did not give it a thought.

As we came up the straight below the bottom lock of 'Corkers Two' we beheld an unusual phenomenon—all four gates were open! Hearts sinking, we nosed into the empty lock. The pound above was completely empty, the pleasure boat crew had left a bottom paddle half up and the water had all run away from the short pound. This explained why there was so much water lower down.

I set off on the bicycle to pedal up the long pound to 'Nags Head', leaving all the paddles up at the top lock of 'Corkers'. I then drew paddles at the bottom and middle locks and left them running. No lock-keeper was to be seen, but at the top lock came the welcome sight of Ray White's empty boats hastening northwards. Ray said he would give Bill a hand if necessary, but he brought just enough water down with him for Bill to creep up the short pound dragging the butty. I biked on to 'Peters Two' in search of a lock-keeper but found none, so returned and shut down all the paddles. Bill had, after an hour and a half, managed to get into 'Corkers' top lock. We then had a long and tedious crawl up 'Nags Head' because all the pounds were now low. At 'Peters Two' there was not enough water over the sill to let us through. Once more I got off and flushed the boats in, another twenty minutes were lost, darkness fell and we knew that we would not now get to 'Maffers' before locking-up time—so much for our plans for the Cowroast that night. It had taken us six hours to come just over three miles! We tied by the Ship Bridge at Marsworth thoroughly exhausted and peeved. Had the pleasure boat been available I think we would have sunk it and murdered the crew. Worse was to come. I walked over to the "Red Lion" for a drink at what I thought was ten o'clock to find it was only nine. British Summer Time had ended the night before and we had not realised. There would have been time to go up Marsworth Locks after all.

Lying half awake in the grey morning light I heard Bill's alarm ring at seven and went through my morning evolutions. Bill had still not appeared, so I got on the motor, peered through the doors and found him still in bed. He groaned piteously, "Stiff neck ... can't move it". I took him a cup of tea, he sat up with his head twisted round. He was stuck with it sideways. I thought the best plan would be to motor just round the corner to bottom lock and get a doctor, so I started up and steered round abreast. Below the lock tied by the pub wall was a pair of Willow Wren fore-ends lying empty. It was none other than George. Bill had emerged by now, swathed in a long brown overcoat, looking very sorry for himself, with his head askew. George came up to the bottom lock and I asked about doctors. "What's the matter wi'you Bill?" rumbled George. Bill explained. George turned to his elder daughter. "Janet, go an' git the jollop." Janet ran off to do his bidding. "Soon fix 'm up," he said confidingly to me. I asked why he was tied up. "Bloody rings is knackered," he replied. "Ain't no compression."

Remembering our experience with "Thaxted" and knowing that his engine too was a National, I brightly asked whether he had tried dropping oil down the intake. "I 'ave," said he and his eyes glittered dangerously at me as he peered over his spectacles. "I throws 'er over, Colin drops the compression, the bastard stops dead, I goes over the top o' the 'andle and smacks me bloody 'ead on the engine

137

'ole side."

Janet reappeared carrying a square can labelled "Goddard's Sweet Oils" and "For Veterinary Use Only", in one hand and some clean engine wiper cloth in the other. George opened the can and an overpowering whiff of horse liniment arose. He slopped some viscous-looking fluid onto the cloth and summoned his patient. "Come 'ere Bill!" Bill sidled cautiously towards him and George clapped the cloth onto his stiff neck. Bill yelled and leaped several feet in the air. George gave the happy chuckle of a successful physician as Bill hopped about the lock cursing and muttering.

By the time we had reached the middle lock, Bill's head was beginning to move and by the top lock he was his old self again. I told George this when next we met, he nodded knowingly: "I know 'tis good jollop. I gargles wi'it."

Just by Bulbourne Depot we met the pleasure boat which had caused us such trouble the day before. I could tell that Bill was feeling better by the way in which he expressed himself upon the subject of not shutting paddles to the pleasure boat's crew as he passed them. I too gave my opinion as they drew alongside, so hopefully they would not make the same mistake again. Although judging by their indignant reaction at being spoken to by "ignorant bargees", I doubt whether they had the faintest understanding of what we were talking about.

Cowroast Lock was a traffic control point and here British Waterways held the 'mill-boats' until there was room for them at the discharge point. The real reason for thus keeping the boats in the Hertfordshire wilds was to prevent congestion in the short pounds by the mills and at the same time to regulate the arrivals at the paper mills. The boatmen, however, did not see it this way and several claimed that one had to cool one's heels in the outback as a punishment for a boatwoman lighting up her portable washing boiler underneath the Esparto Grass Stores. Today there were no boats waiting and Clarkie, the Geordie lock-keeper, came out of his office to say: "Away, marrers, ye can gan on reet doon, the dee", meaning that there was no need for us to stop.

So we sank steadily down, 'strapping' in, 'thumblining' out; 'Dudswell Two', Northchurch, 'Bushes', 'Gas Two', Broadwater, 'Sweeps Two'—all familiar country by now. At 'the Sewerage' we met Mark and Dolly coming uphill empty and giving us a good road to the 'New 'uns'.

A rainy dusk was falling as we went by Boxmoor Common. The lights of cars and buses gleamed on the wet roads, street lights glared and traffic lights blinked. It seemed late. In fact it was only about five o'clock but we had not yet grown used to the shorter day. Somewhere below Fishery Lock George's description of the fouling ability of "Tern's" blades proved once more correct. We slowed appreciably as the whiff of smoke from a labouring engine came back to the butty, a sure sign of a "bladeful".

The motor staggered into Boxmoor Lock, we put her on the towpath side of the lock and spent a fruitless hour in the pitch dark playing 'pull devil, pull baker' with a variety of shafts. We had picked up a car outer tube to start with and this had taken as its companion a piece of tangled fencing wire. One would get a good shaftful of the stuff and then it would slip; alternatively one of us would try to help by giving a touch ahead or astern. When this happened the shaft would shoot forward under the counter, pulling one's arms nearly out of their sockets; or else the shaft would fly the other way and flail one about the head and shoulders. Night and rain fell on two very frayed tempers and we began to debate desperate measures, such as getting in the cut to make a proper job.

Morale was very low when a bicycle came rattling up the slope and a stentorian voice boomed, "Boats a-comin' up!" It was Ernie, mate to Arthur on Blue Line's "Roger" and "Raymond". His massive figure bulked out of the dark by the bottom gates and paused in the act of putting a windlass on the bottom paddle. He pushed the windlass back in his jacket, came along the lockside and peered at us. "You got your blades a-blocked up," he said. Rather shortly we informed him that his surmise was correct. "Gi'us that shaft a minute," Ernie continued. He took it, bent down, thrust it under the counter and twisted it several times. His effort nearly lifted the motor's stern out, then he pulled. There came a tinkling of wire and Ernie staggered backwards pulling yards of wire and bits of chewed-up rubber with him. We had begun to thank him profusely, when out of the dark came a yell.

"Ernie! Why the bloody hell ain't that lock ready?"

"It's me mate," said Ernie, "make haste." He helped us drop down the lock and we decided to tie below for the night since we had had enough and Arthur had given us a good road right down for the morning. Outside the bottom gates our headlights illuminated Arthur's empty pair as he held back slightly to let us get into the bank.

"What was holdin' ye'up?" Arthur called. We told him and he bade us goodnight as he thrashed into the lock. Muffled noises came from Ernie's Mum who was in the butty's cabin. Arthur said, "It's them young fellers, they'm a tyin' up." The lock filled and away they went into the night. They had emptied at Southall that morning. They would go to the top of 'Maffers' that night, a run which made our efforts sink back into perspective!

The following day we met a steady uphill procession of empties and loaded boats, some bound for Wellingborough, some for Aylesbury with timber. We made another of our silly mistakes when leaving Cowroast. We had pulled over Tring Summit on a long line and foolishly had not replaced it with a short snatcher down the short pounds. This would have saved Bill much tedious coiling-in every time we came to a lock. It would also have prevented us from giving an oncoming 'Waterways' pair a free laugh. Just below Lady Capels is the first of the sharp turns in the Parks, put in to gratify the Palladian taste of the adjoining landowner when the cut was built. Bill forged off round this to meet a low fore-end creeping under the change-over bridge. The oncoming boatman saw him, thought he was a single motor and swept closely by. Then he caught sight of "Teal's" fore-end with the long line dipping under water and myself pumping desperately to get her round. He managed to avoid me and said laughingly: "Sure you got enough line? I thought you was another single!"

Suitably chastened we made our way through the russet-tinted Parks, dropped through Cassio Bridge by the great rival railway viaducts and saw the looming sheds and squat chimneys of Croxley Mills crouching on the outside. Two pairs of 'Waterways', one nearly empty, lay ahead of us at journey's end. It was exactly eight days since we had loaded, giving us the breathtaking average speed of twelve and a half miles per day! To be fair to ourselves, we analysed the delays not due to our lack of skill as follows: stuck with 'Waterways' dredging hoppers, two hours; stuck with Dinkum Dredger at Atherstone, one and a half hours; stuck on unidentified object at Mancetter in mid-cut, one hour; empty pound at 'Corkers Two', three and a half hours; bladeful at Boxmoor, one hour—making a grand total of eleven and a half hours. In other words we had lost a full day's boating, plus half a day at Braunston because of the lighting failure, making our actual running time six and a half days. With practice we felt this could be reduced to five days and perhaps a round trip could be completed in ten days including discharging and reloading. Time would tell, but for the present we were to be residents at Croxley.

Fate decreed that we were to have an extended sojourn, for the unloading plant broke down the day we arrived and we had enforced wait of three days.

Ironically, no diminution occurred in the number of tipper lorries coming in with coal. The boats had to be clothed-up, as mentioned before, because wet coal allegedly gummed up the jigger and the conveyor belts. Yet I saw numerous lorries arrive with rainwater streaming out of their loads which shot straight down the same hopper into which the boat coal went. The truth was that the Mills had lost interest in both boats and coal. For this, the Transport Commission and the Coal Board were to blame. The Mills, not unnaturally, found the ease of handling, coupled with the regularity and efficiency of the supply of oil outweighed the advantages of water transport and coal. In particular, the refusal by the Coal Board to allocate coal from waterside installations along with the closure of many such places, was to result not only in the loss of canal traffic but also in the loss of coal sales because, inevitably, the industrial user had had enough of nationalised fuels and turned to oil. The cost was redundant miners, loss of canal traffic, increased road congestion and further depletion of foreign exchange. The scapegoats were, of course, the "antiquated" canal system and its boatmen. It was not a matter of economics, but of who made the loudest noise.

Unloading, though quick when one got round to it, was a labour-intensive business which might have been devised in the 1920's to provide work for the indigent poor. After unclothing and removing planks and stands which were laid on the wharf, the boat was positioned below the jigger. First a wire cable from an electric winch was looped over the fore-end stud, then an upright conveyor was lowered into the hold. Two grinning worthies armed with No.10 shovels clambered into the bottom, then the jigger started. The winch slowly pulled the boat forward, the men guided the pea coal towards the conveyor and the coal was inexorably eaten up at the rate of about twenty tons in half an hour. Then the first boat was shoved out of the way and the second drawn in while the men had a smoke. The winch line was re-run and we were ready to go again. Unloading took just two hours from going under the jigger to sweeping out, mopping down and making ready for orders. It was now Friday midday—we should have been unloaded Wednesday at the latest.

I went to the Time Office to telephone for orders. Stanley told us to go back to Hawkesbury empty. We could draw some money at Braunston he added, for we were now due three days laying money and some empty running money as well. Memory fails me and over the years my settlement slips have disappeared, but to the best of my recollection the previous settlement including clothing up, bow-hauling and laying money on top of the tonnage payment came to about £13, less £2 10s National Insurance stamps plus £3 7s 6d laying money. We could, therefore, expect nearly half as much again to come but of course we had earned the company nothing, while two days had been wasted because of the breakdown. Although on an hourly basis the money seemed poor, it stood comparison with other jobs.

After the trials and tribulations of our loaded trip, empty boating was a lark. In those days empties would run abreast to Cowroast, single out across the summit then go abreast down the fields to Leighton. We had more or less got empty boating weighed up by the time we had gone that far.

We arrived back at Braunston on Sunday evening, our first round trip completed in sixteen days (of which four were waiting days), and later that night swaggered up to the "Nelson" for what we hoped would be a celebratory evening. The entrance bell jangled loudly in an empty pub. A peeved-looking Hubert emerged from behind the curtain to serve us. He hurriedly filled our glasses and disappeared. Someone else came in and Thirza came out, served him equally quickly then went. It was the night of the Royal Command Performance on TV!

The following evening excitement was mounting at Hawkesbury Stop. All day loaded and empty boats had been arriving. Down the last long straight on the Oxford, near Wyken Arm, we had been nearly overhauled by "Kent" and "Hazel" (being wooden boats they were faster than us), but Jim, their captain had waved us on when we slacked down to let him by. Billy Wilson Greasy Ocker and Abel opined that Jim was 'O.K.' like that. "No mate, he'd not come by you as long as you kept ahead. Arthur now, e'd come by you at Tusses Bridge," they affirmed.

We were standing by our boats chatting and exchanging boasts. The narrow channel down to the stop lock was now just a boat's width, with loaded and empty boats stretching back to the sharp turn before the power station. All the three carrying firms were well represented for tonight was an important date in the boaters' calendar. It was Bonfire Night and Joe Skinner's birthday. 'The Stop' was already showing signs of life as in the early darkness excited children let off fireworks and raced round the Salvation Army hut with sparklers. One evil band of youths dropped a jumping jack down "Friendship's" chimney pipe. A muffled series of bangs came from within, the stovelid flew across the cabin and Joe, his face and moustache streaked with black, came energetically over the stern flailing his belt after the departing boys.

By about eight o'clock a knot of children had gathered round the door and in the passage of the "Greyhound", like moths round a bright flame. Jim from "Kent" and his brother, who lived ashore nearby, had ensconced themselves near the bay window and lugged out two large piano accordions. Joe and Rose, beaming at everyone, were settled on their accustomed bench and the fun began.

Mrs Nelson scuttled back and forth with trays of beer, whilst the domino and dart players ceased their playing as the musicians tuned up. Bill was dispatched to bring the ukelele banjo while I was forthwith pressed into the musical ensemble. L.T.C. Rolt remarked somewhere that the boatman's interest in music seemed to have ended with the music hall; my impression was that it had ended with Vera Lynn, though some Fifties tunes were popular. On this night we ranged from "Sailor, stop your Roving" through "Paper Roses" and "Rose of Trallee" to more vintage material such as "Goodbye Dolly Grey" and "Little Brown Jug".

By this time the dancing had started. Boots were crashing out the time on the floor, tables were shoved back and a space cleared. At one point I found myself in what dancers call a basket, a foursome comprising myself, the Skinners and an ample-bosomed, broad-bottomed lady called Elsie. Round we spun, legs going like pistons in a wild step-dance, Elsie's bosoms clouting me like pneumatic cushions until the room was whirling. My breath came in painful gasps and still Jim and his brother pumped at their accordions. Finally we broke apart, the music stopped, I collapsed helpless on a chair and Elsie's not inconsiderable bulk came tumbling down on top of me. People laughed until tears came as I struggled like a Daddy Long Legs beneath a prize heifer. The good lady was eventually hoisted away leaving me drained and exhausted. Joe Skinner earnestly asked if I had had enough. "It do take it out o' ye" he said, fresh as a daisy, draining his pint. He was only seventy then, so considered himself still a 'young 'un.

Bill, by this time, had succumbed to force majeure, but there was no escape for me. News travelled fast on the cut and I was bidden to perform, then, while the accordionists had a rest, it was my turn to take the podium. At closing time a hat went round, my share was nearly two pounds.

Abel said, "Bill'sh gone 'ome, goo 'old Bill. We'll look arrer ye', won' we Billy. Ha! Ha! Goo 'ole Dave, goo 'ole Billy!" The Greasy Ocker was stout in heart, mind and build but not very tall. Abel, by contrast, was both tall and powerful. In spite of my protest the two seized me by an arm each and propelled me, zig-zag fashion past the stop lock to the boats. One arm was high in the air, the other low.

"Shh! Don' make no noishe. Ole girlsh fasht ashleep," said Abel with a finger to his lips, making exaggerated tip-toe movements. At this moment we walked into the knee-high balance beam of the stop lock. The three of us, still linking arms, neatly somersaulted over the gate and ended up sitting on the ground with our backs to the balance beam. Abel muttered, "Billy, are you in a puddle?"

"Yus mate, are you?"

"Thank gawd, I though I'd pisshed meshelf."

3

Grand
Unioning

"Have you got any dunnage?" asked Morton over the telephone. I gazed about in amazement.

"Er, no, at least I don't think so," I reported back.

"Well get some off Alfie Best at 'Stockers Lock' on the way down. I want you in Limehouse for Tuesday. You're to meet a ship. Stan'll give you all the details so have a weekend off. I'll pay you laying money till then."

We walked back from the Croxley Time Office talking excitedly. Ordered to the Docks! Now it was to be something else besides coal. Bill said "What's dunnage?" I thought it was what sailors called bits and pieces, but bits and pieces of what I knew not. Within five minutes we were away, heading downhill for London.

We had followed up our first trip to Croxley with one to Apsley and another to Croxley, but not without incident. "Teal" had sprung a bad leak after loading at Longford. On being patched up at Charity Dock, Bedworth, and limping to Apsley, Morton had arranged for us to exchange it for another butty, "Dunlin", back at Braunston.

"Dunlin" was a large wooden boat—a big 'Ricky'—the same length as, but considerably deeper in the hold than, "Teal". Consequently it had a much lower cratch and deckboard which, while not matching "Tern", meant that it was an easier boat to move about on. "Dunlin" had been built by Walkers of Rickmansworth as "Hadfield" for the Grand Union Canal Carrying Company in 1938. Morton, then the firm's manager, had ordered her and, like all the ex-Grand Unions which came into his hands, regarded her with special fondness. Being wooden it seemed more buoyant than the iron "Teal", though her fore-end lines when empty were more massive than the graceful 'Josher's'. However she steered easily. After "Teal" the cabin on "Dunlin" seemed very roomy. It had been Ray White's and he and his wife Margaret, had left it so spotless that the changeover did not take very long. I bid an unsentimental farewell to "Teal" and settled down with the bed made and the crockery and cooking pots stowed away as if I had been on "Dunlin" for years. This was another strange aspect of boating: a boat, while one was on it, was one's home and everything that that entailed, yet after a few minutes packing it was vacated with all traces of one's occupation swiftly effaced. A few minutes more and another boat was home. One was like a hermit crab moving from shell to shell.

We found Alf at Stockers Lock. He was one of Morton's old captains from both Grand Union and Willow Wren times, an open-faced cheerful man now working for British Waterways as a lock-keeper (as boaters would say, "a Company's man"). He had been warned that we were here and indicated a large pile of old timber on the lockside. This, he explained, was to go below our load when we loaded overside of a ship to enable slings to be placed when we unloaded.

Thus encouraged, we carried on through the short November day, past the Colne Valley Sewage works, down Denham Straight and Cowley Lock, and round Cowley Pound until the side bridge at Bulls Bridge heralded the start of the Paddington Arm and our first new water for several weeks. For the first time since Birmingham we were also entering a lengthy stretch of urban waterway; unlike the Birmingham Canals but like the Cowley Pound, the Paddington Arm was wide and deep. Boatmen are perhaps less concerned with scenic grandeur than with "gettin' 'em ahead", so most welcomed a run down the Paddington Arm to "Lime'us". We found out for ourselves that the Arm had its compensations.

Once we had swung round the right angled turn under the towpath, we saw on the towpath side the entrance to 'Jam'ole', alias Kearley and Tongue's Preserve Manufactory, whence one hundred tons of canal-borne coal went each week. Opposite, the steam cranes of the Western Region sleeper depot chuffed away as barge loads of timber were emptied and removed for processing and kyanising. We wound past the gasworks with their evil, sulphurous tang and grimy tankers floating in the basin; under the Uxbridge Road; past a vast timber yard; by Glaxo laboratories; under Western Avenue; by tips and desirable freehold residences; by a jingling glass mountain made of millions of broken bottles; through momentary open countryside round golf-coursed Horsenden Hill; through Alperton; over the North Circular Road; and into the factories of Park Royal, birthplace of Guinness, Heinz 57 Varieties and McVities biscuits. Darkness came upon us puttering through the power station at

Willesden Green, but there was just enough light to view a breathtaking scene as we ran high above the railway yards of Old Oak Common.

Beyond the long curving wall on the towpath side was a sharp drop into the yards. Old Oak Common running sheds sent a constant fume above the geometric parallels, curves and crossings which gleamed wetly in the light of yellow yard lamps. Semaphores and colour lights winked red, yellow and green, reflecting the multi colours off shining steel. Diesel trains rushed past on the through lines and a steam locomotive sent a roaring column of steam skyward from its safety valves. Beyond the tracks the dark open ground of Wormwood Scrubs led to the bulbous towered prison outlined against the brightness of the London night. Behind this stretched a panorama of South West London, silhouetting with a million points of light the tall chimney on Camden Hill, the towers of St Mary Abbotts and the Houses of Parliament, the clustering bulk of the Shell building and a myriad of lesser spires, towers and chimneys. Above them all, in the hazy distance, red aircraft warning lights picked out the television mast on Sydenham Hill.

Flanked by gasworks on the inside and a huge cemetery on the outside the cut plunged into Kensal Green. Just as we were about to sweep into the bridge Bill yelled and went hard astern. The fore-end of a tug was slowly drawing out of the pitch blackness of the bridgehole into the glare of streetlamps overhead. We promptly jack-knifed across the cut. Furious waggling of the tiller by myself brought "Dunlin" back into line as the tug "Ruislip" slowly drew past revealing a towline tautening over the stern. Out of the bridge lumbered a lighter piled high with timber, then another, then another, then another, then another, and yet another. "Tern" was by now 'stemmed-up' on the side nearest the towpath and the last lighter—apparently being steered by witchcraft for no steerer was visible—came gliding straight at her until at last we realised that the steerer could not possibly see us. With one accord we both yelled "Hold Out!"—meaning steer away from the towpath. Slowly the lighter moved out, its ponderous bulk slipping by with about enough room to slip a postage stamp between us. As he passed us the lighterman, a sort of Cockney Toulouse Lautrec, said reproachfully, "You wuz goin' a bit bloody 'ard weren't yer mate?" Although not usually lost for words Bill was, for once, silent.

The next stretch ran between squalid tenements from the basements of which bleary lights behind iron bars or wire meshes revealed sweat shops with toiling Asians and West Indians; wafts of hot steam puffed out from pressing rooms and machinery hummed. Snotty-nosed, tousle-headed children scampered rat-like in the dark corners; foul mouthed teenagers lurked smoking in bridgeholes; kitchen windows revealed festoons of dangling washing, blue television screens winked behind tatty curtains, as unseen we threaded through this silent, ignored highway into the heart of the metropolis. Considering that our revered Premier had not long before told us we had never had it so good, I found myself wondering with what sort of life this compared favourably. I remembered the shock which London evacuees caused in Abingdon in my childhood; how the town was full of stories of the lack of personal hygiene, rudimentary diet, awful clothes and sheer neglect. I reflected that two decades later, and with State Welfare highly advanced, there was still a long way to go. I also reflected that the critics of family boating used living conditions and the alleged neglect of children as an argument for ending the system. Rarely did I see anything to compare with the lives of the unskilled, urban poor among the people of the boats. Perhaps it was for this reason that boaters were, in such areas, subjected to barrages of bricks, airgun pelleted or spat upon from bridges. If Paddington exposed the hollowness of Tory boasts, it had little comfort for those who proclaimed the brotherhood of man.

Then, quite suddenly, we passed beneath a footbridge. The buildings fell away and trees and moored pleasure boats appeared. We had arrived at the junction with Regents Canal known to the cut as 'Paddington Stop' and to romantics as 'Little Venice'. Slipping quietly past the tollhouse and under the graceful iron bridge at the end of Bloomfield Road, we tied up in the wide basin formed by the meeting of the two canals. Above our heads the London rush-hour boomed and roared but at our level there was an oasis of tranquillity just as we had found in Birmingham. The wind-whipped surface of the basin reflected the dark, bare silhouettes of the surrounding plane trees outlined by hundreds of lights, ranging from the sodium glare of street lamps through the ever-changing headlamps, tail lamps and indicator bulbs of vehicles, to the modest glow of curtained windows.

Paddington Stop is conveniently near Paddington Station. We were not required for loading until Monday afternoon at the earliest so, following Morton's behest, we decided to have a proper weekend off. I agreed to stay as watchman and next morning showed Bill how to get into the wrong end of Paddington Station by slipping across a secluded footbridge near the empty taxi-cab entrance.

While he returned to the bosom of his family, I resolved to make the most of a weekend in London.

The first step was to shed some of the accumulated grime of boating, so banking up the cabin fire of "Dunlin", I made my way to the Turkish Baths in Harrow Road, now long vanished beneath an elevated motorway. Today such places would be called Saunas and Massage Parlours and have an aura of sleezy naughtiness about them, but then, Turkish Baths were about as sexy as a fish and chip shop. There was a powerful 'whiff' compounded of chlorine, disinfectant and steam and, having paid five shillings, I was invited to place my clothes in a steel locker. A near-naked giant with a broad Cockney accent put me in a sort of pressure cooker from which my head protruded. My hair was swathed in towelling and the cooking began. Although I had washed and shaved with particularity each day and thought I was reasonably clean, I was amazed to feel every pore opening up and oozing, right to my scalp. After several minutes the steamy atmosphere and the great heat made me feel both drowsy and as though I was about to burst at the same time. I had really lost account of time when the giant let me out and proceeded to towel me, vigorously removing, I was aghast to note, quantities of filth. Eventually I staggered out into the street feeling like death and, as though sleepwalking, stumbled the few hundred yards back to the boats. Thankfully the little stove was roaring away and, stripping off once more, I collapsed into bed and fell fast asleep.

That afternoon I thought I would investigate a street market which I had heard of in the back streets of Marylebone, beyond the Edgware Road. "Dunlin's" cabin had a bare look which would be improved, I felt, with some plates hung round and in those days these could often be bought off street barrows for a few shillings. I found the market, to the south of Maida Hill tunnel. It never.fails to amaze me that progress has not succeeded in sweeping away these London street markets into that same limbo as the music hall—to which they contributed so much robust life and humour.

It was a raw December afternoon with fog about. The crowds round the stalls shuffled, stamped, sneezed and blew on their hands. There were china stalls (alas with no hanging-up plates), book stalls, fruit and vegetable stalls, old clothes stalls, cheap clothes stalls and stalls selling a most comprehensive selection of women's underwear, from saucy creations presumably for professional ladies to colossal bloomers capable of sheeting up a sizeable lorry. There were hot dogs, toffee apples, lucky charms, balloons and

149

budgerigars, toys and twist records. Cockney voices with a thickening of Yiddish filled the air: "I'm not arstin' a pahnd; not nineteen shillin's; not fifteen shillin's; not even twelve-an'-bleeding' sixpence, but . . ." pause, smack, "ten bob!"

Tilley lamps hissed, glaring yellow as they hung from flimsy wood battens above the heaps of empty boxes, mountains of fruit papers and ricketty barrows. It was all so untidy, such a nuisance to motorists, that I thought then it would soon have to make way for the Supermarket and the chain store, yet years later, against all odds, it survives.

I left the holly garlands and Christmas trees, trays of nuts and oranges, cheap jewellery and dubious furs for the neon-lit Edgware Road. As I walked on, two dogs were snarling over a piece of meat, football editions were being sold on the corner and lights were going on behind the ground-glass windows of pubs. In the orange glare of the Edgware Road street lamps, the yellow gas lamps and pressure lanterns back in the market looked old and feeble. I quickly made my way back to the canal.

Bill returned on Sunday evening and we were ready to start once more. Monday morning was one of those misty, late autumn mornings which impart a melancholy beauty to London. A watery sun gleamed down into the frost-rimed plane trees and elegant stucco of Maida Vale. The water was glassily still, exhaling vapour and flecked with the last leaves of autumn. Our exhaust stabbed cheerfully skywards and smoke rolled from the chimneys. "Tern" slowly drew ahead, the cross-straps jerked and we were away, under the neat iron bridge at the end of Warwick Avenue, down the centre of a wide boulevard between Paddington and Maida Vale. The vision of Beau Nash, that planner of most dignified townscapes who had much to do with the Regent's Canal, survived until we were swallowed up by Maida Hill Tunnel and plunged beneath the roaring Edgware Road.

Maida Hill Tunnel is not long, but it marks a contrast. At its eastern end we emerged into a brick-walled cutting flanked by a power station ("Marylebone Light" to boaters), a municipal rubbish wharf and outliers of Marylebone Station. Above a 'tunnel bridge' just beyond, a dignified old office block looked down on us, then suddenly we came back into Nash's planning as we curved through Regent's Park in a wooded cutting. The graceful, iron columns of Macclesfield Bridge brought to mind the famous Regent's Park explosion of 1874, when a boat load of gunpowder and petrol blew up underneath the bridge one dark morning. This accident, one of the very few serious disasters to have taken place on a British canal, was long remembered by boaters. The bridge was still known unofficially as 'Blow-up Bridge'. I had read that the cast iron columns were re-erected afterwards and turned through 180 degrees in so doing, which explained the rope score marks on the wrong side of the ironwork. I noticed a small detail which I have not seen mentioned before. A mature tree on the cutting side above the towpath had evidently grown from a sapling split by the blast. It was now fully grown, but its trunk had developed in two halves.

High above us the birds and animals in the Zoo made their chirps and grunts. Not a soul was to be seen on the towpath and we met no other boats until we swung round the sharp turn near Cumberland Basin and left the Park behind us. Under Regent's Park Road, then under the railway from Euston at Camden Bank and between warehouses to Camden Town Locks we slipped. In those days these locks were duplicated, as at Hillmorton, and lock-keepers were on duty at each lock. It was the changeover point for uphill traffic from tractor to tug haulage. We had met Friday evening's collection at Kensal Green, now the jumble of downhill lighters which had been collecting there since Friday was being cleared away by towpath tractors to make way for the next uphill lot. We had the distinct feeling that we were not welcome to the lock-keepers.

The canal wound through a succession of warehouses, factories, tenements and bridges, past the 'Waterways' yacht basin on the site of an old coal wharf at St Pancras, down another lock and over the Great Northern railway line out of Kings Cross. At this stage we were uncertain of the whereabouts of all the locks so we were going 'abreast', working on the assumption that if loaded barges could get by so could breasted empty boats. As Islington Tunnel loomed up we decided to stay as we were, since it was clear right through, but it was a foolish mistake and we paid for 'cocking a snook' at the regulations which insisted that narrow boats pass through singled out. There came a graunching clatter in the dark and the motor's chimney was swept overboard by the arch of the tunnel!

Rather a pleasant stretch followed from the east end of the tunnel to the next lock at City Road. Below this another basin, City Road Basin, led off to the right. It was deserted save for a few empty maintenance craft and had little to indicate that once it had been the vitally important terminus of Fellows, Morton and Clayton's flyboat service, successors to the Grand Junction Canal Carrying Company's fleet, who were successors in turn to Pickfords the giants of

151

pre-railway times.

Industry and buildings crowded in again down Sturts and Acton locks. Then, sure sign of the East End, we found ourselves following the edge of Victoria Park. Near here we were hailed from a Woodward Fisher barge which was unloading timber outside the canal and recognised our old friend, the lighterman from Brentford who had had to come and unsheet our barge that first trip. Below Old Ford Locks a hump bridge on the inside marked the junction with the Hertfordshire Union Canal, or Duckett's Cut, which connected through to the River Lea. Now there was a real atmosphere of Dockland. Barges became ever more numerous and tractors rattled back and forth on the towpath.

Typically, in spite of this greater use, the paddle gear was stiff and frequently red with rust. We filled the pressure oil can that we had transferred from "Enterprise" with old sump oil and liberally squirted the bearings. Both lock-keepers and bargemen stared open-mouthed at this practice. Fortunately it seemed that this was not anybody's job, otherwise we would probably have caused a demarcation dispute.

Under Mile End Road, down Mile End and Salmon Lane Locks we dropped. Then suddenly masts and derricks appeared over roofs. The canal split into two channels beneath Commercial Road, leading into the twin Commercial Road Locks, from whence it led beneath a tall railway arch and straight into Regent's Canal Dock. This was journey's end—'Limehouse'.

Now, even the clumsy lighters were dwarfed. The ships in the dock were not very large, being mainly coasters, but they seemed gigantic viewed from a narrowboat. A friendly lock-keeper directed us to a tying place in the wide expanse of water that was the Dock. Above us cranes bowed and rattled, winches heaved, lorries growled and hooted. In the midst of turmoil the dockers carried on in the deliberate manner of a religious ceremony. A nod, a gesture, a sharp word and crates of merchandise dropped neatly down a hold. Sailors peered down incuriously at the tiny canal boats arcing round from the lock, gulls wheeled and cawed overhead. We tied up and I rang Morton to report our arrival. We were, it seemed, to await a Norwegian ship "Sigrid K" due up on the evening tide and to load pallets of hardboard for Olton, Birmingham. Morton issued a stream of incomprehensible instructions about dunnage, side-stowing and quay charges. The gist of which was that the load was to total forty tons and in order to get it all aboard, the pallets would have to go in sideways, not flat. Putting it in flat would result in the boats having too much 'top' (i.e. it would rise too far above the gunwale and thus become unstable). I did not like the sound of this very much and privately wished we had Charlie or some such experienced mate to consult. However, we were on our own.

By now dusk was falling so, after tea, we wandered forth to explore. Just ahead of us was a scrap wharf where a coaster was loading ferrous scrap from a barge by means of an electro-magnetic crane. Behind us was the lock and beyond this the berth for "Sigrid K". Several other ships were berthed in the dock, along the landward side of which ran a railway on tall arches. In the corner near the scrap wharf lay two wooden sailing barges making ready to leave. Limehouse was the one place left on London River where the canal boatmen might meet the sailing barge men, or "sailormen" as boaters called them. We found these last much more affable than their doleful colleagues on the canal.

We walked over to the tide lock, a huge affair capable of taking ships. At nearly full tide both sets of gates were opened to replenish the dock water. This enabled craft to slip in and out without using the lock and also allowed craft that were too long for the lock to enter. We stood on the knuckle where the lock joined the Thames. Tugs and lighters swept upstream on the flood pouring in from the Nore, navigation lights twinkled across the wide reach and sirens whooped in the misty gloom.

As we reached the far side of the Dock, I noticed the swing bridge over the lock was opening and went back in time to see the towering bows of "Sigrid K" entering the lock. A solemn, overcoated man held an outsize fender on a long rope from the inner knuckle as the ship barely touched but the old man's arm jerked suddenly. Loud Cockney rent the air: "Yer clumsy, bleedin', square-'eaded, snot-gobblin' Oslo git!"

The captain leant over his bridge rail, touched his cap and said, "Ah! Goot efenink Harry!"

At first light next morning we pulled alongside "Sigrid K" and made ready for loading. Long lines were dropped to us and a Jacobs Ladder unrolled itself down from the deck. A sailorman of the London and Rochester Company tied astern of us as we cleared away the stands, cross beams and planks of "Tern" and stacked them aboard "Dunlin"; for we had resolved to put as much as possible aboard the motor first then load the rest, which would be the greater part, on the larger and deeper butty. Last night's mist had thickened to fog which showed little sign of lifting as time went on, but work commenced.

Almost immediately a problem arose. The chief stevedore, or ship-worker, was adamant that pallets could not go in sideways, nor would they load above gunwale height. I telephoned Brentford to report this to Morton. His answer was pithy, "Bribe the booggers." I asked how far I should go; he asked what I had in ready cash.

"A fiver between us," I replied.

"That'll do," and the line went dead.

Back then to the shipworker, whose badge proclaimed him a Union official. "Are you trying to bribe a Union official?" he asked threateningly. I explained that we only wanted to ensure that his men were adequately recompensed. After some humming and hawing he agreed that whilst the pallets most adamantly could not go in sideways, a couple of pounds would ensure they would go above gunwale height. The balance would be landed and no amount of pleading would move him further. I pointed out that it was vital for the firm that we took the full load by hook or by crook. Eventually he softened and said, quite kindly, "Look kid, I know you're keen, but it ain't your worry. If there's an accident though it won't 'arf be my bloody worry, and if anything ain't done by the book I'm the geezer wot gets lumbered." So that had to be that.

Whilst waiting for work to begin we had a visitor in the shape of an earnest official from the Public Health Department. He seemed rather upset that we did not have any Registration Certificates and insisted that both boats should be repainted. I think he was secretly disappointed not to find any bugs.

By mid-morning loading began. Dunnage was laid on the floor, then pallet after pallet of hardboard rattled down into "Tern" but after an hour or so an unforeseen snag occurred. The fog was getting steadily denser as the morning went on. Although we did not realise it then, we were being caught in the last of London's famous 'pea soupers'. Since those days bituminous fuels have ceased to be burned in London, steam has vanished from both river and rail and in consequence dense fogs are a thing of the past. The kind of atmospheric conditions which cause chaos on motorways are mild mists by comparison with the choking, yellowish vapour which was gradually swallowing Limehouse as more smoke and carbon monoxide was pouring into the atmosphere. By noon, the dockers on the deck of the "Sigrid K" could neither see us in the boat's bottom, nor the crane driver above their heads. Work in these circumstances was not only highly dangerous, but virtually impossible. A council-of-war amongst the shipworkers was held and all agreed to suspend work until two-thirty, by which time things might have cleared a little.

Rather than cook a meal we decided to investigate the surrounding cafes, but found the fog too thick even to get to the Dock gates. It was impossible to see from one side of "Sigrid K" to the other, so we dined on sandwiches while we waited. By two-thirty it was obvious that the fog was not going to lift. One of the dockers came back from the pub and informed us: "Fick! It's ficker 'an Paddy's napper. Cars 'an lorries is a-tyin' up all dahn Commercial Road."

We gloomily covered up the pallets with a tarpaulin and Bill suggested that we go to the cinema; at least we would be in comfortable seats and out of the fog. This was good thinking, so we cleaned up, banked up the fires and set out. By now it was dark but we managed to steer from light to light until we reached the Dock gates. The gateman directed us to the nearest cinema, which must have been half a mile away across Limehouse and out into the world we groped. The rush-hour traffic was literally standing still, headlights made ghostly patterns and thousands of car exhausts added their quota to the miasma. Dodging across Commercial Road I noticed that the amber globes on the top of the Belisha Beacons had been removed, presumably to lessen the diffusion of light, and they lay at the foot of the posts while overhead a bare bulb flashed. I said jokingly to Bill that one of those would come in handy in the cabin, saving a cold trip out to the hatches in the night when nature called. I should have known better and kept my mouth shut.

The main film was, I recall, "The Amorous Prawn" and the cinema was half empty. During the showing I realised with horror that the fog was invading the cinema every time one of the exits was used. Having seen the programme round and noted how the rather frothy comedy was lost on the East End audience, we headed for home. Just outside the cinema was a Belisha Beacon with its globe on the ground. The streets were completely deserted. Bill taunted: "Go on! I dare you." I picked up the globe, put it under my arm and off we set. The lights of a fish and chip saloon beckoned us out of the gloom so, leaving the globe on the pavement outside, in we went for an enormous meal. Our prize was still there on our return and so I picked it up again. At the Dock gates a hand fell on my shoulder. "Just one moment," said a stern voice. I turned to behold a blue helmet and cape. "Where are you going with that?"

I thought desperately, "Home."

"And where's home?"

"Regent's Canal Dock," said I, realising instantly how silly such a reply sounded.

"I think you'd better come with me," said the constable, gripping my arm. Bill's face looked white.

I shouted to him, "Go on, you're not with me" and he vanished into the murk; the policeman grasping vainly at the fog where he had stood.

"That's enough," he uttered grimly, "now come along." Gripping my arm he steered me over a cross-roads, holding the plastic globe triumphantly in his free hand. A plain-clothes man hove out of the fog and took my other arm.

"What-o cock!" he said conversationally. "Been out on the piss then?"

"Haven't had one all night," I replied truthfully. Both my captors roared with laughter. Soon I was marched into Limehouse Police Station and into a large hall. A sergeant sat at a desk and made me turn out my pockets and a pathetic pile of possessions, which were duly noted, grew on the desk.

"Take him off!" ordered the sergeant and I was marched towards the cells. Realising whither I was bound, I begged to be allowed to keep my copy of the "Evening News" which I had earlier bought. This was allowed, then down a passage we went. I was shown an open door through which I stepped and the door clanged shut behind.

My new accommodation was somewhat larger, loftier and better appointed than "Dunlin's" cabin. It had a WC without any projections or chain, merely a bowl with a handle in the wall, a bunk-type bed with a hard shiny mattress and an electric light flush with the ceiling. I sat on the bed and read my paper, wondering what Morton would say on hearing that one of his captains was in the calaboose. It would not have been the first time, but he would not be pleased at having to bail me out.

I was no stranger to cells, having visited prisoners in police stations, court buildings and remand prisons, but it was novel being incarcerated oneself. The bolt was thrown back and a grinning policeman came in with a steaming mug of tea. "'Ere you are mate, don't smash the mug," he quipped and withdrew. Presumably they had decided I would not attempt to cut my throat with a jagged piece of china.

Time passed, then once more the door opened to reveal my arresting constable who told me to 'come out of it'. We marched back to the hall and stood again before the desk. I was still wearing the gear in which we had been loading; boots, bib-and-brace overalls, woollen muffler, cloth cap and donkey jacket. Thus attired, I faced across the desk, in all his splendour, a uniformed Inspector.

"What the bloody hell's the meaning of this then?" he roared.

"Er-I-er-er," I stammered.

"Ho yes! I suppose you want to tell me you were going to use it as a pisspot."

"Well, yes, I suppose I was . . ."

"WHAAT!" A sausage-like finger wagged in front of my nose. "Look son," he growled ominously, "don't try and be funny with the Law!" He leaned back in his chair. "Now then, what's all this about living in Regent's Canal Dock?" I explained. He seemed puzzled, evidently my accent was unfamiliar. "Well, are you a bargee then?"

"No, I am a boatman."

"What? a canal bargee?"

"No, a boat captain."

"Do-you-live-on-a-canal-barge?" he thundered.

"No, I live on a canal boat," I responded.

"DON'T BLOODY ARGUE!" The desk sergeant was suppressing his mirth with difficulty at this point. The Inspector fixed me with a steely glare. "Look, I've heard about enough from you. Have you got anything to say before I charge you with larceny?"

I thought quickly. The time for fooling was over, I had not studied Law for five years for nothing, besides there were forty tons of hardboard to shift back at the dock. "Yes, I have," I declared. Three mouths opened and three pairs of eyebrows lifted. Before anyone could say a word I went on, "Before you can sustain such a charge, you must be in a position to prove the intent permanently to deprive the owner thereof." Silence. The desk sergeant chortled and hastily stopped as the Inspector whirled round at him. For what seemed an age the Inspector glared at me, then he leaned towards the sergeant and whispered in his ear. The sergeant produced a ledger-like book which the Inspector opened and began busily to write in. My heart sank. This was it. A night in the cells, up before the 'Beak' and get Morton to pay the fine. He finished writing, sat back and surveyed his handiwork.

"Can you write?" he asked. I nodded. He turned the book towards me, placing a finger on a column. "Sign here," he commanded, proffering me a pen. I looked at the book. It was the Lost Property book. There was my name and address and a description of the property I had so kindly handed in. I signed. The sergeant pointed to my belongings, still piled on his desk. I pocketed them. "Now bugger off!" said the Inspector, and for the first time chuckled. "Straight home now," he continued. I asked directions which he gave me and went out of the building a free man.

The entrance was at the front, but the Inspector evidently left straight away by another door, for a few minutes later I saw him by a busy cross roads trying to disentangle a traffic jam. "Go on, keep moving!" he called to me through the gloom.

A few yards further and he had disappeared. There, by the dock gates, was the pedestrian crossing I had first seen. Its globe lay beside it. A wild notion of wickedness came to me and I bent down and picked it up. "Oi!" called a voice, another hand fell on my shoulder. Limehouse was crawling with police that night. "What's all this then?" asked my new acquaintance.

Quickly I said: "You know Inspector Blank?"

"Of course I know Inspector Blank?"

"Well, he's on point duty at the cross-roads, would you give him this," I said, pushing the globe into his hands, "tell him I've found another one!"

As a postscript to this episode, months later Willow Wren received a pro forma from Limehouse telling them that the property handed in had been duly claimed. Morton kept it as a means of blackmailing me into behaving myself when in his company.

The fog lifted sufficiently on Wednesday morning for loading to be completed. In spite of our efforts three tons had to be landed and forwarded by road. Had we had a pair of big 'Grand Unions' we would have been able to load all the hardboard.

There then came the delicate task of clothing-up in the dock. An awkward operation at best and worsened by the prospect of a bath in thirty feet of smelly water. The sailormen watched this with tolerant amusement and offered friendly chaff. When we had finished we had to wait several hours for Customs clearance and documentation, without which we could not leave the Dock.

We pulled back to our old mooring near the scrap wharf and climbed up to the quay for lunch. A West Indian sat on the quayside above a scrap barge eating his sandwiches, his steel-tipped boots dangling over the side. Suddenly the crane driver energised his magnet as the grab came down and one of the boots shot off the West Indian's foot onto the grab. Eyes rolling, he shouted up to the crane driver, "Hey man, dere's ma boot gone!" Obligingly the driver shut off power and the boot descended into the hold of the barge along with a pile of scrap. We went before murder was committed!

Late that afternoon I collected our papers from the Customs Shed, Bill started the engine and we moved into Commercial Road Lock on the first leg of our second trip to Birmingham. It was then that we found the top gates were padlocked and the lock-keeper had gone home so, nothing daunted, we spent the night in the full lock. The lock-keeper was not amused next morning when he found us, but he let us out grudgingly and away we went into the foggy morning on our first trip "Grand Unioning".

The Grand Union Canal Carrying Company, from whom the name was derived, had built up a good long-distance traffic in the 1930's. They saw themselves as a link in a chain of water transport stretching from the industrial Midlands through Limehouse to the Continent and beyond. In this respect they were forty years ahead of their time. Today the unit-freight concept is commonplace, but operated by virtue of motorways and roll-on roll-off ships. The complex and interlocking network of canal companies, road hauliers, warehouses, shipping companies, stevedoring firms and forwarding agents was broken-up by the BTC and quietly disposed of. They were able to prove once more to their own satisfaction that the operation did not pay since the taxpayer was left with the least profitable part of the operation which now existed in isolation. By December 1962 long distance transhipment traffic via Limehouse had dwindled to a trickle. No longer did the motor industry of Birmingham, or the Midlands steel works, or the Northampton boot and shoe industry, or other important consignees receive imported supplies by canal via Limehouse.

The fog was patchy that day. By Kings Cross and St Pancras the combined effects of steam locomotives and cooling water outlets slowed us to a mere crawl. I could just make out the 'loobey post' of the butty in such places. A bridge would only become evident as a darker area in a choking blanket of steamy vapour. Through Regent's Park and Paddington Stop things were a little better, there was even a shaft or two of wan sunlight, but the railways and gasworks at Kensal Green were the densest so far. It was about three o'clock and only by glancing over the side could I tell we were moving. I kept about fifteen feet out from the copings on the towpath, which was just visible, and hoped for the best. I heard the sound of Bill pulling "Tern" out of gear, slowly the noise of the engine drew nearer and the motor's stern loomed up. Bill declared that he had had enough. It would be dark in less than an hour and we needed some shopping. I agreed and knowing that there was a road bridge somewhere near, we pulled in and tied up, taking diligent care not to bang our mooring spikes into subterranean cables which I feared ran below the towpath.

Willesden was even thicker than Limehouse that day. One could have cut the fog into blocks. It was everywhere, dripping off lines and cabin roofs in sooty drops. Somehow we found our way to the road and shops and back again. We listened awhile to the wireless giving details of the traffic chaos all over London, though the continual thunder of trains outside proved that the Great Western's automatic train control system was keeping Paddington trains moving. We drew up our fires to add our quota to the smog and 'turned in' early.

By first light there was some sign of improvement. It was possible to see about two boats' lengths, so we cautiously moved off again. As we came up by Harlesden Power Station the thing I had been dreading occurred. The butty ran over a drum on the canal bed and heeled far over to the left. Normally such a tilt is more frightening than dangerous, a boat generally soon recovers, but to my horror she remained at an angle—our load had shifted. I whistled for Bill, who slowed down to let me catch up. Together we lifted the cloths to find that several pallets of hardboard had keeled over. Two of these were above gunwale level and only the sidecloths had held them. A good hour's grunting and heaving, using planks and tying bars as levers, restored the status quo, after which the tedious business of re-lashing and clothing-up had to be done. By now it was Friday noon. Although the fog began to lift slightly, enabling us to pick up speed, it was nearly nightfall when we came round the turn at Bulls Bridge onto familiar waters once more.

We had a bad road from Black Jack's Lock so I went ahead, lock-wheeling in the dark, while Bill brought the pair up abreast, and in such fashion did we arrive above Rickmansworth Lock to find several pairs tied ahead of us. A steady drizzle was falling, clearing away the last remnants of the fog but I coughed up black sputum for days after. Later we heard that the fog had killed more people than many of London's wartime blitzes.

It made a pleasant change once more to be sitting in a snug bar (at "The Railway") exchanging boating boasts and gossip with other captains. One of these captains, George, we had passed at Fenny a few trips before and he was very anxious not to let it happen again. We, in turn, aimed to get at least to the bottom of Marsworth, if not Leighton, by the next night to try and make up time. George's pair were loaded with barrels of limejuice for Boxmoor but he was also towing a single-loaded 'dust-bin' or 'blue-top' with timber for Aylesbury. This entailed double-locking and bow-hauling all the way from Brentford to the bottom of 'Maffers' (sixty two locks), then the 'dust-bin' butty would be worked singly down the Arm. Just how this was to be accomplished I am not quite sure. I seem to recall some talk of towpath tractors, but the state of the Aylesbury Arm towpath would have made this a somewhat doubtful proposition.

Needless to say, we were not looking forward to getting stuck behind this ensemble, but George beat us to it next morning. The unwelcome rattle of his engine made a grim background to our breakfast. By the time we had finished, George's last butty was vanishing round tne turn at Batchworth Millstream. We kept the boats abreast and pottered off behind him. By the time he was through Lock 80 we had spent a good five minutes dawdling about below it. This was to continue all through the miserable, wet, December Saturday. The only consolation was that we could have plenty of cups of tea and other refreshment and get on with household chores between locks.

At last the 'New 'uns' appeared and we worked steadily upwards in a fine, cold drizzle. George and his eldest son solemnly bow-hauled-in the 'blue-top' at each lock; two more pairs joined the queue behind us. Visions of Leighton faded, but we still had hopes of the Cowroast as George would be tying-up at Boxmoor and beyond that the road was good. The doleful queue arrived at Lock 65, top of the 'New 'uns' and the last before Boxmoor. "Now for a quick run," we thought, resting our fore-ends against the bottom gates as the 'blue-top' rose. It was about three o'clock and getting dark but half past seven should have seen us tied snugly at Cowroast. We stood at the bottom gate paddles ready to draw as soon as the 'blue-top' was half way out. Then came disaster. With about a foot to go, the 'blue-top's' fore-end (which was not vertically rounded like a proper boat) caught under the balance beam as the boat rose and lifted the top gate clean out of its shoe plate. The gate fell over, the lock filled with a rush, George called: "Ta, ta lads!" and the 'blue-top' floated out round the wreckage.

By now the rain had turned to sleet. We stared at the cold and miserable scene dumbly. A bicycle rattled up behind us. It was 'Mad Ted', a 'Waterways' captain, whose boats were behind. "Out o'the way, you bloody pair o' Willow Wrens," he called sternly, then his long face broke into a toothy grin. "Cor boogger! 'Oo've done that? ole George?" he slapped his knee, "'e wants to learn 'ow ter steer them fookers," he chortled.

I failed to see the hilarity of the situation and knocked on the door

161

of the Company house which conveniently adjoined the lock. A Company's man appeared, disturbed from Saturday afternoon television, took one look and told me to go down to Apsley Yard and call the foreman out while he secured the gate.

Luckily Apsley Yard was only a couple of hundred yards away. 'Mad Ted' pointed out that there were some boats following him and they had best be stopped. I got out the bicycle and pedalled back into the murky dark. The foreman was out, but his wife took a message while I went down the 'New 'uns' stopping traffic. Altogether there were now six loaded pairs in the four pounds between Apsley and Nash.

Had it not been dark and dangerously slippery we would have been away that night, but when the foreman arrived he said we would have to wait until next morning in the circumstances. He and the Company's man, however, turned cheerfully to in the dark and slush, lashed the gate to prevent it moving and strained it back to ease the weight on the collar. We decided, therefore, to have a night out in Hemel Hempstead and walked up to Boxmoor before heading 'up town'. George looked sheepish when we came up by his moored boats. I rather fancy he thought we might set about him because he declined coming ashore for a drink and remained warily in the butty hatches while talking. I seem to recall our Saturday night out merely resolved itself into a Chinese meal. Still, it was very pleasant to change clothes and sit in comfortable chairs in a warm restaurant.

Where the practical people are given their head, British Waterways can be relied upon to do a good job and at eight-thirty Sunday morning the foreman and his mate arrived to finish their task. Their tools for the job of moving this heavy gate were no more than spanners, hammers, ropes, block and tackle and crowbars. Quickly and efficiently they buckled to and by ten o'clock all was finished and we were away. George was apparently lying in so we blasted him with our horn and wash as we went past—but he lay 'doggo'.

Because of our late start we were barely clear of 'Maffers' before dark and although we should have gone at least to Fenny, we called it a day at Leighton Bridge.

The next day was a cold and miserable trek through a sleety landscape. At Stoke Hammond Three the lock-keeper had shovelled the slush away and gritted the gates. I managed to persuade the landlord of the pub to part with some nuts and chocolate as he swept out his bar at about eight-thirty and this was all we had to eat until tying-up time that night. Once again, the short day petered out into rainy darkness before we had seemingly got anywhere.

At last the white footbridge below Stoke showed up. We clambered up the seven locks and tied up. Then supper had to be cooked. This was, we both felt, the worst thing about two-handed working. When you tied up at the end of a tiring and cold day you had all the trouble of preparing and cooking food, not to mention washing up afterwards. I was feeling distinctly fed-up by this time and resolved to have a pint at the "Boat". Bill rather grumpily declined. Morale was at a low ebb, so I went in on my own.

A roaring fire lit up the nearly empty bar. The tiny room contained three tables, some stools and benches, a grandfather clock and three customers. They were Jack James the lock-keeper, Colonel Ritchie and a thin, balding man who was sitting on a stool by the fire smoking a long-stemmed pipe. Behind the door was a thin, elderly woman with snow white curls. The men nodded to me and the old lady quavered: "Good evening, my duck."

I took my pint over to where Jack James was sitting. He winked and took a long pull from his glass. The Colonel seemed to have difficulty in fitting his lengthy frame into the low-ceilinged bar and was hunched near the fire, resting one hand above his head on a heavy oak-beam. He and Jack James were arguing about canal politics—a common enough occurrence I discovered—and Jack was saying: "It wouldn't pay me to say what I know. I don't know nothing!"

The Colonel snorted: "Of course you do you silly old bugger. You old boatmen are all the same. Got eyes in your arses all of you."

The others grinned. The old lady said: "Now, now Colonel. I'm surprised at you."

"Oh no you're not Mrs Woodward. You know me well enough never to be surprised. Evening Teddy!" This last was addressed to a newcomer who had just entered. He was a well-built, florid faced man of about forty, wearing brogues, woollen stockings, breeches, coloured waistcoat, check jacket and a tweed cap. He greeted everyone in the bar, nodded to me, ordered his drink, lit a pipe and started to converse with the Colonel. Suddenly the Colonel looked at his watch, then, bidding us adieu, strode out.

Teddy said conversationally after he had left: "How's the pound, Mr James?"

"Up and down, Mr Cook, up and down," replied Jack.

I added: "Outside here, or on the London Market it's much the same."

Teddy threw back his head and laughed: "Well done skipper, have a drink."

Thus the ice was broken and I met for the first time Edward R. Cook, M.R.C.V.S. I was destined to get to know him very well indeed, but my most enduring memory is of him as he was on this quiet December evening; brimming with good humour and generosity, the epitome of a country vet.

A prosperous-looking man, of similar age, had entered meanwhile. There was a by-election brewing in the local Parliamentary Constituency and he had just returned from a public meeting in Towcester. The thin man with the pipe had been joined by another elderly, smaller man with spectacles and a cap. These two began a spirited discussion about the election in which everyone joined with the exception of Jack James and the landlady. It seemed to me that the political spectrum of Stoke Bruerne ranged from a sort of Cromwellian radicalism through Whiggery to Gladstonian liberalism. Of Marxism, Fascism, or even modern socialism or conservatism there was barely a trace. Jack listened sagely and the landlady contented herself with acting as referee when things became heated. At length time was called. The landlady's son beamed goodnight as he ensured that the towel was draped across the handles of the beer pump and we parted in jovial mood.

In order to make Braunston in daylight from Stoke Bruerne, a loaded pair must be away before 8am in winter. We had got into the habit, when not having to get or keep ahead of other boats, of rising at seven and untying by about quarter to eight. We reasoned that this gave us a daylight start and a final tie-up by 8pm at the latest; should further effort be necessary, I have always preferred to start earlier rather than go on later. Since we needed to see Morton at Braunston about the docker's payment as well as oiling-up and some minor engine repairs, we were able, for once, to do a whole day's boating in daylight and to see the attractive countryside of the Blisworth Pound for its whole length.

The time came when, wedged in a corner of the "Nelson's" Bar, I had to explain the matter of the missing three tons of hardboard to the 'Gaffer'. He was fairly sanguine about it, then came the matter of the bribe. I told him that we had paid out two pounds. He was incredulous: "By heck lad, you've got something to learn." It was my turn to look doubtful, he chuckled: "I said go up to a fiver. I thought you'd have gone higher." Privately I felt that a fiver would have meant that we would not have eaten for a week, and any higher would have had even more terrible repercussions—no beer or cigarettes either. "Well," he continued "If I'd have been you, I'd have told me a tenner and settled for a fiver. You can be too honest in this game you know." The upshot was that he gave me five pounds plus two days' laying money extra to compensate for hanging about, plus the pair of us having free beer for the rest of the evening. Honesty, I reflected, was the best policy. Not for some years did I discover just why Morton was so generous. He had calculated that we should only have loaded thirty three tons and had based his quotation for carriage on this. The remaining seven tons he was expecting to forward by lorry at a much higher rate. Of course he and the firm had made a handsome profit by our loading an extra four tons!

Once again we headed across Braunston puddle banks on the road to Brummagem. At Itchington we heard bad tidings. We had been anticipating meeting Clayton's gas boats again and making our peace with their captain. The news was all the more shocking, therefore, when we were told of a fatal accident which had happened while we were at Braunston. The captain's wife had been lock-wheeling and had gone to get aboard at the locktail of 'Capes Two.' She had slipped on the steps in the frosty darkness and gone beneath the fore-ends of the boats. The captain was left with seven young, motherless children a fortnight before Christmas. The starkness of this tragedy added to the general depression of the day. We tied at the bottom of Hatton feeling dejected once more.

Our dismal spirits were not improved the next day when we arrived at Olton Wharf at lunchtime to be greeted with amazement by the yard foreman. He was not expecting us until Monday, thus ensuring yet more hanging about over the weekend. Financially, we badly needed to make another trip before Christmas and time was running out; there were only ten days left. At length it was agreed that we should unload one boat on Saturday morning and finish on Monday, so we settled down to another few days waiting.

The foreman was true to his word and emptied "Dunlin" with a fork lift truck on Saturday. Then at noon work ceased with "Tern" partially emptied. Bill wished to potter about with the engine so I washed, changed and set off for a long walk towards central Birmingham. At one point I scrambled over a broken wall and came out in a side street in what was then an area of decrepit slums. These Dickensian hovels were built in courts which opened off the street beneath an arch.

I plucked up courage and walked through one of these arched alleys. A flickering gas lamp stood at the end of a row of privies facing the houses in the court. Yellow light in downstairs windows showed that these places too were lit by gas, though blue flickering from cathode tubes showed that somehow electricity was available to power a television. The apparent lack of aerials may have been because the landlord would have raised the rent if he saw his tenants had a television, or it may have been because the Sutton Coldfield and Lichfield transmitters were close at hand.

Tin baths hanging on the privy walls and a row of dustbins added to the general air of gloom. It was miserable enough on a raw winter Saturday, what the atmosphere was like on a hot summer's day I dared not think. Once again I realised with a shock that we had far to go with housing problems in inner cities. The sheer ugliness of life when warped by both poverty and the industrial system was like a blow in the face. It was easy to talk of self-help, of pulling oneself up by the bootstrings, of educating oneself out of such a place, but how in truth was it to be done? How does a housewife cope with a steady rain of dirt and grime? How do you encourage your child to learn at school, to work and study at home when you live in a single room downstairs in which all the family activities take place and the two bedrooms are either freezing cold or stuffy? And just where do teenagers get the privacy they need to develop their minds and expand their mental horizons? Not surprisingly the horizons are limited by the factory or dead-end menial jobs. The only real surprise is that, in spite of all the odds, some people have fought their way upwards and out. With all its drawbacks and petty discomforts, life on the boats was certainly no worse and in many ways much better than in these conditions.

Such experiences and conditions had a profound effect on my thinking. It was not the dramatic occurrences which doubtless happened in such places, although I never saw any, but the sheer squalor, emotional bankruptcy and the squandering and waste of human talent and spirit which it engendered that seared and inspired me for years to come. Seeing both the London tenements and Birmingham courts at close quarters troubled me for long after I had returned to the less claustrophobic atmosphere of the canals.

Bill had had an idea. "What about a mate?" he asked as we sat having breakfast on Sunday. The advantages of a third hand were manifold, especially if we were to get a load in before Christmas, while the disadvantages of two-handed boating were abundantly clear, as well as being fresh in our minds. Bill then revealed that he had been in touch with a youngster in Newbury who was about to start his school holidays and, if I was agreeable, he would come up to meet us on Tuesday. He had negotiated terms over the telephone whereby we would feed him and give him a pound at the end of each trip. This far-fetched sounding proposal had been eagerly accepted. I felt it was a first class idea so Bill once more hastened to the telephone.

By nine the next morning we were ready for orders again. I telephoned Brentford to be told by Stan to go to Tyseley, a couple of miles up the canal in the Birmingham direction, for orders. This was good news indeed for it implied another load for the London area rather than a hike round the Bottom Road to the coalfields. Of course 'Waterways' bureaucracy could not make it as simple as that. We were received with amazement at Tyseley, in spite of the fact that Willow Wren had informed Bulls Bridge Traffic Control of our presence and that Stan was sending our starting money and trip settlement there per registered envelope. We were told to go to Sampson Road at Camp Hill. A suggestion that the clerk might telephone Sampson Road to save time and fuel was met with incredulity followed by a blank refusal and the suggestion that we 'took it or left it.' On the way to Sampson Road we met a loaded horseboat carrying rubbish for Sparkbrook tip. We slacked right down because the driver on the towpath said that: "Th'oss day loike they maowters," which translated from 'Black Country' meant that his animal was shy of engines.

The office at Sampson Road greeted our arrival with astonishment and told us to go back to Tyseley where they had fifty tons of cocoa waste for us. Choking back our rage, we expostulated only to be met with shrugged shoulders. Boatmen, we were given to understand, should think themselves lucky to be given work. It seemed futile to point out that the depots were set up to serve the canal rather than the canal built to serve the depots. Seething inwardly, we winded and headed back.

At Sparkbrook tip the boatmen were tossing rubbish out onto a tramway truck to which the horse was now harnessed, so we throttled right back again. Just beyond them a gust of wind caught our high-riding fore-ends causing Bill to rev up sharply to avoid stemming the mud. The sudden burst of staccato throbs from the engine stack proved that the Joey boaters spoke the truth, for the horse promptly bolted down the tramway at right angles to the cut. The wagon rocked behind him, shedding rubbish as the Joey boaters roared Brummagem curses after it.

The Tyseley office had been telephoned by Sampson Road and did at least have the grace to look ashamed. They redeemed themselves by arranging for us to load on that Wednesday morning. It was essential, they said, that our cloths were watertight as the load must be kept dry. We had several splits in "Dunlin's" side cloths which I felt might let the water in, but in view of their treatment of us earlier I kept quiet about it.

We tied up to await our third hand, Keith the schoolboy, who was expected by train the next day. His assistance would more than compensate for loss of time, so Tuesday morning saw us making our way by bus to Snow Hill to await his arrival. Like many inhabitants of Berkshire in those days, Keith had never been north of Oxford and, as he told Bill over the telephone, Birmingham was to him somewhere near Greenland. Snow Hill, unknown to us, was under sentence of death by then, as were the steam locomotives whose steamy breath condensed and wreathed round the superb ironwork of the station. In spite of the cold, trains for far destinations, dignified expresses and fussy locals made the time pass quickly. At last a train from the south arrived bearing Keith, a fresh faced fifteen year old who gaped in wonder at the noise and bustle. We set off to get back to Tyseley before dark.

Next morning we pulled under an overhanging iron roof. Doors in a warehouse were opened, a grinning Asian jumped into the hold, a conveyor was wheeled into position and loading started. The load was one thousand hundred-weight bags of cocoa residue from Cadburys. This was mainly bean husk which was bagged and exported to the Continent, whence crafty Dutchmen and Swiss converted it into cosmetics and similar products. It was due to be dispatched by barge from Brentford on Christmas Eve, five days hence.

By two o'clock both boats were loaded. We clothed up in the gathering dark alongside the place we had tied up with Charlie and George back in the sunny days of early autumn. Now the wind howled and rain lashed the yard where we had watched the horseboat pass in warm sunlight. Without a backward glance we lit up the engine and cracked off into the dusk. We pressed on that night, down Knowle and on to Hatton—Lord knows what time we arrived there for we just had a cup of cocoa and crashed into bed. As Keith was too tall for the sidebed we had rigged up an air mattress on the butty cabin floor. By seven next morning we were up and about. Keith, with boyish innocence, asked what was for breakfast; we, with boating callousness, chorused: "Hatton Locks!"

Wasting no time, I banked up "Dunlin's" fire and set off lockwheeling in pouring rain. There was no doubt about it, a third hand made a difference. It was only nine-thirty at the bottom of Hatton. Keith, who was experienced with boats at Newbury, took the butty tiller while I dried out, cleaned up and got some food. Out of the Avon valley we toiled. The rain eased off near Itchington and, although it was dark again before we reached 'Wigrams', the night was clear and dry. Even so we did not 'whoop it up' too lavishly at Braunston that night for we had to put another good day in for our deadline. We were now planning our trip with confidence; Friday Leighton, Saturday 'Ricky', Sunday Brentford, unload Monday and home for Christmas. We should have known better.

Thursday started well. We were in Braunston Tunnel before dawn, having the singular experience of entering the tunnel in darkness and leaving it in daylight. Into Buckby we swept like old-time professionals. About ten o'clock, with two more locks to go, Bill emerged from the engine hole with a cross expression. The generator belt had been slipping previously and he had taken a link out to keep the dynamo charging, now it had broken. Luckily there was a telephone box by the lock so he rang through to Braunston for a spare. We tied up below the lock in balmy sunshine and waited. It was the shortest day of the year yet the weather was like early spring.

Black Charlie, the fitter, arrived, tutting apologetically, after a couple of hours, but it was not until nearly two o'clock that we got away. Our chances of getting even as far as Cosgrove that night were at an end because the locks at Stoke closed at six o'clock and a deep-loaded pair such as ours took five hours to navigate the Blisworth Pound. Dusk fell soon after High House. We surged along Heyford Deeps in the dark, wallowed through the mud in Bugbrook Cutting, watched a frosty moon rise behind the pinnacles of Gayton Church, called greetings to boats lying at the Arm End, then rattled the bricks of Blisworth Tunnel and tied at Stoke just after seven o'clock. Over a pint in "The Boat" we amended our plans. With luck we could still do it. If we got to Cowroast tomorrow, Saturday, we would get to the top of Norwood on Sunday night and still be in Brentford for the morning of Christmas Eve. Jack James unlocked at six-thirty next morning and said he would give us a knock at six if there was nobody moving on the boats.

In the dim light of the engine hole at about six-fifteen I was pottering about checking oil levels when I became aware of a dull "plop! plop!" from below the gearbox. I dipped the gearbox and called Bill. The dipstick was almost dry. Bill put his hand under the box and groaned. The casing had developed a crack and the oil was draining away. The only chance of moving now was for a spare casing to be rushed out to us from Braunston and there would be nobody in the yard for two hours. It was a grim-faced trio who sat down to breakfast, for all was now in ruins. Even if we got moving again we would only make Fenny or Stoke Hammond that night. We desperately considered 'fly-boating' right through but the fact that Marsworth, Cowroast, Norwood and Hanwell would be locked over night made the proposition doubtful; for even if we got away by two o'clock we still would be brought to a stand at 'Maffers'—in order to clear the latter before lock-up we would have to have been out of the bottom of Stoke by half-past seven.

Jack let us use the telephone in the lock-keeper's hut to ring Dennis at Braunston. He gave us the news that there were no spares: the gearbox would have to be removed and welded, which was a specialist job to be done by a Northampton firm, and that he would be over directly. The Whitlocks came puttering by loaded and shook their heads sympathetically. Bill opined that we had best stay where we were. This was confirmed by Dennis an hour later when he informed us that no repairs could be done until after Christmas for everywhere was shut down. We were faced with Christmas at Stoke and, worse, no money, for we had been banking on our settlement to provide us with some and had spent what we had on Christmas presents in Birmingham.

Jack James solved the problem. "Put 'em over agin the pub stables out of the road and go home," he said. "I'll look after 'em for you. Nobody'll touch 'em, they'll be quite safe." Stanley, when rang, agreed to this plan and told us that if we cared to call at Brentford on our way home he would leave our money with Mark or Ray White who were unloading down there. So, with lighter hearts, we moved over to the other bank, tidied up, drew the fires, locked up and left the boats deserted for the first time in months. The three of us walked to the bus stop by the bridge to catch the Northampton bus. Little did I dream that fate was dealing me a hand which was to change my whole life.

170

4

Frost

I sat in a cafe at Gloucester Green, Oxford, looking glumly at the snow. News had just come through that the Berkshire Downs were still covered in drifts and the A34 to Newbury was impassable. The bus to Bedford via Stony Stratford and Wolverton would not run as the road was blocked in several places and no traffic had come through. It was New Year's Day, 1963. I had got through by train from Reading meaning to meet Bill and Keith and return to Stoke Bruerne by 'bus. Much had happened since we had left the boats at Stoke.

On our arrival in Brentford Mark and Ray had been in a cheerful mood. Ray, in particular, had pointed out that the BTC had just ten days to live before the Transport Act 1962 took effect. This political change had, in fact, escaped us but it was to have a profound effect on the canals before the New Year was very old. We three had parted on the platform at Reading South station, agreeing to get in touch again the day after Boxing Day, when I would ring Dennis for news.

Dennis' news was not good. One thing we had not thought to do before leaving was to drain the engine of cooling water and when he went to remove our gearbox he found the cylinder block split open by the frost. He told us that Braunston had had three inches of ice and the icebreakers were frozen in. I learned later that the BTC had refused to pay the gangs overtime to turn out on Boxing Day and in consequence the icebreakers could not be moved the next morning. The carrying trade — which ceased work on Christmas Day and Boxing Day by long tradition — found itself unable to restart. Dennis said that there would be no hurry as the frost would last several days and the welding would not be ready until the New Year. For this reason I agreed to meet Bill and Keith at Oxford on New Years Day, but 1962 went out with the frost as hard as ever and heavy blizzards swept across the country.

Consequently, I returned to Reading after my fruitless trip to

171

Oxford and we agreed to try again before the weekend. By Friday the roads had been cleared sufficiently to allow regular traffic to move again so, once more, I sat in the cafe at Gloucester Green. The outcome was successful this time. From the top deck of the Bedford 'bus the flat landscape of central Oxfordshire looked bleak indeed. Bicester and Buckingham were swathed in white. Across the snowy meadows of the Ouse valley, beyond the derelict curves of the Buckingham Arm, the chimney of Wolverton Works with its dark plume heralded our arrival back in Grand Union country.

We left the 'bus at Old Stratford on Ray White's advice and, realising that there was a long wait before the Stoke Bruerne 'bus, set off to hitch-hike along the A508. However, nobody in their right mind picks up more than one male and there had been one or two nasty cases in the paper involving hitch-hikers. Not surprisingly, we walked several miles, beyond the village of Yardley Gobion in fact, before catching the 'bus. This stretch of road, which runs close to and roughly parallel with the Stoke Pound from Cosgrove to the bottom of Stoke, is bleak even on a summer's day. Across the open fields and hedgerows the tall spire of Hanslope was etched against a steel grey sky. The drifts piled up at the roadside and the dirty slush at the kerb added its own touch to this wintry scene. It was nearly dark when the 'bus came slithering along and the yellow-lit interior looked quite inviting after the frosty outside world.

A few minutes later we were dropped by the Canal bridge at Stoke and as we walked up to the lock we caught a glimpse of our fore-ends lying on the pub side of the cut in the last glimmer of twilight. The boats were fearfully cold but, mercifully, not damp. Two fires were speedily lit and the cabins soon warmed up, bedding was spread out and aired while we inspected for any damage as best we could in the dark. Nothing was out of place but Bill reported that the gearbox had gone and a nasty sliver of ice was protruding from the cylinder block. One thing we noticed for the first time was the sickly smell of cocoa which penetrated everywhere; defying all attempts to disguise or defeat it. So far the stretch of water where our boats lay had not frozen but ice began just beyond where Colonel Ritchie's boat "Lupin" lay. It was evident that no icebreaking had been done, or was possible. The frost was obviously going to last. Had we known then for how long, I think we would have given up immediately but as it was, we lived in hope of a quick thaw.

Next day we explored the canal in daylight. Apart from an old butty frozen in in the cutting and some carpenters' flats, there were just two other boats at Stoke Bruerne besides ourselves; "Lupin" and a

172

Loftus Bennett fibreglass cruiser called "Julia II". This last was moored some distance astern of us, on the same side and by what was a pleasant-looking landing stage adjoining a large, well-kept cottage garden. This belonged to the vet, Teddy Cook, whom I had met just before Christmas. Further down the locks everything was frozen solid. We walked down to Bottom Lock where an icebreaker lay forlornly locked in the ice. Not a soul was to be seen in the ice-bound countryside. We carried on walking to check whether the ice could be broken to let us move the boats nearer London but soon found that we could walk on it. Past Bozenham Mill bridge, where on a happier day we had first seen the steamdredger at work, to Grafton we walked; sliding and skidding on the surface before turning back. The sun was setting blood red behind the stout Norman tower of Stoke church as we came up the long pound. The Colonel had a pleasant surprise for us on our return for the postman had brought a registered envelope containing fourteen days' laying money at 22s 6d per day, less 2s 6d which Stanley had agreed to keep back for us until the end of the trip. So, with £7 each, less Keith's promised share, we had the wherewithal for a mild celebration in the "Boat", where the locals were rapidly accepting us as part of the landscape.

The frost continued and the following day, after much discussion, we agreed that it was hardly worth all of us waiting at Stoke eating food and costing laying money; besides which Keith's holidays would soon be over. The upshot was that we agreed to take turns in acting as watchman aboard until the thaw came. One of us would remain and the other would go home and find some work if possible. The laying money would be divided so that the one on duty took money out for housekeeping, then split the balance, which worked out at £2 10s each. On this basis we agreed that Bill should return to Newbury first for a fortnight. While he was away the motor could be pushed across to the other side so as to be accessible to Dennis or any fitters, while both Jack James and the Colonel lived near enough to discourage prowlers. We shoved "Tern" across and tied up. The boats were destined not to be reunited for nearly seven weeks.

Bill and Keith duly left on the morning 'bus on Monday. I stoked the fire, cleaned the brass and settled down to what boded to be a long wait. So far the tap by Jack James' office had not frozen which allowed me to fill all the water cans and kettles before settling down to write. I had resolved to set all these experiences down in writing while they were still fresh in my mind. I had been keeping a rough

173

log of our movements, jotted down on the back of an old 'Water-ways' boat tender form and I had bought a large exercise book in which to write. The trouble was, I found that I had lost the ability. I realised that weeks of physical work took their toll when I found that I was mentally worn out after writing half a page and I was sticking my tongue out with the effort, like a child in the infant class. This has always explainèd to me why so many men who do heavy labouring jobs and who have undoubted expressive ability verbally do not appear to like writing. It is indeed a tedious chore in such circumstances.

Over the weeks I came to know many of the locals, none better perhaps than Jack James. He was then in his sixties, a stocky, alert man with a strong blend of shrewdness, craftiness and generosity. Our friendship grew, particularly after he learned that his son John was partly responsible for my being on the boats. One of his other sons, Tom, was a lock-keeper at Braunston, another was at Hill-morton, one at Coventry, a daughter lived in Northampton and one at Roade — the next village to Stoke; the James family had the Grand Union country well covered. Jack came from a similar back-ground to Wilfred, with whom he was very friendly. The family had, he said, "come out of Wales" in the nineteenth century. His grandfather worked the Thames and Severn and other "West Country" canals, while his father had worked these in their declining years and ended up on the Oxford Canal.

Jack had captained his first boats before the Great War, when he had joined the Oxfordshire Yeomanry. He had taken part in one of the rare cavalry charges in Flanders, then had returned to the boats. His experience in the army had left him literate and on his return he had married and set up in business on his own in Reading. He had gone into partnership with his brother-in-law and another acquain-tance of mine, Bill Chivers. During this period he worked right through the Kennet and Avon, navigated the Loddon up to Twyford and performed other remarkable feats. However, a combination of railway competition and the Depression drove the business down. The final straw was a defalcating solicitor who cleaned out the part-nership's profits. Leslie Morton had come to the rescue soon after with the offer of a job with the Grand Union so Jack had swallowed his pride and taken it. For the next ten years or so Jack and his family had had a pair of Grand Union boats, in particular being entrusted with the working of the beer boats. These latter boats ran 'fly' (i.e. non stop) from Guinness's Brewery at Park Royal to Sampson Road near Birmingham. It was a morale boosting part of

174

the 1939-45 war effort to keep the war-workers of Brummagem supplied liberally with Guinness and the Grand Union rose appropriately to the occasion. The operation of the beer boats was entrusted to captains not only of the greatest skill but also of the greatest probity, for liquor was a tempting cargo for boaters. "Sucking the monkey" was always a temptation and accounted for the loss of much beer traffic to rail. This was done by privily obtaining a supply of bungs, a funnel and some tubing. The barrel bung was knocked in, the "monkey" was "sucked" to the boatman's satisfaction by means of the tube, the missing liquor was replaced by canal water via the funnel and a new bung knocked in. To be selected for the lucrative task of beer boating was thus an accolade awarded for honesty and even a suspicion of "monkey sucking" was enough to have the captains taken off the job.

The hard winter of 1946-47 had seen the end of the beer trade and Nationalisation followed close behind so Jack decided to come ashore. He bought a cottage on the canal side at Stoke Bruerne from Sister Mary Ward, taking up his present job of lock-keeper. Stoke Bruerne at the time was an unknown Northamptonshire village whose canalside was generally in a state of decay and neglect. Jack, remembering the smartness of Thames locks before the War, began tidying it up. He painted the double arched bridge white in his own time, put in flower tubs and roses round the top lock, mowed the grass all down the flight, painted lock beams and paddle posts, weeded, gravelled and trimmed until eventually the BTC recognised his work and he was awarded the trophy for the best-kept lock on the entire system. More and more visitors came, attracted by Jack's handiwork, and this, combined with the growth of private motoring in the 1950s, began Stoke Bruerne's popularity. In the little lock office adjoining the pub, where once the leggers had sat waiting for boats to work through Blisworth Tunnel, Jack kept a few mementoes of his horse-boating days, such as harness, painted cans and so forth. This became an attraction in itself and he was asked to lay on an exhibition in the schoolroom at Stoke. The interest that this generated prompted Jack to seek the use of the derelict mill building, used merely as a store, which was on the canal side.

The BTC refused permission and proceeded to plan their own museum in the very same building. The collection of boating items which Jack had assembled, along with a collection of historical and engineering relics assembled by Mr Charles Hadlow, the District Engineer at nearby Gayton, was obtained and formed the nucleus of the exhibition. Mr Hadlow was appointed curator while Jack, who

175

was due to retire as lock-keeper, was to be given the post of caretaker when the museum opened.

Many people regarded Jack as a quaint old character, to be patronised and talked to politely. He was swift to detect such an attitude and would adopt a suitable role, accepting largesse and drinks with a touch of his cap and a becoming air of servility. In such cases, or when asked his opinion on matters of Waterway politics, he would affect an air of senile mysticism. "I wouldn't like to say what I know," was Jack's inevitable reply to prying questions. He had learned the hard way what the public expects of its characters and played the role of a mystic old fool with enthusiasm. Some of the yarns spun to gullible strangers were so outrageous that hearers who were 'in the know' had great difficulty in keeping their faces straight. For instance, I wondered for a long time why I seemed to be treated with respectful deference by some of the Company's men with whom I came in contact. Long after I discovered that he had told them I was an all-in wrestler. On another occasion I heard a rather overpowering middle aged lady ask him the reason for the iron bars which had lately been installed in front of the windows of the Museum as a security measure. He barefacedly explained that boat people were generally law-abiding, but in the old days if one of them broke the law of the canals the others would imprison him in the Mill. Once when he was mixing some puddled clay in order to caulk a hole in a boat some inquisitive stranger asked what he was using. "Marine glue" came the reply and the stranger then informed sundry other bystanders that this was the stuff the real old timers used, the secret of which had been forgotten. I am glad to say that, on hearing this, the old rascal himself had to go indoors before he burst out laughing.

To people who showed a genuine interest and who did not affect to patronise him, Jack was completely different. He had, like many boaters, a phenomenal memory and in many cases where I was able to check, surreptitiously, his statement from other sources, I found him unerringly accurate. In addition his mind was both alert and clear and he possessed a vivid eye for significant detail allied to a natural gift as a raconteur.

He had, not long before, lost his wife and was glad of company. Night after night, I would hear his canalside front door bang and in the light from the old boat headlight mounted outside the pub would see his cloth-capped figure nimbly swinging itself across the lock gates. Presently I would find him in the bar, a pint grasped in his gnarled old hand, sitting with his back to the wall puffing at one of his execrable hand-rolled cigarettes.

As an old soldier who had served in France, Jack laboured under the impression that he was a fluent linguist and would frequently lard his discourse with such soldier's French as "San fairy Ann" and "Napoo", which lent an air of exotic quaintness to some of his tales. Should a foreigner of any nationality be introduced he would burst into a voluble, but quite extraordinary, lingo such as might have been used round Arras or Armentieres in 1914-18. "Ah bongjour mamzelle", he would greet a foreign lady. "Tray bong poor voo raycontray. Avay voo un van plonk ness par? Parlay voo jig-a-jig?" In vain did I remonstrate with him. He was convinced this was the height of foreign urbanity.

Jack was a grand talker — I hope I was as good a listener. He was in very truth my Homer. From him I heard in rich detail what it was to horse boat the West Country; how flash locks were negotiated; of the Cassington murders whose perpetrator was hanged on the Castle Mound of Oxford Gaol and whose passing was witnessed by Jack's father (still alive in 1963); of the Fenny Compton murders where the victim, a policeman attacked by poachers, died in the signal box to which he had crawled; of the great boatmen's fight at Stoke when two steamer crews had battled for hours on the lockside; of Bread and Larders; of the "Tank Hedge Hotel" where the Oxford down-and-outs slept behind the L.M.S. engine shed; of boatmen hiring themselves to aspiring University boxing blues as human punch bags; of the fighting parson of Littlemore; of the boater's parson from St Thomas', Oxford; of towpath Rodneys and latchlifters; of Jumpabout Charlie and Trotting Johnny; of Eynsham Harry (who lived to be immortalised by Temple Thurston) and Black Sam. I heard of the great Heyford Aerodrome scandal of the First World War and of the Grand Union black market scandal of the Second. I learned why 'Greasy Ockers' were so called and what 'mud heelers' were; of strange and violent deaths on the cut and of wedding feasts. In short I encountered the living substance of social history. Jack gave me a precious gift, the value of which I could never begin to repay, that gift is simply the memory of him.

Two other canal characters came into the pub regularly. The first was the jolly, fat man whom I had first seen driving the steam dredger. He was a true Northamptonshire countryman called Frank Smith but better known as 'Craney'. Craney was said to have acquired his name in his youth when his powers of strength were called for by the gang in lieu of a crane on occasions. He had merry eyes, a droll expression and a way with a cigarette. There was always, apparently glued to his lips, a white cylinder which performed amazing evolutions as he talked. It would travel from one side of his mouth to the other and punctuate his conversation by wagging up and down. Craney's wit was pungent and apposite. He wasted few words yet he had a very kind heart. I heard him say many funny things but never a bad word about anyone.

The other local character who frequented the "Boat" was a tall, old man, slightly stooped with bushy eyebrows and snowy hair, a rather beaky nose and bright, twinkling eyes. He was always known as 'Suff', and had been born and bred at Stoke, and was now retired. Suff's father and grandfather were Company's men; his grandfather had been a registered legger in the tunnel, his father a tug man who had died when Suff was quite young. His mother had been granted outdoor relief at Towcester Workhouse whither she had had to walk each week, some ten miles return, to draw a pittance of three shillings and sixpence on which to keep her family. Yet, Suff said, they lived comfortably. They had kept chickens and a pig, had grown vegetables, lived in a Company house and always found odd jobs to do. Suff had done many jobs in addition to being mate on the steam tug which hauled horse boats through Blisworth Tunnel until 1936. Among these (and he was most proud of it) he had been the village privy-digger and cleaner until the unhappy day that main drainage came to Stoke. Suff was the historian's delight for he had a vivid memory for dates and would always preface a reminiscence with the date. "1913, August Bank Holiday", he would start. "Ole lady Wood'ard sent me to Shutlanger fer two casks o' beer . . ." Or: "1929, Old Nat Sarrin'ton's cesspit needed cleanin' . . ."

Another regular in the pub was the thin, balding man who had seemed to be the village radical when I had met him before Christmas. He was known as 'Cruppet' and had been a boon companion of Wilfred, who called him 'the Baron'. Cruppet was a man of some learning and possessed a great store of Biblical knowledge. He seemed to enjoy bad health. Having a weak chest he was currently 'on the box' from the nearby factory at Roade. Cruppet always had an answer for everything and was something of a rogue. He was, nonetheless, a kindly soul and befriended both Bill and myself.

Cruppet was at heart a countryman and he confided to me once that factory work did not suit him. He loved the open air and fields. He knew the names of all the plants in the hedgerows, where mushrooms were to be found in season and when to set beans ("Old May Day, boy, for runner beans. That's the twelfth of May now, you know" — thus unconsciously perpetuating the pre-1752 Gregorian Calendar). He knew why swifts flew low before rain in summer; where fish lurked in the canal and in the river below Bottom Lock; and all the field names of Stoke Parish — Long Stocking, Happy Lands, Breach Furlong. One of his ancestors had been transported with other men of Stoke and Shutlanger for throwing down the ditches and fences when Stoke Plain Common had been enclosed and of this feat Cruppet was very proud. He had the makings himself of a village Hampden, but sadly, there was no work for such as he in the modern village economy. His health ruined by indoor work, he earned good money at the factory and ate his heart out. He once said, "Putting me in there is like picking a flower cut of the hedge and putting it in a bottle. We'll both wither away. You'll see."

He had a close friend and arch enemy called George, with whom he had been arguing when first I met him. George was a Tory, Cruppet a Radical, and many a 'ding-dong' battle they had. George was a small, bespectacled man who possessed a surprisingly loud voice. Frequently the arguments would reach such a pitch that they would address one another only by their surnames. George too was a sick man. He was a skilled hedger and could make anything grow, but now the factory had claimed him.

Presiding over all these — and many other characters — was the landlady, whose name, "Emily Woodward, licensed to sell tobacco", was emblazoned above the door on the canal side. She was known as 'Em' — but always addressed as Mrs Woodward. She had been widowed many years and had thus inherited and run the pub with her only son, Jack. She was a shrewd old lady with a keen business eye. Yet she was very kind to me and, in fact, treated all boat people with great consideration, never with the discourtesy that some publicans were wont to use. She was beginning to suffer from Anno Domini and her hands tended to shake when serving with the result that she would spill the drink and get very cross with herself. The regulars accepted this as a hazard of drinking in the "Boat". Aside from this I only remember her getting nonplussed once. At about closing time one night Teddy Cook, Jack James and myself were discussing property values. I ventured to suggest to Jack that his house had increased immeasurably in value since he had bought it. He said he did not know too much about it. Then Teddy suddenly laughed and said: "What about Mrs Woodward here, I'll bet she's worth a six figure sum now."

There was a silence, old Em looked rather grim for a moment then cackled, "Just for that cheek Mr Cook I'll buy you a whisky". She paused, then continued "And you two can have one to keep quiet!"

The second Friday that I was sojourning at Stoke, Teddy said to me: "Want a day out tomorrow?" He enlarged on the subject, informing me that he ran a shoot and wanted beaters. "Be on the bridge at nine-thirty," he continued and concluded with, "Oh! bring warm clothes and some sandwiches. We don't pay much but you won't go home empty handed."

Saturday morning saw me stamping my feet in the snow by the bridge. Teddy pulled up with a large, green shooting brake, in the back of which sat a black labrador with slavering jaws. After calling at the little shop down from the bridge for cigarettes, he headed up the hill out of Stoke, through two small villages and over the M1. Here we entered wooded country called Salcey Forest through which the road ran straight as an arrow. We pulled off the road into a lay-by near some keepers' cottages to find several more shooting brakes, a couple of Land Rovers and a number of men in breeches, waterproof jackets, green Wellingtons and a variety of country head gear. Gun cases were propped against mudguards, spaniels and labradors rushed about sniffing, country gossip was being exchanged. "Going over to barley beef next . . .", "Should be next Master of the Grafton . . .", ". . . promised him a pair of Purdeys for his twenty first . . ."

Teddy, chairman of the Shoot, moved among them introducing me as his new beater. At length all the guns arrived and we moved off under the direction of a gnarled old gamekeeper in a suit of orange tweed. All beaters were issued with sticks and the first drive of the day began. The guns departed to their prepared and marked positions and the beaters formed a long line at the other end of a woodland ride. The keeper blew a whistle and, taking post in the centre of the line, we advanced, sticks tapping on trees.

"Keep up on the left!" roared the keeper. "Kyup! Kyup! Hey Loss! Hey Loss!", this last to his brown and white spaniel which ran back and forth along the line. "Keep them sticks a-tappin'. Hey Loss! Loss!"

It seemed I was advancing into tangled thickets of briar and matted thorn in the company of a lunatic, but obediently I kept my stick tapping on any trees. There suddenly came a great whirring to one side and a brightly-plumed bird rose skyward. "Cock up!" came a shout. (Privately I agreed with this assessment.) Then from ahead came the crack of guns and shouts of encouragement to dogs.

"Keep up on the right!" bawled the keeper. "You sir! Boogger it, keep up!" This was directed at me, for I was standing gaping at the sound of gunfire. More whirring of wings, another sound of firing and cries of "Mine!", "Blast!" and "Missed!" rang in the air. The noise of guns grew nearer and then we were at the end of the drive, stepping out of the wood to see a row of men sitting on shooting sticks, guns broken open, dogs being fussed and a few bundles of feathered things near their feet.

Another drive followed, then another and another. It grew steadily colder and grey clouds drifted up from the east. Lunch time came. Teddy thoughtfully produced a flask of cherry brandy as we sat eating sandwiches. There was a quiet, elderly man eating his sandwiches next to me. When he spoke it was with a slight foreign accent. He accepted a nip of cherry brandy with urbane courtesy and we exchanged polite conversation. Later Teddy told me that he was now a businessman in Northampton but had been an officer in the Imperial German Army in the 1914-18 War during which he had won the Iron Cross. He left Germany in 1933 and, because he was Jewish, lost nearly everything he had to the Nazis. Taking British nationality, he had volunteered for service in the British Army, had been commissioned and seen action in which he had been decorated for bravery.

The sky looked ever darker and some of the farming members of the Shoot began to look worried. One of them, a lanky man of about my age, drove home and returned about half an hour later with a tractor and trailer instead of a car. "I think we may need this," he rightly forecast.

The afternoon's shooting was poor. The creatures seemed curiously reluctant to come out and be killed and after each drive people began to drift off. By four o'clock snow began to fall and dusk was near. Teddy called a halt and the day's bag, which included a couple of woodcock, a hare and a Muntjak deer, as well as a few brace of pheasants, was divided up. It seemed a somewhat masochistic form of pleasure and a very expensive way of obtaining meat. However, everyone seemed to have enjoyed themselves.

It was quite dark by the time Teddy had concluded the official part of the day's business. The farmer with the tractor and two others in a Land Rover agreed to meet us for a quick drink at a nearby inn. Everyone else made for home as quickly as possible when flurries of snow began to fly on a rising wind.

The pub, called "The Globe", was in darkness as we drove into the yard but a bang on the back door brought the landlord to open up. Into the stone-flagged bar we trooped, dogs milling round legs, a fire roaring in the hearth and Teddy beaming proprietorially from before the bar. I had left Stoke before my laying money had arrived and so privately whispered to Teddy that funds were strictly limited. "My dear chap! No beater ever pays for drinks while I'm chairman." That was that and a costly gesture it proved to be, thanks to the vagaries of nature.

There was great pleasure in sitting in this snug bar over a foaming tankard after a day's 'beating'! It closely resembled one of the joys of boating, when a group would sit similarly in a bar boasting and chaffing, but the weather gave cause for unease and, after an hour, we rose to go. I went first and tried to open the back door into the car park. It was stuck. Shoving hard I pushed it open to reveal a white wall of snow banked up. Struggling through this we reached the car, by now nearly buried in drifting snow. Henry, the farmer with the tractor, managed to start it and pulled the Land Rover out. Then the pair of them pulled out Teddy's car. The two in the Land Rover said they would try the road to Hartwell, a bleak open road at best. Teddy decided we would go back through the forest for it would be more sheltered. The tractor went a third way towards the village of Hanslope.

A short way from the pub the road crossed the M1 on a concrete bridge. By the time we got there the bridge was full of snow up to the parapets and we stuck fast. Teddy, used to country motoring in winter, had a shovel in the back so, with muscles tempered by shifting coal, I tried to clear a way. It was useless. The wind was blowing so hard that my puny efforts filled as fast as I shovelled. Below, the motorway was completely deserted and drifts were creeping across. It was at the highest point of the M1 in this part of Northamptonshire and a grim place to be snowbound. After some minutes I was exhausted and leaned on the bonnet for support. Through the gale I faintly heard an engine and saw the gleam of headlights coming up behind. It was the Land Rover. The direct road to Hartwell was, as Teddy forecast, blocked. We agreed that the only thing to do was to retrace our steps and try to reach the main A508 via Hanslope and Castlethorpe. Back into the hamlet we went, turning left towards Hanslope and there we beheld the red rear lights of the tractor. A monstrous drift was forming across the road and men from the nearby houses were trying to clear it by lamplight. Beyond the drift the Hanslope policeman was trying to get through with a snow plough attached to a tractor. The tractors charged the drift continually but each time they backed off for another run it filled up. At length both tractors met, Henry backed off for the plough to come through and as he did so a vicious blast sent a white curtain of snow over everything. When it cleared the effort of the last half hour had been obliterated. Through the howling wind came the voice of the policeman, "Pack it in, Henry. We'll have to wait till this wind drops."

Back to "The Globe" we went. Not a soul was in the place but the old couple did not seem surprised to see us. Henry managed to telephone his wife but nobody else could get through for all the lines were down. Of course, there were worse places to be stuck than in a pub.

At about nine o'clock we tried again but the wind was blowing as hard as ever and snow was still falling. We hardly got to the end of the street with the tractor this time, so once again back to "The Globe" we went. By now I was very conscious that I had had a hard day in the forest and had been facing a vicious blizzard all evening with nothing more sustaining than a couple of sandwiches, a cherry brandy and three pints of bitter. On staggering back to the pub I stopped short at the sight of a magnificent spread of pork pies, cold black pudding, pickles, cheese, biscuits and hot soup which the old lady had prepared for us — guessing that we would not get through the snow. After this feast Teddy declared a party. He had thoughtfully made me bring 'the music' so the fun began.

Logs and coal were piled on the fire. The dogs were quietened and lay on the stone flags basking in the warmth from the flames. Chairs were pulled up, glasses filled, legs stretched and an impromptu ceilidh began. My fellow prisoners were a jovial bunch. All but Teddy were farmers; one, called Mac, being a farm manager and the other two farming on their own.

The pub doors were locked at eleven but the party went on. Each took his turn at singing or telling a yarn. I heard: the ballad of "Sonia Snell, to whom an accident befell", several quaint, Rabelasian songs, unexpurgated Rabbie Burns, and two fine hunting songs — one a lament for John Peel, the other a lilting tune from the Cotswolds.

About three o'clock we staggered upstairs to the room where the landlord's wife had prepared beds for us. There were two double beds with feather mattresses and the landlord had thoughtfully provided a plastic dustbin against needs arising during the night — there being no upstairs sanitation. We undressed to our underwear for the night. My modest briefs were in sharp contrast to the long johns of my companions; one of whom was tall and knock-kneed and the other was short and bow-legged. Teddy began laughing hysterically and, in the face of dire threats from the rest of us, buried his face in his pillow from which occasional hiccoughs came.

It was not the most comfortable night I have spent, being wedged between two farmers, but sleep came at last and I woke to brilliant light and blue sky glaring in at the window. Overnight the blizzard had blown itself out leaving a perfect, clear, winter's morning.

The landlord's wife had prepared a magnificent breakfast after which we sallied forth with new heart. Teddy and myself had to make a long detour through Castlethorpe and crossed the canal at Thrupp Bridge, Cosgrove to the A508. In several places this main road had only been cleared for single line traffic and many side roads were blocked. It was after two o'clock when Teddy dropped me once more at Stoke. I was dog-tired and did not find the excavation of the butty's hatches a joyful experience. Snow was caked on the now-cold chimney, packed round the water cans, and worst of all, the gale had lifted Willow Wren's flimsy duck canvas in places and driven snow in on top of the cocoa bags. I lit the fire, spent the rest of the afternoon clearing out snow and fell fast asleep soon after tea.

Bill returned the next day and we changed guard. I returned to my parents' home for a few days to face a fair amount of business correspondence and matters that had to be arranged for next summer.

Calling in at Brentford one day, I received three disturbing pieces of news from Morton. The first was that I had been given the sack! I goggled back at him. He smiled and said that it was not him, but British Waterways who were demanding my head on a platter because I had, allegedly, abandoned my load and allowed it to be spoiled. I gave him my version of what happened. He laughed loud and long and said he might have guessed I would have a reply like that. Anyway, he had appointed Bill as captain in my absence and, over the telephone, Bill had in my absence set me on as his mate. "That," said Morton, "will give 'Waterways' something to chew on." I found it incredible that on a Sunday morning at Stoke, in the dead of winter, there should be someone whose business it was to check on whether boatmen were aboard their craft or not. Bitter subsequent experience with officialdom has taught me that such an episode is not unique. Somebody has to be made a scapegoat for official shortcomings. Morton was well aware of the position but as, in this case, Willow Wren were mere contractors there was little he could do but comply with their demand that I should be sacked. Such petty vindictiveness did not really hurt me in any way, we all laughed up our sleeves at the way Morton had outwitted our enemies. What really angered me was that I could just as easily have been a family man and, with a lesser man than Morton as my boss, could have been thrown out of my job and home on the unsupported word of an official.

The second grim piece of news was that 'B-J' was being forced to pull out by a combination of circumstances aggravated by the frost, now in its fifth week. This meant the end of Willow Wren after nine years. Unless something dramatic occurred, the Company would be wound up. Morton had grave doubts that the canals would survive the withdrawal of narrow boat traffic. I pointed out that at least 'Waterways' would have about thirty pairs left in the South East, plus a fair number in the North West. Morton looked at me pityingly: "David, lad, where the Hell have you been recently?"

Then came the third blow. The British Waterways Board which had been in command for only a few weeks had already decreed that their commercial fleet was to be wound up in the near future, probably in March also. I nearly wept with despair and frustration. Was it for this that we had toiled and fought? Was all the effort made by brave and dedicated men and women to be lost? What was to happen to all the families I had come to know and love? Were they to be quietly shoved out of the way? I somehow felt that the smug officials who had dragged the industry down and who now supported this bald decision would not be out of a job. They would not tramp round Coventry or Southall to take a job in a factory eating their hearts out at mindless soul-destroying tasks. They would not have to adjust to life on bleak council estates, or muddy caravan sites, to be sneered at by neighbours as "illiterate gipsies". It would not matter to them if no boat ever again navigated the canal system; their salaries and pensions were safe. It was in a sombre mood that I returned to Stoke Bruerne.

February came and the frost deepened. There were no more blizzards but instead an anticyclone developed. Clear, sunny days were followed by crisp, starlit nights. The ancients declared: "It'll freeze this moon out." Gradually the ice crept over the basin. Two swans were imprisoned in the ever-decreasing circle of water. They swam round and round in desperation until Jack James, Colonel Ritchie, Bill, myself and Jack Woodward from the "Boat" managed to corral them with a rope. Jack Woodward opened up the old boat horse stables adjoining the pub, installed a tin bath full of water so that the birds could eat and thither we installed them, albeit with a great struggle. In spite of Teddy's ministrations one swan died after a few days. It was carried off by him to be cremated in the retorts of

185

Northampton Gas Works. The other swan survived until the Spring.

The old adage of a Green Christmas meaning a full churchyard proved true as the frost began to take its toll of the elderly. Old men felt the cold sear their lungs and gave up; old ladies grew weary of trying to warm mittened fingers.

News came from beleaguered outposts. Ray White was caught in Brentford, where I had seen him twice since the frost began. Mark, George and the Whitlocks were at Boxmoor. Arthur was at the bottom of 'Maffers'. Our nearest neighbours were a 'Waterways' pair at Fenny. There were several 'Waterways' pairs at Braunston along with Charlie and Jack Monk and a great collection at 'Suttons Stop', Hawkesbury. The worst case was Alec Purcell who, returning from Banbury before Christmas, had been frozen in at Marston Doles since Christmas Eve. He was in the middle of nowhere and two miles from the nearest pub! Colonel Ritchie spent much time motoring round to frozen-up boats seeing that they had fuel and Calor Gas and making sure that laying money got through to them.

Stories filtered through. Boatmen at 'Suttons', wearying of idleness had settled an argument over the speed of shovelling by emptying a boat onto the bank and reloading it several times until the champion shoveller emerged. A boatwoman in desperate straits with trying to feed her family on 22s 6d per day had proffered a gold sovereign in a Longford supermarket. The police, investigating a broken-open steam dredger, had followed sledgemarks on the frozen cut for three miles back to some boats whose occupants were warming themselves with 'Waterways' steam coal. Craney said that they had put a drill down at Black Horse Bridge on the Fenny Pound and found solid ice for over three feet. Cruppet claimed that one night was so cold that the brass balls outside Jack James'son-in-law's pawn shop in Northampton had fallen down. Jack said he would not know anything about it!

Musical evenings at the "Boat" had become commonplace at weekends and it was during one of these that I made another acquaintance—a dark-haired, worried-looking man who came from Northampton and was called Brian Collings. He was courting a girl from Coventry and had done some summer boating with Joe Skinner. He was an artist of some ability and had painted some fine scenes of the canals and its working craft. He became a good friend.

Imperceptibly the days were lengthening. No longer did I have to get all the outside work done by four pm, no longer was there pitch blackness over the waterside until the outside light of the pub went on at six. By now it was twilight when the pub opened, snow had long since slid off cottage roofs and had shrunk to a crystalline carpet over the fields. From cottage gardens came the reports of shotguns being discharged at pigeons raiding brussels sprouts in the longer daylight. Yet right into February the frost kept its grip. Teddy brought news one evening of a farmer at Roade who had watched skein after skein of Brent geese land on his fields for roosting, a sure sign of Siberian conditions.

From time to time we had been visited by Dennis. The cylinder block had been thawed and removed and after mid-February bits of engine began to reappear. First the ruptured gearbox casing was re-installed, newly welded, then on a red letter day came the Braunston van with Black Charlie, the cylinder block and Jack Monk and Charlie as assistants.

Black Charlie had finished fitting by lunch time and we attempted to start "Tern". By now the frost had eased sufficiently to release the stern, so there was no danger in turning the blades. We toiled away with the hand starting gear and "Easi-start" but weeks of idleness had thickened the oil and she was very stiff. Black Charlie had brought us a spare battery, so the other Charlie quietly connected it up with ours while Black Charlie got out of the boat and walked up and down, wringing his hands and chanting: "Oh deary me! Oh dear, dear!"

Charlie shoved us both aside, took our cabin shaft and said: "Watch this boogger fer startin'". With which he leant in the doors and pushed the shaft so its point was on the starter button. The engine started to revolve, the starter motor whined, the exhaust began to sound and then, in a monstrous cloud of black smoke she fired and picked up in earnest.

Black Charlie came running along the towpath, "Ooh Charlie! What have you done?"

"Started the boogger," he replied. A happy smile spread across his face. "Med that boogger give us best. 'Er'll goo now Dave." And events proved him right. There was no further trouble with the engine.

Jack Monk and Charlie had news for us. Namely that Morton was going to fight back, that 'Waterways' boats were going to be kept running somehow and that we were all going to be 'Number Ones', subcontracting boats from Willow Wren. This was the first cheerful rumour we had heard for weeks so, that evening, I broached the matter to Colonel Ritchie. He informed me that he and a few other well-wishers were forming a company to take over the assets of

Willow Wren from 'B - J' and that if they were successful in doing so they would run the boats on a sub-contract basis. In other words a skipper would be supplied with a fully-equipped and running pair for which he would pay a nominal rent. The Company would find him work and supply him with the repair facilities, fuel etc—much as they had done with "Enterprise". In the event of another frost skippers would "sign on" at a labour exchange so that laying money, the sore of the company's finances, would not be paid in the future. I agreed that this was a good point, since we were both Insured Persons we would have been far better off if the Company had discharged us during the frost. We could then have drawn Unemployment Benefit and saved the firm over £7 per week. Lastly, the Colonel had reported that Morton was negotiating with a view to taking over all the 'Waterways' boats and the newly-formed Board was considering replacing tolls with an annual commercial licence, such as had long been advocated by many well-wishers. So there was a package of proposals to be mulled over. We argued and discussed it for hours — it could be the beginning of a great revival; it could be a flash in the pan; it was the best thing that had happened for years; it was merely putting off the evil day; boatmen could really make money; boatmen could end up worse off than ever. The main thing was that there were at long last positive proposals afoot. Much would depend on a report that the Board were preparing on the assets or otherwise of what they had inherited from BTC.

As if to underline this new feeling, the grip of winter began to ease with the lengthening days. The iron-bound ground gradually appeared as the sun melted the snow during the day, although the nights were still frosty and starlit. The deep frost of early February, when one night the temperature dropped to -3°F, gradually began to lose its grip. There came a day when, returning from wooding, I found "Dunlin" give underneath me and the ice creaked and protested as she wallowed free. Then came the time when "Tern's" newly restored engine was put in gear and splintered the ice right across the basin. The butty was at last re-united with the motor and we laid once more in our old mooring outside Jack James'. It was evident that soon we should be moving again, but down the locks and up as far as the tunnel the ice still held fast on St David's Day.

Then, on Monday 4th March we were with the maintenance gang 'wooding' up by the tunnel end. It was a sunny morning and the temperature in the sheltered cutting was mild. Craney stood up straight and said "Listen!" From far away came a droning sound which stopped after a few seconds. "Wolverton buzzer," said he: "That's the first time I've heard it since Christmas, you'll be away by Friday."

News came on Thursday that the ice breaker had at long last been freed from its durance below Bottom Lock, so we walked down the locks to see what was happening. It was a sunny day, sheep and lambs called in the fields as we walked the Long Pound, still iced right across, towards the five lower locks of the flight. Suddenly, above the hedges I saw jets of blue smoke rising skywards, a singing noise came from the ice, splintering crashes came from ahead, then round the turn from the next lock shot the icebreaker. It was a small, wooden tug with a short fore-deck along which ran a horizontal rail at about waist height. The gang, including a red-faced Craney, were disposed along this deck rocking the boat violently so that she rolled from gunwale to gunwale. The steerer would go astern and let the boat ride back a few yards then he would clutch in, rev hard and drive full tilt at the hard ice with the gang now rocking the boat almost through 180 degrees. The rounded fore-end would rear up on to the unbroken ice which would sing and creak and break apart. This continued until the accumulated pack ice brought her to a stand, then the process would be repeated. We managed to jump across the ice to the deck of the icebreaker while it was temporarily stuck and so added our weight to that of the gang. It was an exhilarating, if perilous, experience to find one's nose apparently directly above the broken floes one second and then to have to avoid having one's bottom dunked the next. It was definitely not a job for sufferers from sea sickness.

We rocked and rolled up the pound into the lock, roaring in and packing a great mass of broken ice up against the sill. Jack James filled the lock and then we attacked the short pound below the Top Lock. This was soon broken, then it was the turn of the section through the Tunnel. The ice breaker had a clear run across the basin up to Teddy Cook's mooring where the ice started again. The hundred yards or so were covered at the gallop. Up reared the fore-end, we all rocked and it smacked into the squealing ice. Great cracks spread across it, the ice breaker paused momentarily, then we were away again.

At length we reached clear water near the tunnel mouth, where a little stream purled out from a culvert on the towpath side. Everyone then crammed into the cabin for the tunnel. There was no light beyond a row of glowing cigarette ends which faintly illuminated their smoker's faces, making it appear that we were in a company of friendly gargoyles. From time to time thunderous crashes would come as the boat dislodged tree trunk sized icicles below some of the tunnel shafts.

At the end of the tunnel we all piled out to start rocking again. However, the ice at the Blisworth end was less troublesome. We tied the boat up at the old Mill and the gang assembled on the road outside waiting for the foreman to arrive with his blue van to return everyone to their home stations. The foreman assured us that they would have broken the whole section from Buckby to Fenny by Saturday night, but even though the locks were now clear, he did not advise us to go beyond until Saturday when the icebreaker from Fenny would be at Cosgrove to come to our aid if necessary.

We decided that next morning we would go down the locks and lie there. Brian Collings had agreed to come as mate for a couple of weeks, being in between jobs. The contract of service was that we should pay his national insurance stamp and feed him, for which we would work him like a horse some twelve or fifteen hours per day. He could not join us until Saturday afternoon so this all fell into place most conveniently.

Working a loaded pair in ice, even when it is broken, is a tedious job, especially in locks. The ice packs behind gates and has to be raked out, for which the Canal Company provided long white-painted poles with grapnels on the end, called 'ice-hooks'. These were kept in racks beside most locks and had plenty of employment as we painfully plodded down, taking nearly twice the time we normally took. At length we reached the bottom and tied up on the rings recently vacated by the ice breaker.

That night we were having a farewell drink at the "Boat" when Teddy Cook remarked with prescience that a chapter in my life was closing. At that time it seemed apposite enough, with hindsight I can see that it was a watershed. Nothing in my life, or on the cut, was ever to be the same again.

5

Farewell
to the Boats

It was a bright March day. The countryside looked new, bare and clean in the sparkling sunlight. Winter had retreated to an extent which, a week before, would have seemed incredible. The engine sang its deep song and we were in high spirits as we nosed away down that lovely, lonely, unspoiled pound towards Cosgrove.

The "Navigation" at Thrupp Bridge came and went and a cluster of roofs on the valley side heralded our destination. We slipped under the ornamental bridge, past the clustered stone and brick buildings, into the lock. Across the embankment the ice stretched, unbroken as yet, but there was just enough room in the small basin below for us to tie up.

Sitting having tea in the cabin in the fading light, we heard the splintering of breaking ice. Through the dusk I saw the dark shape of the Fenny icebreaker driving steadily through the remaining ice. Cheerful shouts rang out from the crew, who told us that the road was open at least as far as Fenny and that the 'Waterways' pair had started that morning for Leighton.

As soon as the sun was well up on Sunday morning, we left. Although the water was still fearfully cold, the ice was only to be seen in a few exposed places; generally on turns and always broken. A bright morning was a much better time to boat the Fenny Pound than a rainy night and being three-handed transformed the trip into a pleasure cruise. Even the fishermen, with only a week or so before the end of their long-interrupted season, seemed cheerful for once and exchanged chaff with us.

At Fenny Lock we saw evidence of its late occupancy. The fresh water tap casing was charred, a relic of the hardest frost when the only way to get water was to swathe the tap in diesel-soaked rags and set fire to it. Then, just below Talbots, came a heartening sight. Racing round the turns of the river-like Water Eaton Pound came the black hull and white fore-end of a Blue Line motor boat. It was the Whitlocks, released at last from bondage at Boxmoor. News and

191

greetings flew back and forth. Laura on the motor paid us the unwonted compliment of slowing down so that more news could be exchanged. We learned that Mark was close to and sure enough, in the open fields below Stoke Hammond Three we met Mark, beaming happily, white cigarette spiked inevitably in his lips, the children waving to indicate their joy at moving again. Everyone was in high good humour: "for the winter was past and the voice of the turtle was heard in the land." I had never before felt so acutely the ancient significance and symbolism of the death and resurrection of the world. I am certain this is only tangible to those who live close to nature — to those insulated by material comforts such things must be meaningless. At that time I would not have changed my place at the tiller nor the company of the canal community for any riches the world could offer.

At Leighton Bridge Arthur lay with "Roger" and "Raymond". They had been caught at 'Maffers' with some 'Waterways' boats and were to load sand for Paddington on the morrow. As we passed Arthur called: "Best make haste, or we'll be by you." Some hope of that, I thought, we'll show you how to run, and with that in mind we set about Slapton Fields in style, It was pleasant to have the longer daylight now, darkness did not come down fully until about six thirty and it was just after six o'clock when we tied below 'Maffers', having decided not to go up until the morrow.

We talked with a 'Waterways' captain in the bar of the "White Lion". He was not enamoured of the prospect of going back to "number oneing" or sub-contracting. The Barlows (or properly Blue Line) pairs had all said that "Mester Streaks" was not changing his system and, with the prospect of Willow Wren at least continuing, was going to stay trading for the foreseeable future. Sam, the 'Waterways' captain, was of the opinion that some of the best captains—British Waterways and Willow Wren— would not stay on with the proposed new scheme. His opinion proved only too true over the next few months. On a lighter note, the landlady complained that she had not been able to sleep that afternoon for the first time for twelve weeks as she had missed the soothing sound of Arthur and Ernie sawing and chopping logs.

Next morning we woke the echoes up the locks and across the summit to Cowroast, where Geordie booked us through with many a caustic word about our lateness. Then it was an invigorating run downhill, three-handed on a good road, through 'Berko', past Winkwell and Boxmoor and down the 'New 'uns' where the melancholy thought came that nobody would be going to Apsley any more. There was a great heap of coal by the crane, all brought by tipper lorry. Ray White met us with the first loaded pair to come North after the frost and shouted the news that we had a good road all the way to Brentford. In the gathering dusk, therefore, we decided to stop at 'Ricky' for the night and make a really early start next morning to arrive at Brentford for midday. Knowing that we had a good road, but that there might be some night-owlers working up, we went below the lock then backed under the towpath bridge into the side lock, which was rarely used, to give us a convenient mooring that was also out of the way. The only possible pursuit was Arthur's pair which we had passed at Leighton Bridge yesterday and which would have been loading at Leighton that morning. In spite of his threat to get by us if we did not make haste, we were sure of ourselves now and went to bed after a few pints in confident anticipation of a quick run down to Brentford in the morning.

Alas, we had reckoned without Arthur. It was five past four on a chilly March morning. I was just loosing the fore-ends preparatory to starting when there came the rattle of a paddle from the main lock. In the wan light of the street lamps of Ricky Bridge I saw Arthur's fore-end just nosing out in front of us, his Lister ticking away contentedly and he and Ernie grinning like Cheshire cats. Arthur called: "Are you a-goin' to lay there all day?"

To rub salt in our wounded egos, Arthur had now got the road and put the locks against us. It served us right, I suppose, but he was not such a 'bad old stick' really for once he had got ahead, after Stockers, Ernie left all the locks filling for us. This was the nearest I ever came to getting ahead of Arthur. Others better than I have tried but I only know of one man who succeeded.

That hero poled past Arthur at two o'clock one morning at Leighton Bridge, but as he was passing made a splash with his shaft. Immediately the motor's slide went back on Arthur's pair and Ernie's head popped out. The overtaker forthwith abandoned all attempts at stealth and wound up his engine. Before he had gone a hundred yards he saw sparks shoot out of Arthur's exhaust. Both pairs were northbound empty, both were fast swimmers and neither would let up. That evening they carried on and went right through to Hawkesbury, arriving there at about midnight.

Although Arthur lost the race he still had the last laugh. The other captain was so tired that he overslept and missed his turn for loading the next day. Arthur took it instead!

The distant chimney at Firestone's with its trailing scarf of smoke and the tall gasholder welcomed us back to Brentford. The smelly waters of the Brent below Hanwell seemed almost welcome and we managed to wind in Brentford Basin with some style and aplomb; sliding alongside Brent Meadow Wharf exactly eleven weeks and one day after we had been due to arrive. There, leaning in the doorholes of his pair waiting to discharge his cargo, was George, booming and rumbling, cap askew, spectacles well down his nose. The two small boys clustered on the motor's cabin whilst the daughters—in the butty hatches with Marion—chattered like monkeys. The 'Waterways' staff to whom we reported were surprised to see us, for they had only just been advised that Stoke was clear. The cargo was to be transhipped into a barge for the docks and they had not got one available for two days, having just sent one down empty on the previous tide. Once more the dreary lack of urgency in the industry was brought home.

The three of us clambered up the iron ladder of the Willow Wren office to see Stanley and have a Council of War with Morton. Time was beginning to press upon us and, not for the first time, we were becoming aware that for this season at least our sojourn on the boats would have to draw to a close. It was now the 12th March, Good Friday, and the usual start of "Enterprise's" tripping season was exactly a month away. In that time we had to get "Tern" and "Dunlin" back to Braunston, refurbish "Enterprise", return to Reading, make her ready for the season and perform other myriad tasks. Unless we could get a load for Aylesbury, Wellingborough or Birmingham we would have to give our notice in then and there and go back empty. There was just not enough time to go back empty and do another coal trip, much as we would have liked to.

After officially reinstating me—which, as Brian remarked, "Means that you tell Bill when to get up in the morning rather than the other way round!" —Morton did some telephoning but could not find us anything before Friday at the earliest. Then he had an idea. "Stan!" he called, "What about "Romford" and "Ruislip"?" Stan mumbled away in the outer office for a minute or two, then conceded that they might indeed do.

The names seemed vaguely familiar. I recalled them from a 'Waterways' tender list as old butties. Morton had bought them, it turned out, and they were lying at Cowley Tip. If we would take them to Braunston he would pay us £5 per boat on top of laying and empty-running money. We could then finish on Thursday 21st March, which would close his books off neatly. This would net us about £16 for a week's work, quite a princely sum in those days. As we had a third hand, we agreed to undertake this task. Meantime,

Morton was heading for Braunston the next day and would have "Enterprise" brought out of the reservoir and pumped for us.

For the next couple of days we laid in Brentford. This time we were there as part of the scene not as initiates but as boatmen, fully fledged. Now not only could we talk canal gossip knowingly in pubs but we knew the whereabouts of the fish and chip shop as well as the other inhabitants of the canal side. We were even visited by that saintly old character, the Reverend Chapman of the London and City Mission, anxious to save our souls. I asked him, rather to his surprise, what branch of the Faith he preached to boatpeople. For a second he thought, then said: "I just tell them Jesus loves them and leave it at that!" The Reverend Chapman completed the Trinity of Christian ministry to the cut for me. I was once more impressed by the goodness and sincerity of those few rare souls who so faithfully trod the towpaths in the footsteps of their Master.

In the "Six Bells" stories of the frost were exchanged. Jumbo joined us, nodding sapiently as each horrific tale was piled upon its predecessor. Our experience of frost and cold were speedily capped by an old 'Waterways' boatman, reputed to be the Baron Munchausen of the cut. According to him, nothing could compare with the first winter of the Second World War. He was boating for Fellows, Morton and Clayton at the time and they had oil head lamps in spite of black out regulations. One very cold night, the cut was freezing as fast as they could break it but eventually they reached a place where they could ride out the frost. He went to blow out the lamp and nothing happened. He could neither blow it out nor turn down the wick. It was so cold, he claimed, the flame had frozen to the wick. In the end, said he, they had to take the lamp into the cabin and thaw the flame on the cabin range. Jumbo said he should have broken off the flame and kept it in a tin to warm his hands with. The old chap looked quizzically at him: "You knows dam' well, flame won't go wi'out air."

On Thursday morning unloading at last commenced. The bags were lifted out in bundles by crane and swung into the down river barge. There was a slight contretemps when the gang demanded 'dirty money' for handling the cargo with which we had been living for nearly three months. They presumably based this claim on the exaggerated reports of spoiled cargo, which still clung round my neck like an albatross. However, we had taken care to show both Morton and Stanley serried rows of dry bags beneath our cloths. Privately I was worried about a slight weep through "Dunlin's" left side behind the mast although I had made this clear to Morton at the time of loading. With bad grace the gang set to. The motor was cleared first and not a bag was seen to be damaged, then came the butty's turn. On the very last sling of all, the bag which had been lying beside the weep incontinently burst over the heads of the most disgruntled members of the gang. I gazed innocently skyward, life had rarely been so perfect. I felt like the Ancient Mariner must have done when the albatross fell from him.

Early on Friday morning we left on our last trip. The lock-keepers greeted us like old friends as we clambered back up the locks to the Cowley Pound. Near the end of the Slough Arm we found our quarry and two ancient, worn out boats they were too! "Ruislip" was a large 'Ricky' butty, similar to "Dunlin" in build. She had been built in 1936 for the Grand Union and for some years past had been used as a mobile tip. Examination of the bottom indicated that apart from dredgings she had carried old hospital dressings, for a revolting muddle of blood and pus-stained bandages, old plaster casts, soggy lint and other medical waste washed backwards and forwards amid mud, clay and old iron in the empty hold. She had no rudder, no planks, stands, cratches or false floors. There was not even a rope beyond tatty lengths of rotten hemp snubber which tethered her fore and aft, whilst the cabin was stripped bare and rotten. Her colleague "Romford" was a much older iron butty, ex-Fellows, Morton and Clayton. Grass grew along the kelson, ominous holes gaped in her rusty plating while the equipment was even more rudimentary — even a cabin was lacking.

We wasted little time in unloosing these two sad specimens and headed for Cowley Lock. There were ninety locks from here to Braunston, each of which we would have to work twice. Going up through Uxbridge we found "Ruislip" to be thoroughly unstable because of the sloppy muck inside her so, finding a convenient mud-hopper above Uxbridge Lock, we shovelled this obnoxious cargo over into it. While we did so George and his family came up the lock empty. "'Ow far tonight, lads?" he called as the boats rose. We said we were not too sure, but we certainly hoped to clear 'Ricky'. "I shall be at Croxley," he assured us as he chattered off.

In fact two locks had already shown that we were not going to break any records this trip. The two extra boats were being dragged astern breasted up. At each lock the pair had to wait above the gates, the other ones being pulled and held hard against the bottom while the lock emptied. Then they would be dragged in slowly and the lock filled. Three-handed as we were, we needed every hand. Apart from this the drag of the boats slowed us down appreciably.

Painfully slowly we gradually worked up through Denham and Harefield, Black Jacks, Coppermill (where the still turbulent overfall gave us some nasty moments) and Springwell. We decided to press on after Rickmansworth and, as dusk began to fall, tied up near George at Croxley. Heavy rain was falling so the overhanging roof of the grass stores made a convenient and dry mooring for the night.

We tried to persuade George to have a farewell pint with us, but he had 'signed the pledge' the summer before and would not even enter a pub. "But I'll come up the Fish Shop an' 'ave a Vimto wi' you," he condescended. I do not think any of us had ever drunk to another's success in Vimto before, but at least we were able to give George some small appreciation of his little kindnesses and friendship over the months.

The next day saw a long, slow flog up to Boxmoor; shades of last December, but this time without mishap. Through the Parks we met Jack Monk careering southwards, his boats "ring hole deep" and the only sign of his butty apparently being a deckboard, cloths, a row of cans, a chimney and his wife tearing through the water. Jack wished us well and told us Charlie was half a day or so behind. Sure enough we met him at Boxmoor at dusk and spent a convivial Saturday night in the "Whip and Collar". Both Jack and Charlie were dubious about the future and Charlie revealed that he wanted the pair of Clayton gas boats so tragically deprived of crew before the frost.

Sunday brought a gale. Up the final eighteen locks to Cowroast we crept, tempers becoming frayed as the boats obstinately drove into the bank or cross-winded in bridgeholes. Although there was a steady stream of southbound boats, including the Whitlocks and Mark and Dolly, giving us a good road, we were getting distinctly tired of the sight of locks. Never before, except for that first trip with Wilfred, had the climb seemed so endless. It was a full eight hours' work before we dragged those two old boats clear of Cowroast Lock and even then the summit, which normally took about forty five minutes empty, took us an hour and a half — by which time none of us felt like tackling 'Maffers'.

In the "Grand Junction Arms" at Bulbourne we held a conference. At this rate it would take us at least until Thursday to reach Braunston. Bill had fallen in love with an old flat boat of Dickensons at Croxley and wanted to return and negotiate for it before the weekend, while Brian was running out of time as he had a new job to start. Meanwhile more gales were forecast. The only way we could get back in time would be by abandoning one of the boats for another three-handed pair to take on and making our way with one extra boat. Since "Romford" was the smallest and lightest we decided to take her and leave the other in the care of British Waterways at Bulbourne Yard.

Accordingly at nine next morning we were on the telephone to Braunston, busily negotiating with Stan. Morton came on the line, snorting displeasure, but calmed down when I explained that we had at least got over the worst. He mumbled on for a while about payment, but eventually agreed that at least we should have half the money for one boat and the full amount for the other. By the time we had finished arguing and made arrangements with the engineers' department to leave "Ruislip" temporarily, it was close to ten o'clock.

We flung ourselves at 'Maffers', without so much as a cup of tea and grimly bunted "Romford" down the twisting pounds behind the pair. Looking back it might have made more sense to have breasted "Romford" and bowhauled "Dunlin", which did at least have a rudder, but I think we had all become too angry to think very clearly.

As we struggled down the Fields and Leighton Buzzard spire drew imperceptibly nearer the wind dropped and a pleasant sunny afternoon developed. Once on the long Leighton Pound we were able to single all the boats out and make better time. There had been no time whatsoever for cooking or chores so we tied up in the late afternoon sunshine just after five o'clock, in the company of two pairs of 'Waterways' that had come from Buckby early that morning.

An old boatwoman used to haunt Leighton Bridge in those days. A number of boat families had settled on the bank in nearby Linslade and she would appear on the bridge at strategic moments giving news and advice. She greeted me as I bustled about in the hatches and assured me that she would tell us when the fish and chip shop opened. All of us could have eaten a dead horse between two mattresses at that stage, so we felt that this was an excellent idea. Some while later we were cleaning ourselves up when there came a bellow from on high: "They're open!" This was the signal for slides all down the cut to shoot back and for people to come scrambling ashore. I caused a major sensation in the shop by asking for three pieces of fish and seven and six penn'orth of chips. This was when a normal portion cost a shilling!

Breakfast next morning was not improved by "Dunlin's" gas

cylinder giving out. It was possible, given good coal, lots of patience and an hour or two, to boil a kettle on the 'bostin' stove, so by the bottom of Stoke Hammond Three I had managed to produce a cup of coffee. Meanwhile we racked our brains for a source of gas. Today this is not much of a problem. There seems to be a boatyard every few hundred yards or so along the cut, but then Wyvern Shipping were not open and the next boatyard was at Braunston. This was a good day's run for an empty pair and not possible with our cavalcade because we should not reach Buckby before locking-up time. Brian's local knowledge came in handy for he knew of an ironmongers in Stony Stratford which kept Calor Gas. If one of us was to get off at Bradwell he could get a 'bus into Stratford and walk out to Cosgrove. This would minimise any hold up.

All this was arranged at long distance because we had put "Romford" in between the two boats to go round the long pounds north of Leighton. The steerer of "Dunlin" who now had to guide two boats round turns was in rather the same case as the guard of a goods train, for the motor steerer was now one hundred and forty feet away. Brian scuttled back and forth as go-between, for I dare not let go of the tiller except on straight sections.

At length Bradwell Main Road Bridge hove in sight. Leaving Brian at the butty's tiller I leaped ashore in the bridge hole carrying the empty gas bottle.

I was in luck. There was a frequent service to Stony Stratford as Brian had forecast. Moreover, I managed to get the gas bottle aboard the bus before the conductor saw it, for the United Counties Omnibus Company disapproved of carrying such articles, and we lurched away to Stratford. I found that there was another 'bus back in less than half an hour and observed that we passed within a few hundred yards of Galleon Bridge at Old Wolverton. Now I calculated that the boats would take an hour to get from Bradwell to the Galleon, so with any luck I could be back at the cut before the boats had to stop. As it happened there was time to do some shopping for bread, bacon, fresh milk and vegetables so I was well-laden when the 'bus set me down at Old Wolverton. I reached the cut just as the boats came in sight, deposited my burden on the towpath and stretched my aching arms.

In the nine days since we had left Cosgrove on the journey south all trace of ice had vanished. Spring was pressing hard on the tail of winter and although the day was overcast with a chill east wind the sprinkling of snowdrops and crocii in cottage gardens gave colour, while by a sheltered stone wall a row of daffodils nodded their graceful heads. Bill wound open the throttle up the Stoke Pound as the afternoon sun came out, gilding the bare willows and illuminating the lacy tops of distant elms above which rooks were wheeling and cawing. As we rattled up towards Grafton I began to feel a mounting sense of homecoming. The squat chimney of the factory and the two watertowers at Roade looked down the valley towards us. I looked impatiently for Stoke's Norman tower to rise up on its hill as we curved round the green hillside. The long arched overflow weirs of the Tove appeared like old friends. Then came the white footbridge and the steady flog up the seven locks to Stoke basin.

A sign of the advancing year was that it was no longer dark when the locks were closed and we tied outside the Museum with a good hour of daylight to spare. We were welcomed back that evening like mariners who had crossed the wide oceans, but the jollity of the evening was, for me, tinged with sadness. We would be finishing that week. Already we had said our goodbyes to our comrades further south, many of whom we knew would never work the boats again. It was not the imminent departure for the Kennet which saddened me, for I was looking forward to another summer on that happy little river, but I had come to love the countryside and people of Northamptonshire, as well as the life and society of the canal. Although the Thames Valley was my home, I knew that the old-fashioned warmth of the sort of people I had come to know so well had gone forever from its villages and pubs. Commuters' country, however beautiful and however prosperous could never have the richness and satisfaction of this down-to-earth Midland shire. Last year I had felt that, much as I might miss it during the summer, the life, laughter, tears and character of the canal would still be there when I returned. Now I was not so sure. In spite of the optimism of Morton, echoed at Stoke by the redoubtable Colonel, too many good captains were talking of 'finishing' and British Waterways were definitely ending their carrying operations in a couple of weeks time. The hearty laughter and the riotous songs in the "Boat" had a somewhat hollow ring that night.

Wednesday was officially the last day of winter and also the last day that we would be on the books of Willow Wren. By way of compensation the weather was bright and clear, though still with that chilly easterly wind I have since come to associate with the East Midlands. The distant wolds rose clearly against the sky with Borough Hill, crowned by its wireless masts, looking across to the tall, forbidding bulk of the mental hospital at Duston. Our cavalcade wound past Banbury Lane, where a pair had unloaded concrete piles from Marsworth just before the frost, and had narrowly escaped being marooned in that desolate spot. Already some of the piles were being driven and Craney stuck his head out of the flat's cabin, inevitable cigarette in mouth, to shout farewells. Once again, the pleasure of boating in daylight all the time and with an extra hand was evident. It made bearable the inevitable end.

Leslie Morton had been as good as his word and "Enterprise" lay outside the slip waiting for us. A cursory inspection showed that with a little luck she would not take long to make ready. However, her cabin was damp and musty and had to be well-aired before it could be lived in again. Accordingly, that evening I lit the cabin fire for the first time for over five months and began the long process of drying her out.

Sitting in "Dunlin", Bill and myself came to some hard decisions. Ever since the end of the frost the questions had kept recurring and been persistently shelved, now they had to be faced. The unpalatable truth was that we were nearly broke. The poor summer previously had meant that our cash reserves were perilously low at the end of the season. The work we had obtained from Willow Wren had merely enabled us to meet liabilities and commitments until the frost came. Now financial problems, not least those presented by repairing the frost damage and starting a new season, were looming. From a personal point of view the winter's work for Willow Wren had not had the result we had originally hoped for. There had been just enough money on which to exist reasonably comfortably but there had been none to spare. My bank balance at home was severely depleted and I would have to earn something soon otherwise the Bank Manager would become irate. It was increasingly obvious that for the foreseeable future the firm could not support two full-time employees and that severe economy would have to be our watchword until the season began to bring more cash in. In the circumstances we both felt that we would have to return to some form of regularly paid employment, perhaps working the boat at weekends and at times outside working hours. Bill had the opportunity of returning to Newbury and starting a job almost immediately so it was agreed that I should return "Enterprise" to the Kennet on my own; perhaps I could find a part time mate in Reading.

That Wednesday night was a vintage one for the "Nelson". Once again the ditties were sung, once more the 'Gaffer's' eyes became steadily more froglike as the evening advanced, once more Hubert's

201

belly wobbled massively up and down behind the bar as prodigious quantities of snuff mounted on high. The laughter gusted round the cosy little bar, Dennis, Leslie Morton and George, a retired businessman, plotted and planned. We were both offered a pair later on in the year under the new deal and I provisionally accepted, though deep down I somehow felt that it would never be.

On Thursday Brian brought over an old blue van from his home in Northampton and, while I set about the melancholy task of clearing the boats, he and Bill went off to Croxley to see about Dickenson's flat boat. Bill returned happier than I had seen him for days, having clinched the deal. Eventually he had it transported to Newbury where it became the nucleus of a very successful business on the Kennet and Avon.

On Friday I removed "Enterprise's" batteries and put them on a 24 hour charge in the workshops. The mattress, having been turned and re-turned in front of the stove, was now thoroughly aired so I moved most things aboard her, including one or two bits and pieces of Bill's which he did not wish to carry home by train. Brian departed amid much hand-shaking and earnest entreaties to keep in touch. To this day a superb painting by him of a pair of empty Willow Wrens running bracket open through a wintry dusk adorns my living room wall, while some atmospheric murals by him now decorate the bar of the "Boat" at Stoke Bruerne, including a pair of loaded Willow Wrens.

On Saturday morning I collected the charged batteries, made up the fire in the now cosy cabin of "Enterprise" and set about starting the engine after its long rest. I removed the air cleaner and hung a flaming oil-soaked rag over the air intake, then kept my finger on the starter button. The starter motor whirred and whined then began to run faster and faster. I dropped in the compression tap and the engine all but stopped, smoke shot from the silencer gasket, she coughed, fired, coughed and then fired again, steadily taking up the firings and revolutions. The needle on the ammeter swung over from discharge to charge and the engine settled down to a contented chugging. The money spent with Petters so long before proved to have been well spent. Dennis and several other of the yard men grinned and gave me the thumbs-up sign.

Bill was ready to leave. We pulled the slides shut on "Tern" and "Dunlin", mere hulks now, with no chimneys, cans, mopsticks or shafts to indicate human presence, and took the keys to the office. We stood silently for a minute, then Bill walked out of the yard. I was sorry to see him go. We had had our differences of course, mostly quite trivial, but we were a good team. He was very practical and obstinate, unlike myself, and these were both invaluable traits when boating. Now I was on my own. I watched his stocky figure disappear up the hill and returned to the cut.

There was little left to do so I untied and set off. Alec Purcell had tied the previous night at Braunston en route for Banbury Dairy and I resolved that I would try to catch him.

Spring was certainly in the air when I left Braunston. I had worked away at the winter-dulled brasses on the portholes and on the cabin top so they winked back at the sun. The equinox was past and we were in the lighter part of the year although the chill of winter was still evident. However, on this balmy noontide promises of summer were occasionally made in such things as a sudden scent of newly mown grass in a lengthsman's garden by Braunston Stop, a row of hyacinths beneath a hedge at Shuckborough and the joyous birdsong in the towpath hedge. Yet another sign was the removal of covers from moored pleasure craft and even the odd hire boat from Braunston.

From the second lock at Napton I could see the upperworks of a hire cruiser rising further up the flight and, far beyond, the sun glinted off the brass ringed chimney of "Greenshank", Alec's butty. I was somewhat annoyed to find that the hire cruiser had left the top gate open as well as both paddles raised, which gave me extra work to do. I put up with this for three locks then, when it seemed obvious that the hire boat's crew did not appreciate that I was following them up, I decided to walk ahead and remonstrate with them. After all, I felt, they were 'mob-handed' and I was alone. Before I could reach the next lock they had all climbed aboard and were motoring up the pound. They seemed to have had no thought of sending a lockwheeler ahead to get this ready for them. As I came puffing up the slope at the lock, I heard a shout and beheld an irate and red-faced Alec striding down towards them, windlass in hand and blood in his eye. It seemed that they had committed the grievous crime of "drawing against him". This happens when a butty is being worked uphill in narrow locks and somebody draws the top paddles of the lock below. If the butty is still going into the lock, the force of the water pulls it out again, causing much tribulation to its crew. Alec and his wife were two-handed and had had about enough of this.

The hirer of the cruiser was an American. It seemed that this was the first time he had ever been on a canal and if Alec were to have his way it would be his last. Nevertheless he had enough sense to keep his boat in the middle of the cut where neither of us could reach him. Alec threatened to empty the pound on him but desisted when I pointed out that this would not help me. Eventually, with Alec's threats still ringing loud in his ears, he agreed to take things more easily as well as to close his top gate and paddles for me. Returning to my boat I decided to have a cup of tea and let them all get well ahead of me.

As a result it was past four-thirty when I left the top lock at Marston Doles and I realised I would not make Claydon across the summit before dark. This was a blow, for I was hoping to meet Edwina, our secretary, and a friend at Banbury in the morning to go down to Thrupp for Sunday night. Still, I thought, there should be some virtue in spending the night at Fenny Compton rather than Cropredy, and so it was to prove.

There was not a sign of human life on the canalside as I twisted this way and that round the lonely summit contours. The sun was dipping behind Edge Hill and its distant wolds as I came through the arch of Griffin's Bridge to see the sterns of two loaded boats floating in mid-cut, smoke rising vertically into the windless air. I throttled right down and the engine died away to a whisper as I slowly overhauled the pair, their bright Willow Wren colours shining in the afterglow. Alec's wife, Lil, smiled at me out of the hatches.

"Just slacked for some supper, Dave," she called. Alec heaved himself out of the engine hole.

"'ow far tonight?" he shouted across. I told him Fenny Compton. He asked if I was all right for 'grub' and I said I was, but would have supper after I tied up.

"Lily's got plenty if you want it," said he, but in truth I had more than enough to see me home now I was on my own, so I declined with thanks. I asked after the hire cruiser. "Loosed the boogger by," said Alec, "otherwise I'd 'a belted 'im."

I chugged off into the gathering gloom. Although Fenny Compton Wharf was visible across the fields from Griffin's Turn and would have been about fifteen minutes walk, the Oxford Canal winds so much that it was nearly an hour later and pitch dark when I tied outside the "George and Dragon" at Fenny Compton.

I had started some of the supper cooking three bridge holes before arriving. To do this, one stops the boat in the bridge, dives into the cabin, lights the gas and puts on the saucepan or whatever with the flame on low, then dashes back out to regain control before the boat noses into the reeds or blows out of the channel. Consequently my supper was nearly cooked when I tied up. I sat by the fire waiting for the washing-up water to boil afterwards and heard the mutter of an approaching engine. Looking out of the slide I saw the headlights of Alec's pair pulling in behind. As I washed-up there came a thunderous bang on the cabin side and Alec's voice roared, "Coming off?"

I opened the side doors and told him I would not be long, inviting him in out of the cold. He was much amused at my domesticity and told me that he could do with a third hand who could cook. He said that this was his last trip as he would be taking on a pair of hotel boats that summer, but doubted that he would go back to commercial boating afterwards because of his wife's ill health. Only with a young and lively mate could he consider another winter boating, specially now the system was being changed. In fact the enforced idleness at Marston Doles that past winter, though it was spent two miles from licensed premises, had given them both a new lease of life. Having some experience of two-handed boating I could appreciate that.

A canal writer who met Alec a decade or more later stated that he would sooner have gone in the ring with Mohammed Ali than upset Alec, there was some justice in this in his retirement but even more so when he was daily accustomed to shovelling coal, mauling paddles, starting engines and other muscle-building activities. Accordingly, the scene a few minutes later, when we walked into the bar of the pub to see that its only occupant was our American friend from the hire cruiser, may be imagined. I was reasonably tall and weather-beaten, Alec always walked like a boxer, alert and on his toes and while I am no oil-painting, even Alec's kindest friends could not describe him as handsome. I think the American for one dreadful moment thought he was in some Western saloon when the avengers walk in for he blenched ghastly white and gripped his glass. Alec strode over and as he visibly wilted on his bar stool, towering above him demanded in a thunderous tone, "What're yow drinkin'?"

The American blinked nervously and stammered that it was indeed his pleasure so Alec told him that he was drinking Guinness and I was drinking bitter. The landlord came in at that moment, saw Alec and winked at him. Alec burst into loud laughter and told the American to include the landlord. Hastily and with great anxiety he did so, Alec lifted his glass, called "Cheers" and drained it at a gulp. He then insisted on treating the American after which I was prevailed upon to do the same.

After about an hour during which time the atmosphere became progressively merrier, I was sent to bring the ukelele banjo. The American's wife came to find her errant spouse and quickly succumbed to Alec's charm and blandishments. The evening progressed to the swearing of eternal transatlantic friendship. "Sure thing Al, you're the bes' goddam limey, an' you all gotta know it. Anyone shays limeys ain't no goddam good don' know wha' the hell they're talkin' about. Ain't that sho Marylou?"

"Sure thing Irving, I guess you boys are one hun'red per cent OK" and so forth until, long after closing time, the Americans had to be assisted back to their boat and I helped brew strong coffee and Bourbon as a potent night cap for all of us.

Below Claydon there are, at a number of places, lift bridges across the canal. Many original bridges have been removed and many of the remainder are permanently chocked open, but the ones which remain are an obstacle to boats operating with one-man crews. The technique was to stop with the fore-end just in the bridgehole, then rush forward armed with a short cabin shaft which had a short length of rope attached to the end away from the hook. This was the "Banbury Stick". One then heaved the deck of the bridge up by shoving on the handrails and, when it was fully open, jammed in the Banbury Stick, hook uppermost. Returning to the boat one motored through the bridge, grabbing the dangling rope as one passed and taking a turn of it on one of the towing studs at the stern. The way of the boat then snatched the stick away and the bridge, deprived of its prop, came down with a satisfying "kerwallop" astern.

In spite of the slowness of operation, I was in Banbury by lunch time and had the pleasure of female company once more. The two girls bustled about and it was a great boon to have cups of tea and sandwiches passed back. At Kings Sutton one of the girls asked innocently how much longer before we arrived in Oxford. I said that I was intending to get there the following night and they looked at each other in horror. A grave misunderstanding had arisen for they were expecting to be there that night and there were all manner of arrangements to be considered. I assured them that at her fastest speed the poor old boat would not get to Oxford until the early hours, even if we worked all night. Their faces fell so I said we would soon be at Aynho where the station was next to the canal and they could get a train. This cheered them up.

The late afternoon sun was striking across the flooded levels of the Cherwell Valley when the old stone warehouse at Aynho Wharf came in sight. We pulled into what was then a lonely coal wharf and walked round to the station. There were no Sunday evening trains whatsoever. We looked at each other in despair. I was not at all happy at the prospect of two attractive young women hitch-hiking in the gathering gloom along lonely roads but they were determined to go. I walked over the old stone bridge with them towards Clifton Mill and watched them go down the road with a worried heart. I remembered the lack of success that Bill and myself had had, but of course I should have known better. Young women in pairs do not, for some reason, deter lift-givers! The first car along stopped and gave them a lift to Deddington and inside twenty minutes, so they later told me, they were on a bus heading for Oxford.

Next morning was grey and overcast and I grimly set about the long trek down to Oxford. In fact I had a good, if slow, run down the valley until I reached Bakers Lock near Bletchingdon. I had noticed the day before that the Cherwell had broken its banks in many places and frequently the valley was a sheet of steely water with the river's course picked out by brown turbulence as the limestone Wolds continued to give forth their long-pent waters. An old lengthsman hedge-cutting near Pigeon's Lock said it would be as many weeks as the frost had lasted before the river would drop back to normal. On arriving at Bakers Lock, which drops the canal into the Cherwell, I looked in vain for the course of the navigation below. All that was visible was the hedgerow and the iron bridge carrying the towpath across the river by the cement works. Keeping my fingers crossed I set out and swung round the big turn into the river. I went tearing through the water at an unprecedented rate and wondered what was going to happen when I got to Shipton Weir. I kept about twenty five feet out from the hedge and hoped for the best.

I raced under the railway like a plank going down a flume. The hedge seemed to flash past and I throttled down as much as I dared whilst still keeping steerage way. I had no idea of how to stop before reaching the Weir Lock and hoped that I would be able to hold back in time. Round the last turn I shot and, heavens be praised! the lock was full and the top gate open. Jack James and Joe Skinner had both told me that this had been the practice years ago in horse boat days, I did not realise that it was still so. I thankfully nosed into the open gate and stopped in good order. The house by the lock was still occupied and it was the custom in flood for the lengthsman who lived there to fill the lock and keep the gate open in case any boats came downstream. The lengthsman himself came out to greet me, the first boat, he said, to come through since before Christmas.

The afternoon was well advanced when I came at last in sight of Wytham Hill and dropped down through Kings Lock. I resolved not to risk the Dukes Cut and the river at that time of day and, as the pound seemed to be well up, carried on down through Wolvercote towards Isis Lock, near Oxford Railway Station. This route, the original one to the Thames, was not much used at the time and there was some talk of it being closed and turned into a road. The two reasons why it was not used were the amount of rubbish thrown into it and the delays experienced passing through the railway swing bridge below Isis Lock. On the other hand it was, for me, the most familiar length of canal of all since I had known it from early childhood and my earliest memories included narrowboats unloading at Juxon Street Wharf in the war years. There had been no regular traffic to Juxon Street since the Griff Arm near Bedworth on the Coventry Canal had been closed by the Coal Board about two years previously. Accordingly I approached every bridgehole very gingerly, but in spite of this, trouble arose at the lift bridge by the Morris Radiator factory.

Although the factory lay on the east bank of the cut, the car park lay on the west bank and its access to the outside world was the lift bridge. Of course, I had to arrive just as the day shift was going home and the night shift was arriving. Off I leaped and, in a brief interval in the stream of cars, shoved up the bridge and wedged in the 'Banbury Stick'. A chorus of angry shouts from the factory side where home-going workers were being separated from their beloved motor cars, was echoed by a fanfare of horns from the car park side. To illustrate my contempt of such ill-natured impatience I made a rude gesture at both sides, skipped elegantly back along the top plank and motored into the bridgehole, intending to give a virtuoso display of boating and pulling out the stick. Instead I stuck fast in the centre. The shouting and honking of car horns reached a crescendo. Burly donkey-jacketted figures jumped from their motors. Someone suggested dropping the bridge with the boat in it. I said that not only would I belt with my windlass the first person to touch the bridge but that as the boat was already on the bottom, the only result of this would be to jam the bridge open so nobody would get home. At this people calmed down and one sensible character suggested they all got out of their cars and pulled. I took a rope off the stern stud, a long line of men assembled on the towpath, I went hard ahead, hard astern then, as I clutched in, roared "Heave!" The boat wallowed ahead a few feet, I went astern—thus drawing the fore-end down and raising the stern—and we gained some more ground. Another bout of "ahead and asterning" and she was free. I snatched out the stick, coiled up my line and to loud cheers I slipped away into the gathering dusk.

Dropping down through Isis (or Louse) Lock I left behind the Midlands canal system which had been my workplace and home for so long. In the dark my headlight swept round the weedy turn into the backwater of the Thames known as Sheepwash. The swing-bridge which carried the former LMS railway into Rewley Road station was closed, so I carefully nudged upstream until my fore-end rested against the girders and made fast for the night. To make doubly sure of not being loosed-off I drew up the anchor chain from the fore deck, wrapped it round one of the bridge stanchions and secured it with a spare padlock, for I had no desire to navigate stern first down the old navigation to Hythe Bridge in the night.

Once secured I made my way, as directed by a notice, to the Western Region signal box on the parallel main line. From the quiet solitude of the Sheepwash towpath I came out into a world of gleaming rails, red and green lights and towering trains. I picked my way across the ballast, climbed a long wooden ladder and confronted a somewhat surprised but friendly signalman. He paused in an interval between answering tinging block instruments and grasping shiny levers to explain that while he would be able to prevent any train from leaping on top of me when the bridge was opened, I should require the services of a platelayers gang actually to open it. I was bidden, therefore, to see the Up Platform Inspector and make arrangements. He directed me onwards and turned again to his levers.

Down the steps I went again, stepping across point rods, signal wires and rails until I reached the slope at the end of the Up Platform. The Platform Inspector was not in the least put out by my request to pass the bridge and wanted to know if I was going through that night. I assured him that eight-thirty next morning would be fine and he promised that a gang would be onhand. It was pleasant to come up against the traditional Great Western courteous efficiency which had been a byword in my boyhood and I told him so. He grinned from ear to ear and said that Nationalisation was all very well, but what was killing it was all those LMS men at Paddington!

I was up and raring to go by eight o'clock and punctually at half-past eight the 'bridge-gang' arrived in the person of a weedy youth armed with a mighty spanner. As the bridge had not been moved for at least five months, his first task was to oil and then release the 'fish-plate' bolts which secured the track on the swinging deck of the bridge to the adjoining rails. There were two tracks on the bridge, consequently he had to undo thirty two bolts and remove sixteen fish plates. Whilst the lad puffed and struggled manfully I decided to reconnoitre further.

The water was tearing down the main river beyond the Great Western bridge (which was a fixed one with boat headroom) and I walked down to Osney Bridge to find that the weir on the far side, which led off at right angles to the narrow channel, was fully drawn. This meant that I would have to shoot the bridge 'flat-out' to maintain steerage way, but the height of the floodwater seriously reduced headroom under Osney Bridge. Still I judged it several feet higher than the Bridge Street girders in Reading. I walked on to the lock. It was now about ten minutes to nine and the lock keeper came on duty at nine o'clock but since nobody was about I filled the lock and opened the top gate, because yet another weir hole led off under the towpath just above the lock where I would have to stop if the gates were closed. I could foresee some difficulty in getting away from the bank in this case. The lock keeper had not appeared when I had filled the lock, so I left a note on his door which said, "8.55am. Boat coming down on flood. Expect to arrive 9.15am so have filled lock in readiness" and walked back to Sheepwash.

The bolts were by now undone, the securing catches drawn and a hefty crew of platelayers had assembled on the winches which turned the bridge via gearing. I knew that the old LMS station at Rewley Road dated from 1851 and was reputed to have been designed by Joseph Paxton of Crystal Palace fame, so I would hazard a guess that the swingbridge was contemporaneous. It was a massive piece of Victorian engineering and mighty stiff too after the frost.

The gang heaved unsuccessfully, so I said I would show them how to open it. Taking a line from "Enterprise" I carried it across the bridge to the far handrail where I secured it with a thumb-line knot, round the outer end of the near side handrail and back to the fore-end stud. Then, starting the engine I told them to heave when the bridge began to move. I went hard astern, aided by the current, and the whole thing worked like a Grand Union lockgate. There was a slight jerk, the handles spun, flinging the gang backwards, and the bridge slowly opened. I went ahead once the gap was wide enough and the line obediently dropped aboard to the amazement of the gang. I thought they might want me to pull it shut and looped a line from the stern stud round the upstream handrail support and back.

This drew the bridge closed behind me. As it drew back into position I loosed off one end of the rope, which then ran through the handrail and dropped into the water behind, enabling me to coil it in. The ganger called, "That were bloody neat, mate!" and I pressed on, this ultimate accolade swelling my head abominably.

As usual pride had a swift fall. I shot Osney Bridge with inches to spare, and going like an express train, only to find as I hurtled round the blind turn above the lock that the lock-keeper had shut the gates and emptied the lock. Holding back frantically I got a stern line onto a mooring post and stopped only to be sucked against the mooring boom by the force of the weir, as I had feared all along.

The lock-keeper insisted that no note had been left for him. It seemed very strange that in the short space of twenty five minutes it had gone, but further argument was avoided by the Alec Purcell 'Coal Wheeze' which I put into effect. On Alec's advice I had removed the contents of the bunkers of "Tern" and "Dunlin" and put them in plastic bags containing about half a hundredweight. Coal in the Thames Valley was then retailing for about eleven shillings per hundredweight. The offer of a half-hundredweight for three shillings plus a tug ticket worth eightpence plus a telephone call to the next lock to tell him I was coming, appealed to the lock-keeper's business acumen. The news of this spread swiftly down river and, apart from Abingdon, I had every lock ready. Even those who did not buy coal telephoned ahead so I had a swift run.

I timed myself down the half mile from Abingdon Lock to Abingdon Bridge and found I covered it in three minutes from leaving the bottom of the lock to clearing the bridge. This meant my overground speed was ten miles per hour which compared favourably with the Atherstone Pound, or even the Blisworth or Fenny Pounds on the Grand Union. This dizzy speed however, dropped once I got into the wider reaches and became even less in the lock cuts, nevertheless the whole journey downstream was covered at a respectable gallop.

The familiar landmarks of home began to rise up: Streatley Hill, Gatehampton Viaduct, Pangbourne Weir and Whitchurch Lock, Mapledurham Mill, The Roebuck and The Warren. I once more had a feeling of homecoming, but somehow without the triumph of last year. In a way I was coming home with my tail between my legs. Financial problems loomed, narrow-boating was on a knife-edge, the 'Waterways' fleet had only days to live and Morton's scheme was untried. "Enterprise", although in working order, was in a run-

211

down condition. I knew that I would have to go 'ashore' to work—even if only temporarily.

Below Caversham I swung under Horseshoe Bridge. I had last seen it, full of optimism on a foggy October morning, now on a grey, spring afternoon I was returning with most hopes dashed. The full force of the Kennet slowed "Enterprise" right down, and I was forty five minutes punching upstream through Blakes Lock to High Bridge. At long last I slowed down, ran along the top plank and secured the fore end to the mooring hook on High Bridge Wharf. It was five-thirty, eight hours after I had left Osney Lock forty odd miles upstream. I put out the engine, snugged down the engine hole and went into the cabin to pack a few things. It was a melancholy business but I felt it would be best to leave and get home quickly. My work was interrupted by a bang on the slide. I opened the door.

"'Ullo coz" said the voice of faithful Peter, our watchman: "Good to see you back again!"

EPILOGUE

It was not, as it turned out, the end of my boating career. That, I hope, will occur only when I am firmly nailed down in a coffin and even then, as Jack James would have said, they'll have to put it in the ground wrong way up in case I wriggle back out again. But many things changed. A mere two months later I met the woman who was to become my wife. We were married within the year and some eighteen months later I entered the teaching profession. Eventually I sold "Enterprise" and came to rest at Stoke Bruerne in a house just a few feet from where "Dunlin's" stern was tied for so many weeks. Today I still manage to boat, occasionally with loads too, but can no longer claim to be a full-time professional.

"Tern" and "Dunlin" never again carried regular loads. They both eventually became pleasure boats—though "Tern" worked honourably for another fifteen or so years for Willow Wren as a camping boat. She now has a full-length cabin and has been sold into private hands.

Bill Fisher's business went from strength to strength and our friendship has ripened over the years. Our children now wonder how their fathers could have done such mad things, but our wives grumble at the amount of gossiping we still seem to get through when we start talking.

British Waterways ceased carrying in the Spring of 1963, as forecast. Their boats were leased by a revived Willow Wren Canal Carrying Company and the new British Waterways Board gave them a helping hand by introducing craft licensing instead of tolls. Unhappily this well meant gesture proved to be too little, too late.

Leslie Morton continued to run Willow Wren until his sudden death in September 1968. My last dealing with him was to buy a boat from him the week he died. After his death things deteriorated rapidly. It is in no spirit of disrespect to the surviving directors that I write this. Morton was a rarity in the modern world; he was an all-rounder. His ability, dogged persistence, quickness of mind, shrewdness, humanity and above all experience, were qualities seldom found in one man. His loss left a void both in my life and in the world of the waterways. The directors of Willow Wren and a devoted administrative staff, which included the infallible Stanley, struggled on but the odds were against them. Their last contract, to Croxley Mills from Gopsall Wharf on the Ashby Canal, terminated in August 1970. The same month saw Blue Line's last load to the 'Jam Hole' and so ended regular long distance carrying on the Grand Union Canal.

Towards the end the once-proud Willow Wren boats became almost a byword for shabbiness, though several captains kept up a brave appearance. The trouble was that the boats were worn out, there was no capital for replacement and frequently boatmen who were not of the highest calibre got hold of them and thrashed them to death. Even the best and most worthy of the surviving captains became more and more disillusioned as the emphasis shifted away from canals as a serious carrying industry towards the idea of the system as a playground for holiday cruising.

The truth is not always easy, or palatable. The economic arguments in favour of carrying goods by canal are even more relevant in a world of looming energy crisis than ever before. Although a single narrow boat is, as I have perhaps shown, labour intensive and a pair should have at least a crew of three, the sheer economy of fuel consumption has surely to be considered. In the 1950s and 1960s fuel was cheaper than human labour so narrow boating died, a future world may well see the positions reversed. A tipper lorry will transport twenty tons of coal sixty miles and consume eight gallons of diesel fuel—giving a consumption of 150 ton/miles per gallon. A pair of narrow boats will transport fifty tonnes the same distance and consume ten gallons—a consumption of 300 ton/miles per gallon! It may well be that we ignore the transport potential of our

213

canals at our peril.

Another unpleasant truth is that bureaucracy is the enemy of efficiency. The canals were not so much strangled by railway or even road competition, as by an evil combination of red tape and Luddism. The following table shows the appalling decline of waterway traffic in the decade prior to the abolition of the British Transport Commission in December 1962.

	1952	1955	1958	1961
Total tons carried on B.T.C. canals. (millions)	12.442	10.477	9.298	9.272
S.E. Division Miles open	410	410	410	406*
Tons carried in the S.E. (millions)	3.068	3.177	2.586	2.327

S.E. Division included Birmingham and Fazeley, Coventry, Oxford, Ashby, Grand Union Canals and Lee and Stort Navigation.

*4 miles of Ashby Canal, connecting with collieries, closed 1959.

Staff Figures	1952	1962
Administrative, technical and clerical staff	637	770
Boatmen	518	323

Total staff (including boatmen) in December 1962 was 4.051.

Allied to the question of a narrowboat revival is that of crew. The family boat system which I saw and lived with could not realistically be revived today. It had its benefits of course. Speaking with the experience of many years teaching adolescents I would hesitate to condemn a system where the extended family was so strong a unit as either socially or educationally undesirable. The children I knew grew up, as their forebears had done, to be sturdy, independent and intelligent—or at least those whose parents had these qualities did. Some grew up ignorant and stupid but even these had a spark of individualism and character one looks for in vain among youngsters of a similar social background in towns today.

However, I think it both doubtful and unrealistic to think that men and women would voluntarily choose to live with a family in a minute floating box, no matter how comfortable, or that they could ignore the needs of that family for the benefits of education and its concomitant opportunities. It is fine to have a romantic dream of the good life and of a hard but satisfying life style, of which boating has a fair measure admittedly but the problems beyond this cosy, bourgeois illusion are real indeed. If such a revival should come, the crews will perforce be single men and women without families and perhaps with a permanent home on the bank. This is how it frequently was in the heyday of canals, and this is how both 'Number Ones', such as Wilfred's family, and large concerns, such as Fellows, Morton and Clayton, ordered things well into the third and fourth decades of the twentieth century.

Finally, as for the starting and finishing point of this Odyssey, the Kennet and Avon Canal, its future at the time of writing seems assured and it will be only a matter of time before boats once more pass between Reading and Bristol. The resultant canal may not be that for which Gould and the early pioneers hoped, but something of the old idealism remains in a new generation of waterway warriors.

One thing is certain. The way of life, both on the canals and in the surrounding villages and towns, which I have described and which was recognisably the same world that L.T.C. Rolt so eloquently pictured in "Narrow Boat" twenty years earlier has passed away for ever. Change there must be, otherwise humanity will atrophy; though whether it is for good or ill is debatable. Many of the characters are dead and most of the places have changed out of all recognition. One thing still endures, the cut. May its real friends ever increase and cherish it.

Appendix 1. Willow Wren boats Autumn 1962-Spring 1963

MOTOR BOATS

Name	Construction	Engine Type	Origins	
Avocet	Wooden	Seffle	F.M.C.	"Raven"
Bittern	Iron	Seffle	F.M.C.	"Lion"
Crane	Iron	Twin Bolinder	F.M.C.	"Crane"
Curlew	Steel	National	G.U.	"Seaford"
Dipper	Steel	National	G.U.	"Bristol"
Egret	Wooden	Twin Bolinder	G.U.	"Mimas"
Flamingo	Steel	National	G.U.	"Letchworth"
Grebe	Iron	Twin Bolinder	F.M.C.	"Antelope"
Mallard	Steel	Seffle	G.U. (Erewash) "Elm"	
Moorhen	Wooden	Single Bolinder	F.M.C.	"Briar"
Rail	Steel	National	G.U.	"Hadley"
Redshank	Steel	National	G.U.	"Reading"
Quail	Wooden	Twin Bolinder	F.M.C.	"Quail"
Swan	Steel	National	G.U.	"Dunstable"
Warbler	Iron	Single Bolinder	G.U.	"Libra"
Widgeon	Steel	National	G.U.	"Thaxted"
Tern	Iron	Twin Bolinder	F.M.C.	"Emu" (1926)
Sandpiper	Iron	Twin Bolinder	F.M.C.	"Falcon"

BUTTY BOATS

Name	Construction	Builders	Origins	
Bunting	Wooden	Walkers, L. Rickmansworth	G.U.	"Dudley"
Coot (sold Sept '62)	Wooden	Walkers, Sm. Rickmansworth	G.U.	"Ursa"

Cygnet	Composite	F.M.C. Saltley	F.M.C.	?
Dabchick	Iron	Yarwoods "Station"	L.M.S.	Rly boat
Drake	Wooden	Walkers, L. Rickmansworth	G.U.	"Taunton"
Dunlin	Wooden	Walkers, L. Rickmansworth	G.U.	"Hadfield"
Godswall (sic)	Wooden	Walkers L. Rickmansworth	G.U.	"Denton"
Greenshank	Steel	Harland, Wolff, L. Woolwich	G.U.	"Bawtry"
Heron	Iron	Yarwoods "Station"	L.M.S.	Rly "Caleb"
Kestrel	Steel	Yarwoods M. Northwich	G.U.	"Triagulum"
Kingfisher	Wooden	F.M.C. Uxbridge	F.M.C.	"Florence"
Smew	Wooden	Walkers L. Rickmansworth	G.U.	"Norton"
Snipe	Iron	F.M.C. (Braithwaites)	F.M.C.	"Kildare"
Teal	Iron	F.M.C. (Saltley)	F.M.C.	"Minnie" or "Grimsby" 1910
Shoveller	Wooden	Nurser Braunston- for F.M.C.	F.M.C.	"Bascote"
Wagtail	Wooden	F.M.C. (Uxbridge)	F.M.C.	"Freda"
Elton	Wooden	Walkers L. Rickmansworth	G.U.	"Elton"

L=Large   M=Middle   Sm=Small

APPENDIX 2
Glossary of some Canal Terms

Agen	Against, or near, e.g. "Agen the gas", "near the gasworks".
Ahead (to get) vb.	To keep going, keep moving.
Answer Pins or answers	Hooks and shackles at the stern of a boat used for "strapping" q.v. or "breasting up" q.v.
Apsley Mills	The works of John Dickenson Ltd, paper manufacturers near Hemel Hempstead, Herts.
Arm	A branch of the main canal.
Back Door	A door in the back end of a boat's hold (or fore end of cabin!)
Back End beam	See "cabin beam".
Back End rail	An iron rail on a motor boat running from side to side on the leading edge of the cabin, usually having an iron ring on it. Used for tying-up in awkward places, storing Wellingtons and similar tasks.
Back Flush	The result of a flush (q.v.) of water hitting the gates of a downhill lock and rebounding.
Banbury Dairy	A user of coal just below Banbury Lock, supplied from Pooley Hall Colliery until 1965.
Banbury Stick	A pole or shaft used for propping open a lift bridge.
Barge	Technically, a vessel used on inland waterways with a beam of more than 14 feet. Incorrectly used to describe canal boats, but more properly a river or estuary craft.
Bats	The blades of a propellor.
B.C.N.	The Birmingham Canals Navigation.
Beam	The maximum width of a vessel.
Bell Oil (to give it)	To hit something or someone very hard; to work an engine hard. A Black Country expression, possibly derived from the sea battle of Belle Isle.
Blade	The propellor.
Blis'orth (the)	The pound (q.v.) from Buckby Locks to Stoke Bruerne.
Blue Top	(or 'dustbin'). The last commercial boats built for the British Transport Commission 1959-60, so called because of their blue plastic hatch covers.
Boat (Narrow)	A boat of approximately 70 feet in length and 7 feet or slightly less beam intended for working on narrow canals.
Boat's Bottom	An empty hold.
Boat Control	The system originated by the Grand Union Carrying Company of keeping a check and control over boat movements. It involved reporting the daily movement of loaded and empty craft past given points to a centralised Control Office at Bulls Bridge (q.v.). It was operated by the British Waterways Board until the cessation of nationalised carrying in 1963.
Bobby Dazzler	A small light bulb fitting to a motor-boat's chimney or to a stalk, used in tunnels or at night to help guide a butty's steerer.

Bolinder	An early type of diesel engine, usually single cylindered and with a distinctive beat. Standard fitting for Fellows, Morton and Clayton boats.
Bostin Stove	(from "slow-combustion stove"). A small stove used for heating rather than cooking.
Bow Haul, to (vb.)	To manually pull a boat by means of a line from the bank. So called because one makes a loop, or bow, in the rope to fit over the shoulders. Sometimes called "bow hanking".
Bracket Open	Driving a motor boat at full speed.
Braunston Pound	The pound from the top of Hillmorton Locks to the bottom of Napton Locks.
Braunston Summit	The level from Braunston top lock, through the tunnel to the top of Buckby Locks.
Bread and Larders	Boatmen who worked the Oxford Canal south of Napton.
Breasting up	Drawing two boats together side-by-side.
Bugby	Boaters' name for Buckby Locks and Wharf.
Bulls Bridge	The onetime administrative and engineering depot of the Grand Union Canal Company at Southall, Middlesex.
Bull Nose (see "Knuckle")	
Butty to (vb)	To work in company with another person or boat, to be 'mates' (c.f. American 'buddy').
Cabbage Turn	A sharp outside turn (q.v.) between Wormleighton and Marston Doles on the Oxford Canal Summit. So called because the nearby fields were used for growing cabbages.
Cabin Beam	(or Back End Beam) A plank across the hold just forward of the cabin.
Capes Two	Two locks adjoining the "Cape of Good Hope" P.H. near Warwick.
Centre paddle	(or Fly, gate paddles or ranters). A paddle (q.v.) in a top gate usually arranged so as to throw water clear of a loaded boat's fore end. When fitted they save much time in locking uphill, but many have been removed in recent years because they are alleged to be expensive and because some idiots in pleasure boats have been known to sink themselves with them.
Chimley Pipe Side	The left hand or 'port' side of a boat.
Chimley Tins	Usually old Dried Milk tins thrust in the top of cabin chimneys to carry smoke above the steerer's head and to improve the draught.
Clocks, between the	The canal between Hartshill Depot and Nuneaton, so called because of prominent clocks on the Depot and a mill at Nuneaton.
Company	The owners of a canal (usually the British Waterways Board) although, generally speaking, the canals have been nationalised since 1947.
Company's Man	An employee of the canal owners.
Control Chart	(see 'Boat Control'). Changing records of fleet positions kept by carrying companies.
Corkers Two	Two locks (Nos 32-33) between Horton and Marsworth, called by B.W.B. "Ivinghoe Locks". I was told by George "They calls Corkers Two 'Ivan' O Two' now".

219

Counter	The rounded stern of a motor boat which lies above the blades. It is intended to protect them from knocks and contact with coping stones, gates etc.
Cratch	The triangular covering of the fore part of a canal boat, originally where fodder for horses was kept (c.f.Fr. Crèche 'a manger') but latterly used for storing ropes, tarpaulins etc.
Cross Beam	Wide planks across the hold of a boat, slotted to hold stands.
Cross straps	Two short ropes used to haul an empty boat from a motor boat's studs.
Croxley Mills	Dickenson's paper mills near Watford, Herts.
Cutter (or titch)	A small pipe with a vertical loop of brass, fitting above the upright exhaust pipe of a motor boat. Its function is to break the force of the exhaust when passing beneath bridges, tunnels etc.
Dannell	Thames Valley dialect word for 'water' or 'river'.
Deck	The forepart of a narrow boat generally entered by a hinged hatch or 'deck lid'.
Deck board	The triangular fore part of a boat's cratch (q.v.) nowadays generally painted, but in commercial boat days more often covered with tarpaulin. Some 'number one's' and the boats of S.E. Barlow Ltd and Samuel Barlow Coal Co Ltd had painted deck boards.
Dolly	1 An iron stump on a motor's counter used for towing 2 An implement used by boatwomen for washing clothes 3 Short for Doris or Dorothy
Downhill Runner (or strap)	A rope used for checking boats when going down in a lock.
Drudger	A dredger.
Dukes Cut	1 A short canal connecting the Oxford Canal near Wolvercote with the Thames, built and for many years owned by, the Duke of Marlborough. 2 The Bridgewater Canal.
Dunnage (or Dennage)	Bits of waste timber intended to raise cargo above the floor of a hold in order to pass slings underneath.
Dust bin	See "Blue Top".
Economisers	See "Side Ponds".
False Cratch	"A"—shaped wooden uprights forming the rearward part of the cratch, sometimes painted with diamond designs.
False floors	Sectional floors raising the cargo space above the actual bottom of a boat.
Fan hold	The grip of a motor boat's propellor in the water, essential for power, especially when 'holding back' (q.v.)
Fellows, Morton and Clayton	The doyen of canal carrying companies. Sold out to British Transport Commission 1948.
Fenny Pound	The long length from Cosgrove to Fenny Stratford on the Grand Union, now greatly befouled by Milton Keynes.
Fields, the	The section of the Grand Union between Marsworth and Leighton Buzzard.
Flush	A sudden rush of water.
Fore end	The front or 'bows' of a canal boat.
Gas	A gasworks.

Gas Boats (or 'gassy')	A decked-in canal boat used for transporting gas liquor or tar in bulk. Similar to a miniature tanker.
Gas Two	Two locks (Nos 51 and 52) adjoining Berkhamstead Gas Works, Grand Junction Canal.
Ganzies	1 Rushall Locks, B.C.N. 2 Blue jerseys or sweaters worn by boaters c.f. "Guernseys".
Gear Wheel	The large wheel in a Grand Union Motor boat's door holes which operates the gear box via worm or bevel gearing.
Gettin' em ahead	Not hanging about, moving boats onward in a brisk fashion.
Girder	A thin rope used for lashing down top planks when "planked up". It runs from the planks to the cross beam.
Grand Union	1 Canal connecting Buckby with Foxton, so called in 1815 when opened. Sometimes called "Old Union" or "Leicester Line". 2 Canal formed in 1919 following amalgamation of Regents, Grand Junction, Warwick and Napton, Warwick and Birmingham and Birmingham and Warwick Junction Canals. Line later extended via R. Soar to Erewash Canal. 3 (a-s). A boat once belonging to the Grand Union Canal Carrying Co. formed 1933, nationalised 1947.
Greasy Ockers	Fellows Morton and Clayton boaters called because either a they carried cargoes of tallow and fat to a depot at Ocker Hill near West Bromwich or; b the horses which used to pull butties through the pre-1930 narrow locks between Itchington Top Lock and Hatton Top Lock had their hocks specially greased against the mud of the towpath. A boatman leaving the bottom of "Wigrams Three" (q.v.) might send his mate on ahead to "get the 'greasy ocker' out". Whichever is the correct explanation, the name was given to a F.M.C. man who was regularly on the Birmingham run from London.
Ground Paddle	See "Centre Paddle".
Guard	A semi-circular section iron strip protecting a boat's hull.
Hanging-up Plates	(or Ribbon plates). Plates with pierced edges, much prized by boaters as wall decorations.
Hatches	1 Boating. The well deck and its surround at the stern of a butty or horse boat. 2 R. Kennet. Large vertically rising sluices, generally raised with a handspike or winch c.f. "bucks" on R. Thames.
Hayes Cocoa	Nestlés chocolate factory.
Hayes Gramophone	The E.M.I. factory.
Hold back	Go astern, from horse boating days when boats could literally be stopped in an emergency by holding the line back.
Hold "in"	(or Hold "out"). An instruction to steer towards or away from the towpath.
Inside	Towpath side.
Inside turn	A bend in the canal where the deep water is near the towpath.
Ippey Cut	The Wilts and Berks Canal.
Jackdaw Pound	The pound (q.v.) from Leighton Buzzard lock to Soulbury Three Locks (or "Stoke Hammond Three").

221

Jam Hole	Kearley and Tonge's jam factory, Southall.
Josher	A boat once belonging to Messrs Fellows Morton and Clayton.
Junction Cut	The main line of the Grand Junction Canal from Braunston to Brentford.
Knuckle	(or "Bull Nose"). A dockland term for the rounded stonework at the entrance to a lock. "Bull nose" is used by Thames lock-keepers for the same thing.
Light	A power station e.g. "Uxbridge Light".
Lighter	A large barge used for loading or discharging cargo overside of ships.
Lime'us	(Limehouse) Regents Canal Dock.
Lock Wheeler	Someone who goes ahead to get locks ready, strictly speaking on a bicycle, hence the name, but nevertheless applied to persons on foot.
Loobey	The swivelling piece of iron at the top of a boat's mast, sprung so as to return to a vertical position.
Loose by·	To allow an overtaker to "come by".
Maffers	Marsworth.
Marsh Mills	Water mills belonging to Wallis, Son and Wells Ltd near Henley-on-Thames.
Mast	A hollow, square wooden post about 14 feet or so from the fore end of a boat's hold. Used for bowhauling (q.v.) occasionally for towing a butty. In horseboat days always used for towing.
Mast beam	The cross beam just ahead of and into which the mast fits.
Mast rope	A rope from the loobey used to pull lock gates open, sometimes to breast a boat.
Meet (to) vb.	To pass a boat travelling in the opposite direction. "I met 'im in Blis'orth tunnel".
Middle Beam	The cross beam next behind the mast beam, slotted to take a stand.
Middle Stand	The stand which slots into the middle beam.
Mill Boats	Boats carrying coal to John Dickenson's paper mills.
Moira Cut	The Ashby de la Zouch Canal (often, aptly, pronounced "Miry").
Morton Pound	The pound (q.v.) from Hawkesbury Junction to Hillmorton, Oxford Canal.
Moshes Two	Daw End locks, B.C.N.
Motor	A mechanically propelled canal boat capable of carrying cargo.
Mud heelers	Boatmen who worked the Northern section of the Oxford Canal.
Nash Mills	One of Dickenson's mills between Kings Langley and Hemel Hempstead, Herts.
Nags Head	Three locks (Nos 34-36) near Cheddington, Bucks.
New 'uns	Locks 65-68 at Apsley on the Grand Junction Canal.
Noble	Newbold on Avon. Oxford Canal.
Northampton River	(also "Wellingborough River") the river Nene (pronounced "Nen").

Northwich	A boat built for the Grand Union C.C.C. by Yarwoods Ltd, Northwich, Cheshire.
Number One	An owner-boatman, analogous to a sub-contract lorry driver.
Old Thirteen	Farmers Bridge Locks, B.C.N.
Outside	The side away from the towpath.
Outside Turn	A turn where the deep water is on the side away from the towpath.
Oxford River	The Upper Thames from Reading upstream.
Paddington Armer	A lady of doubtful virtue.
Paddle	A sluice.
Parks (the)	Section of the Grand Junction Canal through Cassiobury Park, Watford, where the canal company landscaped the canal to please the adjoining landowner, the Earl of Essex.
Parks Two	(also 'Alberts' Two). Two locks (Nos 75 and 76) close together in Cassiobury Park.
Peters Two	(also 'Two Below Maffers'). Two locks (Nos 37-38) at Marsworth, Grand Junction Canal.
Pigeon Box	A small, detachable skylight, generally above the engine room of a motor boat.
Pound	The canal "impounded" between two locks. One goes 'up' or 'down' a pound, or 'round' a long pound, a summit or a bottom pound such as the Fenny Pound, but never 'along' one.
Ribbon Plates	See "Hanging-up Plates".
Ricky	a Rickmansworth. b A boat built by Walker Bros. of Rickmansworth.
Ring hole Deep	Well-laden. So low in the water that the ring holes on the gunwale are awash c.f. "sparrers drinkin' off the gunnels".
Road	a The canal route to a place c.f. "The Oxford Road". b The state of the locks ahead of one, a good road signifying all locks ready for one, a bad road being that they are against.
Runner	a An official who transmitted boat control orders to crews. b Another word for a check strap—e.g. Downhill Runner (q.v.).
Running Blocks	Half moon-shaped wooden blocks, with a central hole through which a towline passes. These are fixed to the top plank of a butty to guide the towline. Virtually obsolete by the 1960s.
Sailormen	Men or barges which traded round the East Coast and Thames Estuary.
Shaft	a A boat hook ("hitcher" on the Thames). b (to) vb. To propel by means of a pole.
Sheepwash	The channel from the mainstream of the Thames to the Oxford Canal in Oxford.
Side Bridge	A bridge carrying the towpath over a branch canal.
Side Ponds	(or Economisers). Basins adjoining a lock into which lockage water can be run and subsequently reused. Rarely used or usable today and frequently modernised into rubbish tips, the authorities then evincing surprise at water shortages.
Single out (to)	To work boats in tandem (i.e. one behind the other).

Slack	a Small coal for industrial use.
	b (to) vb. To take a break.
Slide	A sliding hatch over a set of doorholes (q.v.).
Snatch	A tow.
Snatcher	A short rope used for towing.
Snubber	A thick rope used as a towline.
South Eastern	In B.T.C. days the waterways were administered in four commercial divisions roughly centred on the Black Country. The South Eastern Division thus included all the canals navigated in the story save the Thames and the Kennet and Avon.
Star Class	Boats of the Grand Union C.C.C. named after stars or constellations.
Stern	(Pronounced 'starn'). The rear end of a boat.
Stinko	Maple Cross Sewage Works, near Harefield, Bucks.
Stop place	A narrow part of the canal, frequently at a junction, where boats' cargo was gauged and tolls paid.
Straight Shoot	Running straight into a lock with a pair of boats singled out, as against having to 'come above' or 'below' and get it ready.
Strap	a A thick rope used for checking the way of a boat.
	b vb. to stop a boat by means of checking the way with a rope round a bollard or stump.
Strapping Stump	A bollard on a lock used for stopping a boat's way.
Strings	Thin ropes used for tying-up or lashing down planks or cloths.
Stud	An iron projection used for tying-up or towing. Fore end studs are invariably tee-shaped.
Suttons stop	Hawkesbury Junction, Oxford and Coventry Canals.
Sweeps Two	Locks Nos 54 and 55 Berkhamstead, Grand Junction Canal.
Talbots	Lock No 23, Grand Junction Canal.
Tall pipe	A long, detachable exhaust pipe, fitted with a cutter (q.v.) used when loaded to carry exhaust smoke over the steerer's head.
Target Turn	A wide inside turn near New Bradwell, Grand Junction Canal.
Thick	Several locks very close together.
Town Class	Boats of the Grand Union C.C.C. named after towns or villages.
Trainees	Outsiders (like myself) learning the job of boating.
Tug	A mechanically propelled boat with no carrying space.
Uprights	Painted detachable wooden pieces running from a boat's gunwale to the gang plank above the hold.
Wind (to) vb.	(to rhyme with "sinned"). To turn a boat round.
Winding Hole	A part of the canal wide enough to turn a full length (72 foot) boat.
Windlass	The metal crank handle used to operate lock paddles on a canal.
Wobble	(to make the water w-). To navigate at high speed.
Woolwich	A boat built for the Grand Union C.C.C by Harland and Wolff Ltd, North Woolwich.

224